GETTING TO YES IN KOREA

WALTER C. CLEMENS JR.

With a foreword by Governor Bill Richardson

Paradigm Publishers
Boulder • London

Copyright © 2010 Walter C. Clemens Jr.

Published in the United States by Paradigm Publishers, 2845 Wilderness Place, Suite 200, Boulder, CO 80301 USA.

Paradigm Publishers is the trade name of Birkenkamp & Company, LLC, Dean Birkenkamp, President and Publisher.

Library of Congress Cataloging-in-Publication Data

Clemens, Walter C.
  Getting to yes in Korea / Walter C. Clemens, Jr.
     p. cm.
  Includes bibliographical references and index.
  ISBN 978-1-59451-406-7 (hardcover)
  ISBN 978-1-59451-407-4 (paperback : alk. paper)
  1. United States—Foreign relations—Korea (North) 2. Korea (North)—Foreign relations—United States. 3. Nuclear nonproliferation—Korea (North) I. Title.
  JZ1480.A57K6 2010
  327.7305193—dc22

                                                                2009025317

Printed and bound in the United States of America on acid-free paper that meets the standards of the American National Standard for Permanence of Paper for Printed Library Materials.

Designed and Typeset by Straight Creek Bookmakers.

14 13 12 11 10   1 2 3 4 5

For Anna Sophia Ho Clemens

CONTENTS

ACKNOWLEDGMENTS

Many individuals have given wise counsel and encouragement over the years: Peter M. Beck, Bruce Cumings, Roger Fisher, Choong Nam Kim, Donald Gregg, Lloyd Jensen, Stephan Haggard, Brad Grosserman, Stephen Linton, Marcus Noland, Terence Roehrig, Scott A. Snyder, Robert A. Scalapino, Seung-Ho Joo, and Yurim Yi, who read and improved the entire manuscript. Jennifer Knerr backed the project from the outset. Valuable insights have also been provided by Boston University students who have taken part in three simulations of the six-party talks in PO 577, Negotiation in World Affairs.

This project began long ago when the U.S. State Department had funds to send U.S. lecturers abroad. In recent years institutional support came from Boston University, the Harvard Davis Center for Russian and Eurasian Studies, and the East-West Center at the University of Hawaii. The research facilities of many institutions proved invaluable: the Woodrow Wilson International Center for Scholars, the US-Korean Institute at SAIS, the Korea Economic Institute, Pacific Forum CSIS, the International Institute for Strategic Studies, the Harvard University Korea Institute, and the Peter G. Peterson Institute.

Valuable suggestions came from the editors and reviewers of journals in which earlier versions of some chapters were published: *Asian Survey, Bulletin of the Atomic Scientists, Financial Times, Global Asia, International Negotiation, Journal of East Asian Affairs, Journal of East Asian Studies,* and *Pacific Forum.*

The book is dedicated to Anna Sophia Ho Clemens. For her sake and for billions of other children, let us hope that the world's politicians get to yes.

FOREWORD BY GOVERNOR BILL RICHARDSON

In December 1994, as a congressman from New Mexico, my plane touched down in Pyongyang some two months after U.S. and North Korean diplomats in October signed an Agreed Framework to freeze North Korea's plutonium production. My mission was to discuss implementation of the framework agreement, raise issues of human rights, and foster a dialogue between the two Koreas. My job changed overnight when a U.S. helicopter was shot down over North Korea. For nine days and nights I worked to learn the circumstances of this incident and the condition of the two servicemen—all the while striving to keep these issues from interfering with the October agreement. My most urgent task became to repatriate the two U.S. servicemen in the downed helicopter. We learned that one of them, David Hilemon, had not survived the helicopter's crash landing; we informed his family. On December 21, North Korea's Vice Foreign Minister Song offered that, if I left the next morning, I could escort Hilemon's remains across the demilitarized zone (DMZ) into South Korea. The minister added that the sole survivor, Bobby Hall, would be released "very soon." I pressed for Hall to be released before Christmas. Upon the advice of Colonel Ray Miller in Seoul, I escorted Hilemon's remains into South Korea. Hall was released to American officials at the DMZ just before the New Year after the U.S. government expressed "sincere regret for this incident."

Following the 1994 events, I returned to North Korea several times in the 1990s and 2000s. The Democratic People's Republic of Korea delegation to the United Nations also visited me in Santa Fe several times during my tenure as governor. Our dialogue was never easy, but helped to secure the release of an imprisoned American, Evan Hunziker, and obtain the return of the remains of six U.S. soldiers from the Korean War. I believe that our meetings probably helped my North Korean counterparts to understand U.S. interests better and provided for Americans a clearer window into North Korea's goals and interests.

Despite past and present conflicts, there is some reason for hope about the prospects of improved U.S relations with North Korea. In 2009 former president Bill Clinton accepted an invitation to Pyongyang and obtained the release of two young journalists sentenced to twelve years of hard labor for their brief entry into North Korea. After the Clinton trip, the Democratic People's Republic of Korea (DPRK) delegation to the UN visited me in Santa Fe and emphasized their government's interest in direct talks with the United States. Since then the authorities in Pyongyang have welcomed a visit by top U.S. envoy, Ambassador Stephen W. Bosworth. However, the DPRK authorities have defied UN pressures and sanctions and continued to develop their incipient missile-nuclear arsenal. Still, there is little choice for any of the parties concerned with Northeast Asia but to continue negotiations.

My dealings with North Korean officials over the years since 1994 support the main contention of Walter Clemens in this book: Negotiations between the United States and the DPRK are often difficult, but can lead to outcomes useful to both sides. My experiences also confirm other themes of this book: How misperception as well as deep conflicts of interest can complicate relations among all parties concerned with the future of Northeast Asia; also, the importance of fostering trust and mutual understanding in bridging differences.

In *Getting to Yes in Korea,* Professor Clemens explains how Korea became critical to U.S. and world security. He points to a long history of misunderstanding between Koreans and Americans. He details how and why recent U.S. negotiations with North Korea have succeeded or failed. He notes that North Korea's poverty appears to have sometimes increased the government's intransigence. He points to features the DPRK shares with other authoritarian regimes and the ways in which it is distinct. He suggests that the leadership in Pyongyang may have more reasons for resisting accommodations with Washington than those in the former USSR or China.

This book points to valuable lessons from the approaches to North Korea taken by Jimmy Carter and Bill Clinton compared to those taken by George W. Bush and his entourage. Drawing on the value-creating/value-claiming framework of the Harvard Negotiation Project and his own studies of security negotiations with Moscow and with Beijing, Professor Clemens suggests guidelines for moving the Korean peninsula from a flash point to a zone of peace and cooperation. As his book makes clear, negotiations are not just possible but essential to avoiding war in Northeast Asia.

CHAPTER ONE

HOW KOREA BECAME CRITICAL

Getting to yes in Korea will never be easy. But all parties to tensions there owe it to themselves and the world to try. The actions of a militant but nearly failing state in the north could intensify arms buildups and even spiral into war involving the world's greatest powers. The confrontation between North Korea and the United States over nuclear and other issues marked "the first 21st century conflict between a failed state relying on the threat of nuclear weapons and their proliferation to ensure regime survival, and a world power intent on preventing such flexing, blackmailing, and transfer of weapons of mass destruction (WMD) to potential terrorists."[1] Behind this confrontation, of course, is a long history of enmity, misunderstandings, and crossed signals. The past is not past. It continues today and will shape the future. Nonetheless, this book inquires whether—and how—a multifaceted conflict could be transformed into multifaceted cooperation advantageous to all parties.

Neither Pyongyang nor Washington nor their other negotiating partners could be sure of one another's intentions or capabilities. When former U.S. president Bill Clinton went to Pyongyang in June 2009, he received red carpet treatment. He dined and talked with Kim Jong Il for several hours before bringing home two U.S. journalists jailed by Pyongyang for "illegal entry" and efforts to conduct a "smear campaign" against the Democratic People's Republic of Korea (DPRK).

The government's Korean Central News Agency (KCNA) said Clinton held "candid and in-depth discussions on the pending issues between the DPRK and the United States in a sincere atmosphere and reached a consensus of views on seeking a negotiated settlement of them." It also reported that Clinton had delivered a verbal message from President Barack Obama, a claim denied by the White House. But whether or not Clinton carried a message from Obama, DPRK media could boast that a former U.S. president had come and met with the Dear Leader. Concurrently, Pyongyang initiated a series of conciliatory gestures to Seoul, including renewed but limited family reunions.

Did all this signal that North Korea was ready to "get to yes" on nuclear and other controversial issues? Or, as cynics suggested, did Pyongyang merely seek relief from recently tightened UN-approved sanctions? Did it conciliate and promote negotiation just to neuter outside pressures? Was Pyongyang ready to give up its incipient nuclear arsenal, or did it strive to win international recognition as a nuclear weapons state? Did it intend to open the DPRK to economic and other reforms or only encourage more relief shipments of food and fuel? Did it want to normalize relations with all its neighbors, including South Korea, or to deal one on one with the White House while diminishing the Blue House in Seoul? Some experts on the DPRK opined that the regime would *never* open up because the ensuing revelations would erode the system and devour the ruling elite. Others said that North Korea had no choice but to risk liberalization and hope for a "Chinese" solution. The tea leaves permitted both interpretations.

North Korea's leaders also had to question the intentions of their interlocutors. Did China and Russia wish to bolster old comrades in Pyongyang or reestablish their imperial influences? Did Washington and its ROK and Japanese partners seek a modus vivendi with the DPRK, or were their tepid handshakes and fuzzy promises aimed at regime change? Even if the Obama administration did not plot regime change, it reiterated the George W. Bush administration's dual mantra: The United States would not reward bad behavior and would insist on "complete, verifiable, and irreversible denuclearization" in North Korea. Pyongyang had to consider whether, if DPRK denuclearization became irreversible, Obama or his successors might renege on U.S. commitments.

These and other uncertainties paired with an unquestioned reality: *Nuclear war, even on a "limited" scale, would bring catastrophe to Northeast Asia and perhaps to the world*. Policy-makers had reason to prepare for the grimmest scenarios but even more reason to find solutions to the security dilemmas facing each party. They needed to develop structures and build habits to foster cooperation and make "defection" unlikely. In the decades between Josef Stalin and Boris Yeltsin, the Kremlin and White House transformed their relations in a positive direction. Could Pyongyang and Washington—despite asymmetries of power and much bloodletting—do the same? Could they get the other concerned players, especially those in Beijing, Seoul, Tokyo, and Moscow, to support the peaceful transformation of Northeast Asia?

The path to a harmonious transformation faces major obstacles within each actor and across the world stage. Some features of politics and culture within South Korea, Japan, China, and Russia as well as the United States favor accommodation with Pyongyang, but other agents and structures in each country work against a deal. The weakness of the United Nations coupled with asymmetries of power and values among the key players add to the difficulties. But even if most concerned actors labored in unison for harmony on the Korean peninsula, they would still face a tough and often defiant partner. North Korea's regime has long been among the most aggressive players in international affairs and the most repressive at home—doing little even to address mass hunger. North Korea— officially known as the Democratic People's Republic of Korea—became the first country after World War II to invade and seek to annex a neighbor, South Korea (the Republic of Korea, or ROK). The DPRK may hold the modern record for state sponsorship of terrorism and assassination. The Pyongyang regime has dealt harshly not only with its own subjects and with the ROK but also with its patrons in Moscow and Beijing. No other government has defied the UN Security Council for so long and so resolutely. None has accepted and then stepped back from formal commitments so often and so dramatically. No other government has treated so shabbily the relief agencies whose programs save millions of its citizens from acute hunger and disease. Would any other government kill an authorized guest and then demand an apology? (See Box 1.1)

Recognizing these and other problems, this book asks, *Is it possible to transform the divided Korean peninsula from a cockpit for nuclear war into a zone of cooperation for mutual gain? Can bitter and distrustful adversaries deal with their differences by diplomacy, or can they be resolved only by brute force?* If a negotiated settlement is thought to be potentially useful and feasible, how can it be achieved? What approaches have proved useful, and which have failed? Are there lessons from these interactions that could be applied to other confrontations between avowed antagonists—even to those between nuclear weapon haves and have-nots aspiring to join the nuclear club?

Box 1.1 Shoot First and Add Insults Later

In July 2008 a DPRK soldier shot and killed a South Korean woman as she walked along a beach in an area that Pyongyang later claimed was marked as off limits to foreigners. The killing took place on the very day that ROK president Lee Myung Bak spoke in favor of more North-South engagement without preconditions. Not swayed by the president's message, Pyongyang's authoritative newspaper *Rodung Sinmun* (July 27, 2008) asserted that the "Lee Myung Bak group of traitors is touting 'pragmatism' and the policy of confrontation with the DPRK based on it," which the DPRK oracle called a "fundamental factor bedeviling north-south relations." Pyongyang expressed no regret for the incident but demanded that Seoul apologize for the transgression.

The bellicose words and deeds of North Korea's leaders raise doubts about whether other governments can ever reach an accommodation with Pyongyang about "high" politics (security issues such as nuclear weapons and boundaries) or even issues of "low" politics (trade, the environment, culture). For Pyongyang, nearly everything is high politics—from energy to human rights. The regime's behavior challenges any view that DPRK diplomacy arises merely from a "high context" culture that requires polite and patient nurturing to settle differences. North Korea's diplomacy seems driven by deeper aspirations than maintaining "face" (*cheymyeon*) and nourishing the "inner spirit" (*kibun*) of negotiations.[2]

As the twenty-first century began, the Republic of Korea offered a model of economic dynamism, self-government, educational excellence, and "wired" infrastructure. Its pop culture animated Japan, China, parts of the United States and Europe, and even—underground—North Korea. By contrast, the Democratic People's Republic of Korea menaced the world not only with its weapons but also with its economic and political fragility. Washington and Tokyo worried about North Korea's military strength; Beijing and Seoul feared its weakness. Both concerns were justified: The DPRK could become a failed state equipped with nuclear weapons.

But why worry about Korea—a small corner of Northeast Asia dwarfed by its neighbors? Not long after the Korean War halted, Secretary of State Dean Acheson gave this answer: "Never has fate been secreted in so unlikely a receptacle." Reviewing recent history, Acheson wondered: How could so much in world affairs depend on what happened in Korea?[3] More than half a century later, in a world more closely interdependent than ever, a smile or a grimace in Korea reverberates far and wide.

"Location, Location, Location"—in a Tough Neighborhood

Size is not everything. But in world affairs, as in real estate, value is often shaped by location. Korea is the hub of security concerns in Northeast Asia and beyond—a crossroads for commerce but also a cauldron for war. A map of the peninsula shows a potential dagger pointed at Japan, China, and Russia. Indeed, Koreans at times have ruled Manchuria, but they have seldom encroached on their neighbors. Instead, outsiders—Chinese, Japanese, Mongols, Manchus, Russians, Americans—have taken turns trying to dominate Korea. As CIA analysts put it: "Victimized by its strategic location throughout history," Korea has been and continues to be "the scene of competition for dominant influence by its powerful neighbors."[4]

Proximity counts. As a Chinese general noted: "China and Korea are separated by only a river. They depend on each other like lips and teeth. What concerns one concerns also the other. The security of China is closely connected with the survival of Korea."[5] China, followed by Japan, sought hegemony over Korea and exclusion of other external influences. Japanese forces left in 1945, but Japanese interest in Korea remained. An early Japanese version of *Encarta* had 216 articles on Korea—compared to just 46 in the U.S. edition.[6] A single comic book on North Korea's "dear leader" Kim Jong Il (portrayed as a depraved despot) published in Japan in 2003 sold half a million copies in a few months—probably more than all the books ever published on Korea in English.[7]

Patterns in U.S. Policy toward Northeast Asia

How has the United States responded to the challenges and opportunities in Northeast Asia? Despite long distances and dangers, Americans have engaged in trade and in mortal combat with Koreans for nearly two centuries. U.S. actions and inaction were inspired by what policy-makers conceived to be the realities of power—bolstered by pressures from firms hoping for business in Asia. For most of America's aspiring realists and merchants, however, Korea was less important than its neighbors. Washington readily sacrificed Korea to America's larger concerns with Japan and, later, with the USSR. American officials paid little heed to U.S. diplomats, missionaries, and educators in Korea wishing to preserve its independence.

Some of America's first encounters with Korea were violent. As we shall see in Chapter 3, a privately owned gunboat in 1866 and a U.S. naval flotilla in 1871 sought to "open" Korea to commerce. Despite these bloody encounters, Korean leaders were soon looking to the United States for help in modernizing and protecting their country. As Japan took over Korea, however, official Washington turned a blind eye. No president spoke publicly of Korea from 1911 to 1942. When the Japanese departed in 1945, one Korea became two—divided north and south—in part because Washington did little to foster a free and independent Korea. The outbreak of the Korean War in June 1950 soon changed all that. President Harry Truman and his secretary of state saw Korea as a battleground between the free world and the communist. For some observers, Korea became a test of collective security; for others, the first in a string of unwinnable wars pointlessly chosen by U.S. presidents.

Despite an armistice in 1953, more than half a century passed with no formal peace agreement between the belligerents in the Korean War. Instead, U.S. and ROK troops confronted DPRK forces along Korea's demilitarized zone (DMZ). The presence of U.S. troops in Korea reassured some South Koreans but angered others. Some South Koreans wanted closer ties with China to counter U.S. influences. North Korea's leaders usually demanded withdrawal of U.S. troops from the Korean peninsula but on occasion allowed that American forces might stay. A near constant in DPRK policy was a quest for normalized ties with the United States. One motive was to offset China's heavy presence. "It would be good for the United States," a visitor to Pyongyang was told, to have North Korea "as a buffer state in this dangerous area. Who knows, perhaps there are ways in which the United States could benefit from our ports and our intelligence if we become friends."[8]

Following some brief respites in the 1990s, tensions flared again in the early twenty-first century as North Korea moved to join the nuclear weapons club. Washington worried not only that Pyongyang might acquire the means to destroy portions of South Korea, Japan, and North America, but also that DPRK actions would encourage Iran, Japan, and other states to go nuclear. It might also sell nuclear materials and know-how to aspiring terrorists.

As Washington applied more muscle, Pyongyang resisted. In May 2009 the ROK became the ninety-fifth country to join the U.S.-led Proliferation Security Initiative (PSI), aimed at stopping the trafficking of weapons of mass destruction. In response, the Korean People's Army (KPA) Mission to Pyongyang challenged the validity of the 1953 armistice. The KPA asserted that "the Lee group of traitors" in Seoul, "steeped in sycophancy and submission to the marrow of its

Box 1.2 First Impressions of North Korea and the World

December 12, 1952. Soviet troops patrolled their zone not far from central Vienna, where Jean-Paul Sartre gave the opening address to the World Congress of the Peoples for Peace. Sartre later called the congress one of the three experiences in his life that gave him hope.[9] For me, a nineteen-year-old foreign student with a press pass, the congress provided my first opportunity to meet people from Asia and Africa. Drawing on my high school French, I translated for Vietnamese anxious to tell English-speakers about their national liberation struggle. We saw a North Korean film purporting to expose U.S. germ warfare—rats stuffed into canisters dropped from airplanes by American soldiers whose huge noses outdid some stereotypes. The propaganda was primitive but persuasive for many viewers. Later I had dinner with some Japanese students. They were slim and ate little, they said, because of tight budgets in Japan. Nevertheless, they sold their blood every month for U.S. soldiers wounded in Korea. The grand finale of the congress helped me appreciate groupthink. When more than a thousand delegates applauded anti-U.S. slogans, I could barely resist joining the crowd even though I disbelieved and disagreed. I described all this in essays mailed to my hometown paper, the Cincinnati *Times-Star.* I suggested that the United States take part in such congresses to make its position known, but my thoughts went unpublished.

Meanwhile, some of my peers were fighting in Korea, while I held a student deferment. More than half a century later, I still see a few of them bearing scars from their time in Korea. One has a bumper sticker reading: "The Chosin Few"—named for a reservoir where U.S. troops defied a much larger Chinese force in late 1950 before retreating. Their experiences in the early 1950s were less uplifting than Sartre's. My year in Vienna, however—including some close encounters with Soviet troops—gave a new direction to my life and pushed me to learn Russian.

Of course, the war changed things for millions. The author of *Angela's Ashes,* Frank McCourt, thanked Mao Zedong for an education. After China joined the fray, McCourt left his job sweeping the lobby of the Biltmore Hotel to join the U.S. Army and later used the G.I. Bill to get into college without a high school diploma.[10]

bones," blindly yielded to its U.S. master. As a result, the KPA would "regard any hostile actions against the DPRK, including checkup and inspection of its peaceful vessels, as an unpardonable encroachment on the DPRK's sovereignty and counter them with prompt and strong military strikes." The KPA "will not be bound to the Armistice Agreement (AA) any longer since the present ruling quarters of the United States, keen on the moves to stifle the DPRK, plugged the south Korean puppets into the PSI at last, denying not only international law but the AA itself and discarding even its responsibility as a signatory to the agreement." Waffling on its position, however, the KPA also said that "*in case* the AA loses its binding force, the Korean Peninsula is bound to immediately return to a state of war from a legal point of view and so our revolutionary armed forces will go over to corresponding military actions." Hence, *"for the present,"* the KPA would not "guarantee the legal status of the five islands under the south side's control ... in our side's territorial waters ... and safe sailing of warships of the U.S. imperialist aggression forces and the south Korean puppet navy and civilian ships operating in the waters around there." The KPA concluded: "Those who provoke the DPRK once will not be able to escape its unimaginable and merciless punishment" (emphases added).[11]

Of course, we cannot evaluate diplomacy in a vacuum. Diplomacy must be studied in the context of the policies it serves. Thus, arms control negotiations may seek to reduce the danger of war, save money, and limit damage if war erupts. But if policy-makers do not *want* an accord, negotiators do not *fail* if they reach no agreement. Their assigned task may have been to buy time by dragging out the talks or merely to save face and embarrass the other side. In this spirit, Vladimir Lenin portrayed disarmament diplomacy as a way to defend the Soviet state and to spread revolution by other means.[12]

Some neorealists say that nuclear spread is inevitable and desirable, because nobody attacks a nuclear power. Furthermore, they say, any dangers from proliferating nukes can be managed. No matter how North Korea's leaders sometimes appear, they do not want to perish in a nuclear exchange.

Arms controllers object that the emergence of any additional actor equipped with nuclear weapons raises the danger that nuclear arms will be used—whether by an accident, by a miscalculation, or by a madman. Nuclear spread can be stopped and even reversed. South Africa, Kazakhstan, Ukraine, and Belarus have given up nuclear arms. Iraq was disarmed by force. Libya surrendered its nuclear plant in a grand bargain. Other states such as South Korea, Taiwan, and Japan have abjured nuclear arms, despite their ability to produce them. Arms controllers hope that North Korea will also renounce and eliminate its nuclear weapons and capacity.

How can we get past mutual recrimination to a real peace in Korea? As the Barack Obama administration succeeded that of George W. Bush, most security experts agreed that it was important to resolve U.S.–North Korean differences without war. None doubted it would be difficult to do so. Negotiations to control and perhaps eliminate North Korea's weapons of mass destruction appeared to achieve positive results in the mid- and late 1990s under the Bill Clinton administration. The collapse of the U.S.–North Korean accords in the first term of President George W. Bush posed serious dangers. In Bush's second term, however, glimmers of hope returned. The two main protagonists and their four negotiating partners gravitated toward a broad accommodation, though every one or two steps forward were often followed by one or two steps back. Nonetheless, several confrontations gave way to limited détentes and even to some elements of an entente. Our investigation here asks how this happened, how it affected the deep interests of each side, and what the lessons are (if any) for foreign policy making and the arts of diplomacy and negotiation.

Get to Yes, but How?

The perennial best seller *Getting to Yes* by Roger Fisher and William Ury offers a roadmap to negotiating mutually advantageous deals "without giving in."[13] But can its recommendations apply to life-and-death confrontations such as those among North Korea, its neighbors, and the distant superpower? Fisher and Ury disparage "positional bargaining" because it can obscure the deepest interests of each participant.[14] The authors recommend instead that each side focus on its own deep interests *and* on those of the other side. Each party needs to understand how the conflict looks from the other's vantage point. If disagreements remain, Fisher and Ury recommend "principled negotiation"—an objective examination of the case based on the *principles* at stake. This makes sense for a boundary dispute arising from a new curve in a river formerly divided down the middle. *But what if each party starts from a very different principle?* What if one side seeks to prevent the entry of more powers into the nuclear weapons club while other actors demand weapons "equality"? What if one side pursues regime change and the other looks for stability? What if one side presses for political and civil liberties while the other sees "order" as fundamental?

Negotiators may try to *claim* values (utilities of any sort) or to *create* values useful to each party.[15] Value-claiming is a *distributive* competition for larger shares of a limited supply of goods, whereas value-creating is *integrative* bargaining to expand supply. These alternatives generate three approaches to negotiation. Hard-line unilateralists see politics as a zero-sum contest in which one side wins and the other loses. Win-win optimists expect positive rewards for all parties. Conditional cooperators try to create values for mutual gain but take precautions lest others fail to reciprocate.[16] Value-creators see most situations as open-ended—variable sum. This means that one or even both sides can lose (as in a nuclear war) but that there is also a possibility—though no inevitability—of joint gains.

So they look for ways to expand the pie to generate positive outcomes for each party. Unilateral gains are sometimes possible but are likely to be short-lived, whereas mutual gains are more likely to endure. Compare, for example, the results of the 1919 Versailles Treaty and the 1947 Marshall Plan. Conditional cooperation and value-creating helped to improve U.S.-Soviet and U.S.-Chinese relations. We shall ask whether this approach can help resolve differences with North Korea and benefit all stakeholders.

Implications of Interdependence and Complexity

A wise policy must take account of growing interdependence across borders. Mutual dependence signifies mutual vulnerability—a relationship so close that moves by any party can harm or help the other. The realities of global interdependence reinforce the logic of a strategy aimed at creating values for all parties.

Interdependence is rarely symmetrical. North Korea occupies slightly more space than South Korea but possesses less than half the ROK population and just a fraction of its gross domestic product. The DPRK is far smaller and weaker than any of its other negotiating partners—the United States, China, Russia, and Japan. Nevertheless, the DPRK and each of these parties share not only vulnerabilities but also a potential for mutual gain. Such asymmetries are not unique. Actors on the global stage are seldom equal. Even the U.S. and USSR "superpowers" had very different assets and liabilities. One was more than twice as rich; the other, twice as large. Nevertheless, Washington and Moscow recognized their shared needs and the utility of collaborating in many realms.[17]

In our world of escalating interdependencies, an effective foreign policy needs to follow three axioms. First, those who make and carry out policy must develop and apply a "smart" mix of hard and soft power plus conversion power—the ability to apply hard and soft power effectively.[18]

Second, each actor's deepest interests are more likely to be advanced by policies meant to create mutual gain rather than achieve unilateral gain. Exploiting others may achieve short-term gains but will tend to boomerang over time so that the costs outweigh the benefits. The time in which exploitation could pay becomes ever shorter, thanks to modern communications and interdependence. Evolution shows that the capacity to cooperate is vital for species fitness.

Of course, a mutual gain strategy requires reciprocity. If any actor merely pockets the other's concessions and then asks for more, value-creating will be a losing strategy.[19] How to induce reciprocity in relations between longtime antagonists, quite different in asset and outlook, is explored in the chapters that follow.

Third, the more that all actors communicate with each other and with their own publics, the greater is the prospect of finding solutions useful to all sides. The most successful U.S. foreign endeavor of all time, the Marshall Plan, was planned, organized, and conducted in full view. Both its inputs and outputs were mutual. The fuller is the public discussion of policy (based on *accurate* information); the lower is the danger of counterproductive adventures such as the Iraq war. For a dictatorship, open discussion of the facts and policy alternatives may not be feasible, but even an authoritarian regime can profit from sharing its objectives, assets, and needs with foreign interlocutors. Without shared knowledge of each side's desiderata, their optimal accommodation is unlikely.

The prospects for better mutual understanding are improved by the fact that in today's world countries communicate not only through their government officials but also through their unofficial representatives—rock stars, basketball players, evangelists, au pairs, bloggers, and ordinary tourists. We have not only Track 1 diplomacy, meaning official diplomacy between governments, but also Track 2, or "private citizen," diplomacy. With North Korea we have also Track 1½ diplomacy conducted by private or semiprivate citizens. Thus, representatives of the Nautilus Institute have discussed energy issues with North Korean specialists while U.S. officials have observed and taken notes.[20] President Barack Obama's choice as U.S. special representative for North Korea policy, Stephen W. Bosworth, visited the country along with other scholars just before his appointment in February 2009.

The many forms of diplomacy now available contribute to a major hope for peace—relationships of complex interdependence. Although interdependence could exist in just one area of vulnerability (e.g., nuclear deterrence), *complex* interdependence is marked by three features. First, the parties interact on many levels—not just at the summit. Second, their agendas touch many shared concerns with no clear hierarchy. Third, given these linkages, discord over any particular agenda item or items could never give rise to war. Where complex interdependence is strong, as in today's Europe, violence as a way to resolve disputes becomes unthinkable.[21] The ROK "Sunshine Policy," initiated in the late 1990s, aimed to create such relationships with the DPRK but encountered many obstacles.

An understanding of interdependence combined with insights about complex systems could contribute to a new paradigm for social studies more useful than realism or idealism with all their "neo" variants.[22] The fledgling science of complex systems suggests that every society's well-being—its overall fitness—depends on its ability to cooperate as well as compete. To sustain life-support networks, humans need to collaborate—not free ride or otherwise exploit one another. Harnessing complex interdependence can make participants stronger than the sum of their parts. Their interlocking ties can resemble a coral reef where diverse life forms find mutual protection in a sustainable ecosystem.[23] Self-organization and self-healing are processes found in nature that can also be nourished and enhanced by humans.[24]

These truths are evident within the European Union (EU) and in U.S. relations with Canada. U.S. and Chinese officials also recognize the growing interdependence of their countries. Their cooperation existed only as a thought experiment in the 1960s. A decade or two later, it became a reality. Between the United States and the DPRK, meaningful cooperation now exists only as mental image—a vision that could push policy in one direction or another.

Each actor in Northeast Asia can utilize interdependence to seek unilateral advantage or mutual gain. If the Korean peninsula became a zone of peace, it could radiate economic benefits in all azimuths. The industrial South could utilize some of the North's mineral riches, whereas the North could benefit from the South's agriculture and technology. All Koreans as well as Japanese, Chinese, and Russians could gain if the oil and gas riches of Siberia could flow freely down the peninsula instead of being first loaded on and then unloaded off heavy ships. Railroad links between Pacific ports and those of inland Russia could be improved. Higher levels of prosperity and human development across Northeast Asia could be reached if political conditions encouraged investment, education, and commerce. No country needs such conditions more than North Korea, where the "military-first" policy shortchanged every other aspect of life.

Détente in Northeast Asia would make regional integration far easier. Protection of rare and threatened species—whooping cranes and fishes—could be facilitated.[25] North Korea's disciplined labor force could become another ingredient in lowering production costs for multinational firms—while raising living standards in the North. These and other alternative futures are noted in later chapters. Worst-case as well as win-win scenarios are also discussed. For example, a nuclear-armed North Korea could trigger an Asian arms race and war. If the lessons of recent history are absorbed by all sides, however, the prospects for achieving mutual gain may improve. Whatever we learn about negotiating with North Korea may have broader implications. Hostile antagonists around the globe need to learn how to manage their differences, create mutual gain, and convert swords into plowshares.

Caveat lector: Any study of foreign affairs must recognize the limitations on what we can know and understand. Outsiders may think they see alternations in North Korea's policies akin to movements in a Beethoven symphony—allegro to andante and scherzo leading attacca to a grand finale. But the realities of North Korea are complex, more like a Bach concerto with constant point and counterpoint. For Bach, melody, harmony, and counterpoint intertwine so that a listener can hardly know where one leaves off and the other takes off. So, too, could North Korea sell missiles to Libya in 2000 at the same time it offered to curtail missile development and proliferation. Some DPRK "counterpoint" was planned and orchestrated; some resulted from decisions by diverse actors; some arose from momentum or coincidence.

Individual actors and their interactions are difficult to penetrate—even in one's own circle or in well-reported Washington. This difficulty is magnified several times when we study a rather closed society. Decades after Stalin's demise, his rule does not appear so monolithic as it once did. We discover fractures within his system and contradictions within his policies. Over time we learn of similar complexities in "Stalinist" North Korea. Whatever is written about North Korea and the world in one decade will need to be reevaluated in future years. But this is so in most fields, including medicine. When a problem is as critical as North Korea, we must seek to understand what we can and then act with greater wisdom.

CHAPTER TWO

HOW KOREA BECAME KOREA

Korea's history, stretching back more than four millennia, anticipates many of the conflicts and opportunities confronting policy-makers and diplomats in the twenty-first century. Facing powerful neighbors on all sides, the smaller fish, to survive among sharks, often tried to play one against the other. The techniques by which Koreans manipulated both adversaries and nominal allies emerged from centuries of life-and-death struggles.

Even though Koreans have long constituted one of the world's most homogeneous peoples, with distinct culture and a unique language, they have often been at war among themselves.[1] Usually they labored under top-down, authoritarian rule. After the Japanese withdrew in 1945, Koreans in the north endured a harsh communist dictatorship. Their "brothers" in the south lived under authoritarian rule for decades but, starting in the late 1980s, came to know the push and pull of free elections.

Two Koreas in Comparative Perspective

Korea is neither a small city-state, like Hong Kong, nor a vast empire, like China or Russia. Divided since 1945, the Korean peninsula is home to two medium-sized states. The Republic of Korea (ROK, or South Korea) was founded on August 15, 1948; the Democratic People's Republic of Korea (DPRK, or North Korea), on September 9, 1948. Early in the twenty-first century, the South had nearly 50 million people living in an area a bit larger than Indiana—38,000 square miles, with a coastline of 1,500 miles. The North had just under 24 million people inhabiting 46,540 square miles—nearly as much land as Nebraska, with a coastline of 1,551 miles. Thus, the North had less than half the South's population but occupied a somewhat larger territory with a slightly larger coastline. The North is more mountainous and less arable than the South.

Analyses by the United Nations and several nongovernmental organizations put the two Koreas in comparative perspective. The United Nations Development Programme Human Development Index (HDI) aggregates ratings on income, public health, and education. As we see in Table 2.1, the ROK ranked twenty-sixth in the world in 2007 on the HDI, just behind Singapore and ahead of Slovenia, whereas China ranked eighty-first, behind Armenia and just above Peru. The ROK in 2007 moved up two places from 2005; China, four places. Still closed to outside scrutiny, the DPRK was not listed at all.[2] Adult literacy in the ROK reached 98 percent in 2007 (much higher than in the United States), with 96 percent of young South Koreans attending school or college. If modernization correlates with infertility, South Korea is a world leader. In 2007 and again in 2008, the country experienced one of the world's lowest birthrates—an average 1.2 babies per woman, down from 1.6 in the 1990s and well below replacement level of plus 2. Per capita gross domestic product (GDP) in the South was about $22,000 in 2007—probably thirty to fifty times higher than in the North. Even though the U.S. GDP per capita was nearly twice that of South Korea, the ROK achieved more with its money for human development than did the United States.[3] Life expectancy in the ROK reached 77.9 years in 2007 (tied with the United States, though well below world leader Japan, at 82.3).

In the North, life expectancy was at least eleven years less than in the South—68.8 years by UN estimates, with an under-five mortality rate of 55 per 1,000 (compared to 257 in Afghanistan). In the early twenty-first century at least one-third of the DPRK population was undernourished (compared to half in Liberia). Malnutrition left one-fourth of young men in the North too mentally retarded to be accepted for military service. North Korean teenage boys were five inches shorter and twenty-five pounds lighter than their South Korean peers.[4]

Unlike the relatively vibrant ROK, the DPRK state by 2010 was close to collapse. In 2008 the Fund for Peace placed North Korea seventeenth in the world

Table 2.1 Human Development Index 2007 Rankings

1	Iceland
8	Japan
12	United States
21	Hong Kong
25	Singapore
26	ROK
[26?]	[Taiwan?]*
67	Russian Federation
81	China
128	India
[185?]	[DPRK?]*

Source: http://hdr.undp.org/en/statistics/, accessed June 10, 2009.
*Bracketed references to Taiwan and the DPRK are author's estimates. Neither Taiwan nor the DPRK is ranked by the United Nations Development Programme.

on the failed state index—just behind Ethiopia and ahead of Bangladesh. (With a deeply fractured Somalia topping the index, North Korea's public services and key institutions—leadership, military, police, judiciary, and civil service—were graded "poor.") Health care was free, but the health care system was understaffed and lacked sufficient resources. Only 59 percent of the population had access to improved sanitation, and 17.7 million lacked electricity. Infrastructures were old and poorly maintained.[5]

After decades of authoritarian rule, the ROK moved quickly toward political freedom in the 1990s. On civil liberties, however, it lagged behind the United States and some other Western countries. Table 2.2 shows their ratings. Meanwhile, the DPRK remained a leader in political repression. All candidates for office were nominated by the ruling party, which also held all seats in the legislative assembly. Human rights abuses were pervasive—state-sponsored torture, starvation, rape, murder, medical experimentation, forced labor, forced abortions in prisons, extrajudicial killings, public executions, and arbitrary detention. Every aspect of society was under state control. All citizens were classified into groups based on the family's perceived loyalty to the regime.

In the first decade of the second millennium, the DPRK gulag contained some two hundred thousand people, confined to political prison camps for arbitrary reasons and without due process of law. "Not only are they imprisoned in unspeakable conditions—fed starvation-level rations, forced to labor under brutal conditions, and subject to torture and execution for trivial offenses—but so are their relatives, including the elderly and children, under a three-generation

Table 2.2 Political Freedom Index 2008 by Freedom House*

	Political Rights	Civil Liberties
United States	1	1
Japan	1	2
ROK	1	2
Taiwan	2	1
India	2	3
Hong Kong	5	2
Singapore	5	4
Russia	6	5
China	7	6
DPRK	7	7

Source: http://www.freedomhouse.org/template.cfm?page=25&year=2008, accessed June 10, 2009.
*Ranked from 1 to 7.

guilt-by-association system instituted by North Korea's founder, Kim Il Sung."[6] Entire families suffered if one family member was suspected of dissent. The regime was close to committing democide—mass murder of its own people.

Kim Il Sung was thought to tolerate Christian practices so long they did not challenge or interfere with his policies. But in 2009 reports increased of the DPRK state persecuting individuals and their families for owning a Bible. One report said a woman was publicly executed for distributing Bibles. The rulers in Pyongyang, as in Beijing, seemed to fear any potential rival organization or way of thought. DPRK citizens were schooled to worship Kim Il Sung and Kim Jong Il at home and in public. Outsiders estimated that, despite persecution, some thirty thousand North Koreans practiced Christianity secretly in their homes.[7]

Due to heavy government support for business conglomerates (*chaebŏls*), South Korea placed only forty-first in the world in economic freedom (see Table 2.3), but North Korea placed at the bottom. In South Korea, most *chaebŏls* were family owned, but the entire North was controlled if not owned by one patriarchy. Bloodlines and proximity to elites in Pyongyang determined who got what to eat in North Korea. Faced with famine in the mid-1990s, the regime instituted what it called the "Arduous March." Under this rubric, the regime let ordinary citizens fend for themselves. Relaxed rules helped people to survive but in a much loosened social order. Desperate and disillusioned, defectors mounted in number nearly every year (two-thirds of them women). Some members of the power elite, including Hwang Jang Yop, a regime ideologue, defected, whereas others were purged and not seen again. Four years after his father's passing, Kim Jong Il in 1998 promulgated a new constitution with power centered in the National Defense Commission, which he chaired. Hoping for hope, the regime in 1998 designated 2012 the "Year of Opening the Door to a Strong, Prosperous Great Nation." On October 12, 2000—the fifty-fifth anniversary of the founding of the Workers' Party of Korea—the regime staged "a grand proud festival of victors who have overcome the unprecedented 'arduous march.'"

But the country still needed a solution to what the regime called the "livelihood problem." On July 1, 2002, the regime proclaimed a new economic management improvement policy. The "7.1. Policy," as it was called, resembled the New Economic Policy that had restored economic life in the USSR from 1921 to 1928. The 7.1 Policy legalized from above the changes already coming from below—an increase in prices and wages, business decentralization, and markets.[8]

Worried that 7.1 fueled social deviation and fanned individualism, the regime became unnerved. Beginning in 2004–2005, it tried to change course and stamp out the beginnings of self-organization.[9] Like Josef Stalin's regime in 1928, the DPRK leadership began to constrict and even ban most elements of free enterprise. The effect of these restrictions was, by 2009, to reduce cash income for most North Koreans by one-third or even one-half. Apparently indifferent to human suffering, the regime also took steps sure to reduce foreign food aid. Pyongyang rolled back the UN World Food Programme's (WFP) capacity to monitor where international food aid was distributed and who received it. Pyongyang slashed the WFP's geographical reach inside North Korea, cutting the number of counties where it could operate from 131 to 57. In spring 2009 the regime abruptly canceled a deal to accept hundreds of thousands of tons of food aid from the U.S. government delivered by the WFP and five American aid agencies. The cuts came

Table 2.3 Economic Freedom Index 2008 by the Heritage Foundation

Hong Kong	1
Singapore	2
United States	5
Japan	17
Taiwan	25
ROK	41
India	115
China	126
Russia	134
DPRK	157

Source: http://www.heritage.org/Index/, accessed June 10, 2009.

during a year when the WFP estimated that 37 percent of North Koreans would need food aid. WFP officials said they were able to deliver about one-tenth of the 45,000 tons of food a month needed to avert severe malnutrition.[10] The regime also changed the rules for monitoring UN food distribution, demanding seven days' notice before it would permit WFP monitors to inspect a food warehouse or distribution site—in contrast to 2008, when DPRK authorities agreed to 24 hours' notice. In June 2009 Pyongyang ordered the WFP and the UN Children's Fund out of Ryanggang Province, one of the poorest parts of North Korea, with traditionally high rates of underweight and stunted infants.[11] Military service used to be a way to get three or at least two meals a day. By 2009 only the upper ranks in the Korean People's Army had such assurance.

When food shortages loomed in the USSR, Nikita Khrushchev and his successors did what they could to produce more food and/or buy it. By contrast, official DPRK attitudes toward mass hunger resembled those of Stalin and Mao Zedong. Kim Jong Il may have sought to bolster his regime's security, but his policies looked almost calculated to inflict a death blow on a comatose system. This was not his intent, however, and the Dear Leader made a show of visiting factories, farms, and military bases in spring and summer 2009, even though his own face and body looked gaunt and frail.

Despite its mediocre rating on economic freedom, South Korea was deemed to be the eleventh most competitive economy in the world—ahead of Hong Kong and Taiwan (see Table 2.4). Some potential investors worried about the potential dangers from the North—an influx of migrants or a military clash—but the South Korean stock market rose and fell with little correlation to developments in the North.

One reason for South Korea's high competitiveness rank was its high networked readiness—also ahead of Hong Kong and Taiwan (see Table 2.5). The ROK tapped the self-organizing resources of the Internet—highly censored in China and off limits to most North Koreans. While authorities in Seoul tried to narrow the urban-rural digital divide, however, experience showed that "wiring" the countryside brought negative as well as positive impacts to rural communities.[12]

On the negative side, Table 2.6 shows South Korea ranked only thirty-fourth in perceived honesty—no better than Taiwan and far below Singapore and Hong Kong. The country's low rank for honesty is linked to its even lower ranking for economic freedom (forty-first). Where politics depends on business and vice versa, the incentives and opportunities for corruption run deep. Two former

Table 2.4 Global Competitiveness Rankings 2007–2008 by the World Economic Forum

United States	1
Singapore	7
Japan	8
ROK	11
Hong Kong	12
Taiwan	14
China	34
India	48
Russia	58
DPRK	[120?]

Source: http://www.weforum.org/pdf/Global_Competitiveness_Reports/Reports/gcr_2007/gcr2007_rankings.pdf, accessed June 10, 2009.

ROK presidents, Chun Doo-hwan and Roh Tae-woo, were imprisoned in the 1990s for collecting millions of dollars from *chaebŏls*. Likely to be indicted for soliciting $6 million for himself and his relations, Roh Moo-hyun, ROK president from 2002 to 2008, committed suicide in 2009. As we see in Chapter 8, a top Hyundai executive committed suicide in 2003 after exposure of his role in bribing Kim Jong Il to host a summit with Kim Dae Jung in 2000.[13]

Given that the DPRK regime is a kind of cult-based family business interdependent with a network of cronies (similar to Saddam Hussein's regime), corruption is pervasive. Apart from the sale of missile technology, the North's

Table 2.5 Networked Readiness Rankings 2007–2008 by the World Economic Forum

Denmark	1
United States	4
Singapore	5
ROK	9
Hong Kong	11
Taiwan	17
China	17
Japan	19
India	50
Russia	72
DPRK	[120?]

Source: http://www.weforum.org/pdf/gitr/2008/Rankings.pdf, accessed June 10, 2009.

major sources of foreign income have been drug trafficking and counterfeiting—altogether bringing in more than $1 billion a year in the early 2000s.[14] A Macao bank said to have laundered illicit earnings of DPRK firms was blacklisted by the U.S. Treasury in 2005, but South Korean sources charged in 2009 that North Korea still maintained some twenty accounts in China and Switzerland for its counterfeiting and other illegal transactions. Wishing to hide corruption as well as economic and military weaknesses, Pyongyang resisted outside demands for greater transparency. Meanwhile, North Korea in the 1990s and early twenty-first century experienced a breakdown in public order and a sharp increase in crime and corruption at all levels.[15]

South Korea is a relatively fit society. It enjoys a high ranking in most domains except in economic freedom and business integrity. The DPRK places close to the bottom in all dimensions where data are available. Its shortfalls do not facilitate negotiations. Whereas a fit country can afford to make some concessions and even some mistakes, an impoverished and beleaguered country has little margin for error. The Pyongyang regime has cause to be defensive—a point made manifest in Table 2.7.

Although South Korea placed fairly high on global measures of development, it did much less well in 2008 when compared against twenty-nine other industrial democracies. The Bertelsmann Foundation assessed indicators of "sustainable

Table 2.6 Honesty Rankings 2007 by Transparency International

	World Ranking	Perceived Honesty Rating*
Denmark	1	9.4
Singapore	4	9.3
Hong Kong	14	8.3
Japan	17	7.5
United States	20	7.2
Taiwan	34	6.7
ROK	34	5.1
China	72	3.5
India	72	3.5
Russia	143	2.3
DPRK		No info.

Source: http://www.transparency.org/policy_research/surveys_indices/cpi/2007, accessed June 10, 2009.
*10 best to 1 worst.

Table 2.7 Composite Rankings of Korea, Its Neighbors, and the United States

HDI	Political Freedom	Economic Freedom	Competitiveness	Networked Readiness	Honesty
Japan	United States	Hong Kong	United States	United States	Singapore
United States	Japan	Singapore	Singapore	Singapore	Hong Kong
Hong Kong	ROK	United States	Japan	ROK	Japan
Singapore	Taiwan	Japan	ROK	Hong Kong	United States
ROK	India	Taiwan	Hong Kong	Taiwan	Taiwan
[Taiwan?]	Hong Kong	ROK	Taiwan	China	ROK
Russia	Singapore	India	China	Japan	China
China	Russia	China	India	India	India
India	China	Russia	Russia	Russia	Russia
DPRK	DPRK	DPRK	DPRK	DPRK	DPRK

Source: Compiled from Tables 2.1–2.6.

governance" for each member of the Organization for Economic Cooperation and Development (OECD). As of early 2008, South Korea placed well below average—twenty-fourth of thirty countries. Of course, South Korea started from a much lower base than the higher ranked countries. At the top came Norway, the United States ranked fifteenth, Japan ranked twenty-second, and Mexico and Turkey placed last. The study found that as President Roh's administration ended, democratic norms and social policy were faltering. On the positive side, a nuanced awareness of reform issues aided attempts in the Roh administration to foster institutional learning. South Korea's management performance was average (seventeenth) in the OECD. Prodigious R&D investments braced the outlook for sustainability. For better or worse, the incoming Lee administration was expected to turn away from Roh's emphasis on social justice and shift back toward the earlier priority on fast growth with distribution later.[16]

One last comparison: Measures of "happiness" in South Korea on a scale from 1 (not at all happy) to 4 (very happy) showed the strongest upward trend of twenty-four countries surveyed by the University of Michigan—from 2 in 1980 to nearly 3.2 in 2005—nearly as high as in affluent Finland. Again, South Korea started from a lower base than most of the countries surveyed. The trend might be interpreted to mean that happiness grew along with per capita income, but happiness among comparatively poor Mexicans rose from 3 to 3.4 in the same period and among Indians, from 2.7 to above 3.[17] Judging by interviews with defectors and other data, levels of happiness in North Korea probably ranked among the world's lowest.

All these rankings must be taken with a grain of salt, but the variables they attempt to measure form part of the context in which negotiations take place on arms control and other issues. Having surveyed some not-so-tangible features of both Koreas, let us review some crucial tangibles while keeping in mind that many defectors from the North found themselves alone and miserable amid the individualist ways of the South.

Borders and Resources

A unified Korea would be a medium-large state with a population less than that of Germany but slightly larger than that of Turkey and much larger than that of the United Kingdom, France, or Italy. By 2000 the ROK was the seventh major trading partner of the United States, generating nearly half as much value as U.S.

trade with much larger China. By 2006 the ROK had slipped to eighth place, but it accounted for more trade on a per capita basis than most U.S. trading partners.[18] Meanwhile, China became the ROK's major trading partner. South Korea in 2007 and 2008 became the world's largest arms importer, as it stocked up with American weapons in response to its increasingly belligerent neighbor, the DPRK.[19] Pyongyang wanted Russia to update the DPRK arsenal, but Moscow demanded cash payments that the North could or would not provide.

The 600-mile-long Korean peninsula is bounded by water—to the east, the East Sea (or Sea of Japan); to the south, the Korea Strait; to the west, the Yellow (or Western) Sea and Korea Bay. The border with China runs along the 491-mile Yalu (Korean *Aprok* or phonetically *Apnok*) River and the 324-mile Tumen (Korean *Duman*) River. Both the rivers originate near Mount Paektu, a still disputed territory where Chinese and DPRK soldiers fought each other in 1969. The mountain (a volcano with a large crater lake) is sacred to all Koreans, but especially to the ruling dynasty in Pyongyang. For the DPRK, it is the "sacred mountain of the revolution"—site of guerrilla exploits led by Kim Il Sung in the 1930s. DPRK legend says that Kim Jong Il was born in a guerrilla camp on Paektu in February 1942—not, as outside historians say, in a military camp near Khabarovsk in the Russian Far East, where his father served in the Red Army. Countless pilgrims visit what guides say is the exact spot of Kim Jong Il's birth.

The last eleven miles of the Tumen form Korea's border with Russia before the river enters the East Sea. North Koreans fleeing to China attempt to cross the Tumen. But refugees seldom cross the Tumen into Russia because that government patrols its stretch of the river more actively than China does, and the refugees have no large ethnic Korean community in which to hide. Russian and DPRK control of these eleven miles could block Chinese access to the East Sea, although neither Moscow nor Pyongyang has ever done so. Since 1949 Beijing and Pyongyang have agreed on joint management of the two rivers and China has conceded most Yalu and Tumen islands to North Korea, but many points of control and ownership are still disputed. Pyongyang's declaration in 1977 of an economic and fishing exclusion zone of 200 miles off the coast of the Yellow Sea has generated another boundary dispute with Beijing. So long as the maritime border is disputed, it stalls economic development at the mouth of the Yalu.[20]

North and South Korea have clashed many times over their boundary in the Yellow (West) Sea. The Northern Limit Line into the sea established by the United Nations after the Korean War is respected by the ROK but challenged by the DPRK since 1999. The North wants fishing rights far below the armistice line. Ways forward could include creating a military-free joint fishing zone with an agreed code of conduct for fishing vessels operating there.[21] But several ROK-DPRK efforts at negotiation ended in rancor.

Another important river is the Taedong, some 248 miles long, which flows past Pyongyang into the Yellow Sea. Despite some reforms in the early 2000s, North Korea's development continued to suffer from a weak transportation system and inland logistics. An analysis of vessel movements at North Korean ports between 1985 and 2006 showed increased use of maritime transport to overcome inland blockages, but that evolution of port traffic reflected a general economic decline, a westward shift of population, and concentration of economic activities around Pyongyang.[22]

The Sino-Korean border has been changed a great deal over the centuries. The kingdom of Koguryo (37 BCE–CE 668) controlled Manchuria and the region around present-day Vladivostok. Koguryo's successor, the kingdom of Balhae (698–926) dominated Manchuria and the Liaodong peninsula. In the seventh century, however, China's Tang empire extended as far south as Seoul. North Korea's present borders with China correspond roughly with those of the Yuan empire (1279–1368).

Deforestation under Japanese rule—and since—has contributed to flooding, pollution, and other environmental problems in both North and South Korea.[23] One-third of the North's forests disappeared between 1995 and 2009.[24] But the peninsula houses great mineral wealth, most of it in the North. Of Korea's five major minerals—gold, iron ore, coal, tungsten, and graphite—only tungsten and graphite are found principally in the South. South Korea has only 10 percent of the peninsula's rich coal and iron deposits. Neither South nor North has oil or natural gas—a pressing need in modern times.

Chinese Legend and DPRK Mythology

Korea's past and present are illuminated but also distorted by legend—much of it inspired by Chinese sources. Works by Japanese, Russian, and other foreign authors with axes to grind add to the difficulty of understanding Korea. Even place-names reveal bias. What many outsiders call the Sea of Japan is for Koreans the East Sea. The deeper one plumbs, however, the stronger appear the indigenous roots. Many finds by Korean archeologists are not yet well known outside Korea. Confusions are compounded as North Korea's rulers adapt Chinese legends to legitimate dynastic rule in the DPRK.

One legend says that the first king to rule the "Dragon-Backed Land" of Korea was Dan Gun, son of the Spirit King and a "she-bear" who had mated at Mount Paektu. Dan Gun is said to have founded the first Chosôn Kingdom in 2333 BCE—the first year in Korea's traditional calendar—and reigned for one thousand years. Dan Gun taught a previously wild and untutored people all the arts of living, including how to make kimchee (fermented cabbage and spices). Pyongyang, his capital, was shaped like a boat. Because a boat will sink if a hole is bored into its bottom, it was "forbidden in those early times to dig wells inside this boat city. That it why the people there had to carry all their water a long way"[25]—a harbinger perhaps of hardships to come under Japanese and then under communist rule.

Kija is called the "Father of Korea." Legend says that Kija, a high official in China, was unhappy with the wicked emperor there and wanted to rule where people could live safely and in peace.[26] Kija crossed the "Duck Green River beneath the Ever-White Mountains [the Yalu]," bringing with him five thousand "good Chinese"—doctors, scholars, mechanics, carpenters, fortune-tellers, and magicians; also, the precious worms that spin silk, plus rice and barley. If so, Chinese influences became strong early in Korean life.[27] Kija founded a colony at Pyongyang in 1122 BCE and gave his subjects the Five Laws laying out their duties. Those were golden days when travelers were safe from robbers and gates could be left open.

Many historians doubt whether Kija ever existed. The story of Kija and his five thousand "good Chinese" may well have originated as Chinese propaganda, but today it has been adapted to fit North Korean mythology. The tale confirms the idea that a father figure has created a great dynasty. Thus, DPRK guides assert that Kija's tomb can still be seen near Pyongyang, where the founding father of today's DPRK, Kim Il Sung, reposes in a mausoleum much grander than that of Vladimir Lenin or Mao Zedong.

Korean kings wanted sons as successors and sometimes acquired them in strange ways. A legend told in the North but not in the South relates that one heir to the throne was conceived when the wind of a passing cloud placed an egg inside the dress of a royal wife. This boy's jealous brothers tried to kill him, but he fled south. He used magic to cross the dark-green waters of the River Aprok (Yalu) and then charm its waters to swallow up his pursuers. Later, this boy's name—Chosôn, "Light of the East," became the name of the entire country.

Perhaps these legends help explain why North Korea is the only communist country that has experienced a dynastic succession—father Kim Il Sung, son Kim Jong Il, followed perhaps by one of his children or relatives—and why these ostensible demigods can adorn themselves in superhuman superlatives even as they exploit and abuse their subjects.

Emergence in the Shadow of China

The first ruler of Korea recorded in contemporaneous records is Wiman, a Chinese or Chinese-born Korean, who seized power in the old Chosôn kingdom in 194 BCE. Chinese forces subsequently conquered the eastern half of the peninsula and made Lolang, near modern Pyongyang, the chief center of Chinese rule.

By the first century CE, a native Korean kingdom, Koguryo, arose on both sides of the Yalu River. By the fourth century CE, Koguryo conquered Lolang and occupied much of what is now Korea and northeastern China. But two rival kingdoms emerged in the south: Paekche in the west side of the peninsula and Silla in the east. Allied with Tang China, Silla conquered both Paekche and Koguryo by 668, and then expelled the Chinese and unified much of the peninsula. Under Silla's rule, Korea prospered and the arts flourished; Buddhism, which had entered Korea from China in the fourth century, became dominant in spiritual life. In 935, however, the Silla dynasty was overthrown by Wang Kon, founder of the Koryo dynasty (an abbreviated form of Koguryo and source of the name Korea). During the Koryo period, literature flourished and, even though Buddhism remained the state religion, China's Confucian bureaucracy became the model for Korean government.

As in China and Russia, Mongols dominated much of Korea in the thirteenth and fourteenth centuries. A Mongol-Koryo alliance lasted until 1392, when Taejo Yi Seong-gye, a general who favored the Mings (who replaced the Mongols in China) seized the throne and established the Chosôn (or Yi) dynasty. This dynasty endured from 1392 until 1910. It made Seoul the capital and changed the state religion from Buddhism to Confucianism. Allied with an army from Ming China, Chosôn drove back Japanese invaders in the 1590s. When Manchus replaced Mings in China, however, Chosôn was compelled in the seventeenth century to become a tributary state of Manchu China. In the eighteenth century, Chosôn experienced material prosperity and a cultural rebirth. Korea limited its foreign contacts during this period and resisted, longer than China or Japan, commerce and other influences from the West, which led to it being called the Hermit Kingdom.

Koreans imported much of their religion, science, and technology from China, but chafed at their dependency—an attitude that persisted in communist North Korea vis-à-vis China and Russia and in South Korea toward the United States. In the early twenty-first century, China became South Korea's leading trading partner even as it remained the North's main patron—unhappy that its client so often disobeyed.[28]

Confucianism and Risk-Taking in Korea

Confucianism became the state religion of Korea in the late fourteenth century. In the spirit of Max Weber,[29] political scientist and Asian scholar Lucian W. Pye pondered the impact of Confucianism on Korean culture. If Pye's analysis is correct, it helps us understand not only "how Korea became Korea" but also why Koreans—in the North and South—behave as they do. Reading Pye's analysis of centuries past, we must remember that Confucianism in Korea was not a static phenomenon. It changed over time and shared ideological space with folk religion, Buddhism, and various forms of Christianity. Each faith shaped and was shaped by the state and its activities.[30] Because Pye's analysis is controversial, however, we should probably take it as a hypothesis or a heuristic rather than as a proven theory.[31]

Pye argued that Confucianism in Korea contributed to a risk-taking style of behavior unlike its analogues in China or Japan.[32] "The Korean model of government was a peculiar combination of the Chinese ideal of dignity, secure in its monopoly of authority, and the Japanese reality of competitive authority."[33] Uncertainty about who constituted the legitimate elite created a dynamic insecurity and produced people who were self-starters—risk-takers like the Protestant entrepreneurs described by Weber. According to Pye, Confucianism made the Koreans aware of standards of excellence foreign to their culture, to which they could aspire, but in so doing it created aspirations for acceptance and anxiety about unworthiness that have made them audacious in carrying out enterprises that test and prove their worth. Those in power tended to have a vivid sense of their own virtue and the wickedness of their opponents, so that it was proper to strike the foe and make him suffer. The brutality of the Korean War and the postwar insecurities "legitimized" the use of harsh methods by Korean officials against perceived foes. Confucian confidence that spirit can overcome physical limitations may also have contributed to the war's excesses.[34]

Pye saw a Confucian background in Koreans' strong attachment to discipline and formal manners, to deference, and to a stiff and aloof style of authority. However, he noted, Korean culture also tolerates brashness and cockiness toward authority, boldness of action by leaders, and self-assertiveness by practically everyone. The gentle Confucian scholar-superior could at any moment become a brusque and cruel authority. "Koreans came to see power, even in its Confucian-ethical guise, as entailing a series of struggles unrelated to either serious policy choices or ideological disagreements."[35] Such behaviors, of course, have occurred in many times and places outside of Korea.

Pye pointed to ways that Korea differed from other Confucian cultures. The *yangban* class was supposed to be a harmoniously united brotherhood of scholarly officials, but in fact the *yangban* was an arrogant aristocracy, torn by rivalries and conflicts. It included both scholars and, ranked lower, army officers. Thanks both to the adoption of competitive exams and to increasing corruption, the number of aristocrats increased. The *yangban* quickly became too numerous for the land available for estates, which the new aristocrats expected to possess, and the bureaucratic posts available for assignment. Seeking to contain the explosion in numbers, factions of scholars conspired with the Korean king to exterminate other *yangban*. Several "massacres of scholars" ensued in the sixteenth century. Having accepted that their special privileges depended also on royal approval in the form of bureaucratic appointments, the *yangban* could no longer opt out of the struggle at the capital.[36] A Korean academic, Yurim Yi, however, believes that Pye's view reflects Japanese colonial propaganda meant to disparage Korea and that the massacres resulted from political and ideological disagreements.

Times change and meanings evolve. Part of the *yangban* heritage may be seen in the determination of today's young Koreans to acquire a higher education. The term *yangban* has come to signify a gentle person. It is also used by a wife who speaks of her husband.

Pye noted another feature he said was particularly Korean. In the Korean family there was no mistaking the superior role of the patriarch, expected to make decisions without the restraints customary in Japan. Korean rulers, like family patriarchs, were expected to be embattled but masterful at all times—lone figures, aloof and able to cope single-handedly with problems, while demanding total obedience. Korean mothers, however, played a more autonomous decision-making role than mothers in China or Japan. Hence, Korean children learned early the art of playing off the two authorities against each other. Nevertheless, children also saw home as a sanctuary to which they could retreat after going out and assuming high risks.

The Confucian sense of family underscored the differences between the internal "we" and the foreign "they." The norms that govern relations among the in-group need not apply to outsiders. As the two Koreas became estranged under anticommunist and communist rule, each side increasingly saw the other as foreign.

Confucian tradition became a tool for those in South Korea, Japan, and China who oppose regional cooperation and integration with a globalized world. For centuries, Gilbert Rozman writes, Confucianization fostered universal values in China, Japan, and Korea—in some ways abetting premodern development. But it also served to entrench particularism and block modernization when it arrived from the West—prompting reformers and revolutionaries to call for de-Confucianization. But some elements of Confucianism survived and contributed to modernization and the rise of Asia's "tigers" in the 1980s and the 1990s.[37]

Confucian along with Christian and other traditions have shaped all of Korea, but many vestiges of hierarchy have been eroded by the forces of "modernity" in South Korea—as has happened in Hong Kong, Shanghai, and many other Chinese cities.

The blend of precommunist traditions with borrowings from Stalinism adds to the roadblocks to modernization and liberation of North Korea. Indeed, the Kim Il Sung dynasty perverted the Confucian emphasis on discipline and reciprocal obligation to help it to command and control. The dynasts saw obligation as a one-way street by which to extract goods and services from most North Koreans to benefit a few. To be sure, the patriarchal system clashed with the forces of modernizations and with competing institutions. In the early twentieth century, however, the Kim Il Sung–Kim Jong Il family business prevailed over incipient pluralism.[38]

Language, Power, and Politics

By the twenty-first century, the ROK had become a leader in science and technology. South Koreans were granted 1,113 patents for every 1 million citizens compared to 857 granted in Japan, 367 in Sweden, and 244 in the United States. South Korea's eminence in science and commerce stems in part from a strong tradition of academic excellence and universal literacy. Buddhist texts were printed in Korea as early as CE 751 using wooden blocks. By the early thirteenth century, Koreans printed books using metal type—some two hundred years before Johannes Gutenberg printed his Bible.[39] Some of the culture's dedication to learning remained in the communist North, deadened however by a pervasive system of mind control.

For a thousand years before the fifteenth century, the Korean language was written using Chinese ideograms—Korean sounds represented by Chinese characters with similar pronunciations. Because the Chinese writing system is not phonetic, this system was very difficult to learn, and few Koreans were literate. The Chosôn dynasty's King Sejong in the 1440s commissioned scholars to invent a phonetic and phonemic script that common people could quickly learn and use.[40] The scholars devised a system called *HunMinChongUm*—"Correct Sounds for the Instruction of the People." Originally it comprised twenty-eight letters, but the modern system, known as Hangul, contains just twenty-four letters. Hangul means "unique, great, and correct." Korea's Japanese rulers saw Hangul as nationalistic and tried to suppress it. Koreans celebrate Hangul day every October 9—probably the only people who commemorate the invention of their writing system.

Despite Japanese repression, some 78 percent of Koreans were literate in 1945—a percentage that quickly rose to 95 percent in 1955. When I visited Korea in 1970, determined young people were selling cigarettes—one at a time!—in bars to pay their college expenses. I also met workers who had moved from the countryside into Seoul, hoping to obtain education for their children. Because they had to pay tuition after the first several grades, however, some children joined their fathers in hard manual labor to survive in the capital city.

After the Korean War, the ROK adopted Hangul as its official script. Up to the 1980s, however, children in South Korean schools continued to learn Chinese characters (*HanCha*) because they were still used in some newspapers and in academic manuscripts. The use of Chinese characters was discouraged by ROK leaders in the 1970s and 1980s, but it was given more scope under Kim Dae Jung. The continued use of Chinese characters in South Korea has been criticized by linguistic nationalists and defended by cultural conservatives, who fear that the loss of character literacy isolates younger Koreans from their cultural heritage.[41]

The "Standard Language" (*p'yojuno*) of South Korea is derived from the language spoken in and around Seoul. Korea's partition since 1945 has led to linguistic divergences north and south of the demilitarized zone. The North's language has become more Orwellian and has developed a system of honorific deferences to refer to the Kim Il Sung dynasty. The DPRK has attempted to eliminate as many foreign loan words as possible. Pyongyang regards Chinese characters as symbols of "flunkeyism" and has systematically eliminated them from all publications. *Kullo-ja* (The Worker), the monthly Korean Workers' Party journal, has used only Hangul since 1949.[42] The DPRK government has introduced new words of exclusively Korean origin and encouraged parents to give their children Korean, rather than Chinese-type, names. Nonetheless, approximately three hundred Chinese characters are still taught in North Korean schools. North Koreans refer to their language as "Cultured Language" (*munhwa*), which uses the regional dialect of Pyongyang as its standard. North Korean sources vilify the Standard Language of the South as "coquettish" and "decadent," corrupted by English and Japanese loan words and full of nasal twangs.[43] North Korea's rejection of Chinese characters and other foreign influences is part of an "oppositional nationalism" that feeds both the ideology of self-reliance (*juche*) and a historical revisionism suggesting that Manchuria belongs to Korea.[44]

Insights from Complex Systems Theory

The history of evolution, human as well as general, shows that survival requires fitness. Complex systems theory holds that for human societies fitness means the ability to cope with complex challenges and opportunities. Optimal fitness flows from *self-organization*—not from top-down dirigisme. Societal fitness requires a polity that is neither too rigid nor too disorderly.[45] In the twenty-first century, however, the creative energies and strengths needed for fitness are likely to be found close to the edge of chaos, as in the United States and, since the 1980s, in South Korea, and very far from the hierarchy of authoritarian regimes.

Self-organization has done much to boost South Korea's social and economic development. In the late 1960s, the Planned Parenthood Federation of Korea began to organize "Mothers' Clubs" to promote family planning and community development. Women in Oryu Li, one of South Korea's poorest villages, used their club not just for family planning but also for transformation of their way of life. A few years later, the husband of the club leader observed: Our "village was once known for its lack of cooperation. . . . But now, because of the Mothers' Club activities, there is much better cooperation."

The Mothers' Clubs minimized the role of clan membership and enlightened women to the advantages of cooperation—working in the fields together, planting trees, and even starting a weaving facility so that girls could earn as they studied. Injections of material resources and information were important, but the Oryu Li experience showed the importance of changing the old ways of communication. What leaders of the club said and did at key junctures was critical to the direction and rate of change. Women became not just followers but also change agents in a traditionally hierarchical and male-dominated society.[46] In 1970 politicians followed civil society as the ROK government launched the New Village Movement (*SaeMaul Undong*) to mobilize the human and material resources of villages

By the end of the twentieth century, labor unions had become very powerful in South Korea, and women's rights in the work place had been radically

---

Box 2.1 How Politics Can Change Culture

From 1987 to 1995, the first democratically elected government of South Korea built dams and other major public works projects without consulting anyone affected by the projects—not the local industrialists, not the local farmers, not even the local governments. Steamrolling these projects appeared more efficient than consulting with stakeholders. A major dam project in 1987 elicited almost no opposition even though it compelled some eighteen hundred persons to relocate. Ten years later, however, another dam, proposed at Youngwol, met protest from civic, environmental, and even religious organizations. Instead of ignoring the opposition, the Ministry of Construction and Transportation set up a joint government-civilian task force. When this group recommended canceling the project, President Kim Young Sam promptly did so.

Why had this transformation come about? Neither the party system nor the constitution nor the citizenry had changed. A series of administrative laws, passed in the mid-1990s, dictated that the government could not lay the first brick on a new construction project until it consulted everyone affected. Administrative procedural reforms "democratized" Korea's infrastructure construction process and made the ROK government far more responsive. All citizens acquired a say in the government's decisions on specific projects—not just on which president should govern. This increasing popular voice reflected the transformation of institutional democracy into a more *responsive* democracy.

How and why did this happen? Briefly, the country's rulers wanted to forestall challenges from their political rivals and to stop bureaucrats from following their own agendas. In Korea, as in Taiwan and some other fledgling democracies (but not in the Philippines), citizens could practice *ex ante* and not just *ex post* democracy. They acquired a voice in decision making before policies were implemented.[47]

improved. Union activity was repressed during and after the 1997–1998 financial crisis, but unions continued to use the Internet to promote resistance to *chaebŏls*, the business conglomerates such as Samsung and Hyundai, often backed by the ROK government, active in Korea and transnationally. Speaking truth to power, the word *chaebŏl* combines the words for "wealth" and "clan." The Samsung Group in 2007 had revenues comparable to Malaysia's GDP; Hyundai, to New Zealand's.

Along with other forces, greater self-organization—for both genders—helped convert South Korea from a society averse to change to one that seeks progress on all fronts.[48] Civil society organizations influenced political processes, shaped public opinion, and compensated for weaknesses in political institutions.[49] The downside, however, was evident in 2009 as backers of former president Roh Moo-hyun blamed his recent suicide on persecution by the current administration (for economic crimes). "Democracy," imported from abroad and deformed for decades by authoritarian presidents, lacked mature roots. A cult of opposition to the government emerged in the early twenty-first century, often blind to the merits of its alliance with the United States and the cruelties of the dictatorship in the North.

Self-Organization and North Korea

Self-organization is antithetical to hierarchical organization, as in the Confucian-communist system of North Korea. Across most of Asia, traditional people see power as residing in the person of a high official—not in offices or in institutions. Respect for the paterfamilias prepares people to esteem the country's supreme leader. Nowhere in today's world have leaders been treated more like god-kings—or simply like gods—than in North Korea. Where else would people die and risk the lives of their children in a flood to save a portrait of their leaders?[50] Where else would they thank their Dear Leader for restoring their eyesight rather than the Nepalese ophthalmologist and his team who performed hundreds of operations during a short visit to Pyongyang?[51] The fusion of politics and religion in North Korea offers people a great scope for fantasies about cause and effect. Political leaders are expected to have superhuman powers. If they do not deliver, some answer must be found. It is convenient to blame North Korea's problems on the machinations of the United States and its Asian vassals.

The DPRK system is profoundly unfit. Confucian culture instills discipline and respect for authority and has been exploited by the communist rulers of North Korea to control and command their subjects.

The implications of all this for peace and prosperity were mixed. The highly confident and dynamic South balked at directions from the United States. The highly centralized but stagnating North needed outside help, but its first priority was to preserve the existing system. Both ROK and Chinese leaders wanted stability on the Korean peninsula, but they also saw enormous business opportunities if North Korea opened up and became more pragmatic. Russia and Japan also perceived vast commercial prospects but kept their distance as from a hot stove. This was the broad context facing the Obama administration as it deliberated policy toward a deeply divided Korea.

CHAPTER THREE

How Korea Became Japan

Starting in the 1860s, Washington's usual stance on Korea amounted to less-than-benign neglect. Until the Korean War in 1950, official U.S. policy generally followed the rule set out in 1888 by Secretary of State Thomas Bayard: U.S. interest in Korea is "merely the protection of American citizens and their commerce."[1]

As outsiders hovered over Korea, a U.S. adviser to the Korean emperor described the struggles for influence by China, Japan, and other actors in "the weakest of Far Eastern countries, not only weak internally but also by having no undisputed official protector or friend among the Western powers."[2] To be sure, many American diplomats, missionaries, educators, and businesspeople based in Korea wanted to help Koreans resist domination by outsiders. The *Korean Review* (published in Seoul) informed readers in 1902 not only about the price of sorghum but also about the success of the Bible Society in distributing the Old and New Testaments in Korean.[3] A British adventurer made several grueling trips across Korea and described in 1897 how her own feelings turned from abhorrence to affection and admiration.[4] Letters home from missionaries in Korea helped spur U.S. newspapers to editorialize against Japanese encroachments.

Although some Americans in Korea—missionaries, diplomats, educators, businesspeople—wanted to help Korea resist domination by outsiders, Bayard pronounced agitation for Korean independence to be "neither desirable nor beneficial."[5] Notwithstanding many U.S. rebuffs, Korea's reformist King Gojong told Washington's minister in Seoul in 1890 that "we feel that America is to us as our Elder Brother."[6]

U.S. policies toward Korea were often conflicted by contradictory impulses of idealism and realism.[7] Idealistic fervor fed on official proclamations such as the Open Door in 1898, the Fourteen Points in 1917, the Nine-Power Treaty in 1922, the pact to outlaw war in 1928, the Stimson Doctrine in 1932, and the Atlantic Charter in August 1941—all implying that law and morality trumped greed and power in U.S. foreign policy. When push came to shove, however, official Washington usually bowed to realpolitik. Top U.S. policy-makers tended to relegate Korea to the status of a rook, a knight, or even a pawn, while treating the region's major powers as queens, if not kings. Thus, President Theodore Roosevelt did not object to Japan's absorbing Korea—provided Tokyo permitted the United States untrammeled control of the Philippines. Forty years later, another Roosevelt— Franklin D.—seemed ready to give Josef Stalin whatever he wished in Asia to secure Soviet entry into the war against Japan. When World War II ended and communist forces crossed into Korea, the United States did nothing to stop the Sovietization of North Korea.[8] Once the great divide hardened in Korea, the free world's hegemon took roughly the same stance toward South Korean politics as it did in Central America: "The top leader is an S.O.B., but he is our S.O.B." Free elections did not become the norm in South Korea until the 1990s—nearly half a century after partition—whereas they never took place in the North.

Why did the United States issue idealistic pronouncements while cutting deals on spheres of interest? For starters, there was ignorance of and disdain for Korea often bordering on racism. Next was the difficulty of projecting finite military muscle halfway around the world. And, not least, there was greed—a belief that business opportunities in China and Japan far outweighed any economic gains available in Korea. Partisan politics in the United States also undercut any hope for a consistent and enlightened U.S. approach to Korea. Top officials devoted their energies to other causes. Whatever they did in Korea could be held against them, whereas hardly anyone would condemn a ban on war or a call for "freedom."

Where Do We Come From? What Are We? Where Are We Going?[9]

As China's sway over Korea weakened in the nineteenth century, Korea's regent, father of the boy king Gojong, sought to resist penetration by foreign powers.[10]

In 1866 shots from a Korean fort at the approaches to the Han River, passageway to Seoul, forced a French naval expedition to retreat. Meanwhile, the United States also sought to open up Korea for commerce—much as Commodore Matthew Perry had done in Japan in 1854. Already in 1834 a U.S. agent advised the secretary of state to open Japan to U.S. commerce so that Korea could also be opened. In 1845 the House of Representatives discussed (but did not pass) a resolution to open both Japan and Korea to trade.[11] Meanwhile, many American ships were wrecked on the Korean coast in the years 1855 to 1866. Usually their crews were well treated and eventually sent to their own consul in China. But an American-led expedition to Korea in 1866 (just a year after America's Civil War ended) met a worse fate than the French. The entire crew of a privately owned gunboat, aptly named General Sherman, was killed as it tried to sail up the Taedong River to Pyongyang and persuade Korean authorities to permit Christian proselytizing and foreign trade.[12] Secretary of State William H. Seward learned of the incident in January 1867 from the French, who had discovered the destroyed vessel while investigating the massacre of French missionaries in 1866. Seward proposed to the French minister in Washington that the two powers unite in a joint expedition to Korea, but this scheme did not materialize.

The same fort at the straits leading into the Han River that drove off the French in 1866 also fired on six U.S. gunboats in 1871. The Americans shot back and silenced the fort. A U.S. officer noted that the Koreans fought until they were overwhelmed and died at their posts heroically. "The men of no nation could have done more for home and country."[13] Three Americans and at least 250 Koreans died—the largest body count of Asians killed by Americans until the Filipino insurrection at the turn of the nineteenth century.[14]

Ulysses S. Grant reported the incident to Congress in December 1871—the first occasion when a U.S. president spoke publicly of Korea:

> Prompted by a desire to put an end to the barbarous treatment of our shipwrecked sailors on the Korean coast, I instructed our minister at Peking to endeavor to conclude a convention with Korea for securing the safety and humane treatment of such mariners.... Admiral Rodgers was instructed to accompany him with a sufficient force to protect him in case of need.... A small surveying party sent out, on reaching the coast was treacherously attacked at a disadvantage. Ample opportunity was given for explanation and apology for the insult. Neither came. A force was then landed. After an arduous march over a rugged and difficult country, the forts from which the outrages had been committed were reduced by a gallant assault and were destroyed. Having thus punished the criminals,

and having vindicated the honor of the flag, the expedition returned, finding it impracticable under the circumstances to conclude the desired convention. I leave the subject for such action as Congress may see fit to take.[15]

Grant's report in 1871 captured the leitmotif of American policy for nearly eight decades to come. He disparaged Korea but paid deference to Japan and China. In Grant's words: With Japan we continue to maintain intimate relations. The cabinet of the Mikado has since the close of the last session of Congress selected citizens of the United States to serve in offices of importance in several departments of Government. I have reason to think that this selection is due to an appreciation of the disinterestedness of the policy which the United States have pursued toward Japan. It is our desire to continue to maintain this disinterested and just policy with China as well as Japan.... There is no disposition on the part of this Government to swerve from its established course.

In the nineteenth century, as in the twenty-first, the United States looked to Korea's neighbors to mediate its relations with Korea. In April 1878 Senator A. A. Sargent of California introduced a joint resolution to appoint a commission to negotiate a treaty with Korea *"with the aid of the friendly offices of Japan"* (emphasis added). This resolution failed, but the treaty by which the United States entered diplomatic relations with Korea was drawn up in 1882 in Tientsin by U.S. commodore Robert W. Shufeldt and the Chinese governor-general, Li Hung-chang. China, however, did not wish to surrender suzerainty over Korea. Li wanted to include in the treaty the phrase "Chŏson being a dependent state of the Chinese Empire," which Shufeldt did not accept. These differences were finessed by a compromise: a letter from the king of Korea to the U.S. president stating that the treaty had been made by consent of the Chinese government.[16]

By signing the treaty of peace and commerce with Korea in 1882, the United States became the first Western power to recognize Korea's independent statehood. China, however, continue to assert its suzerainty. In 1887 the Chinese government demanded that Washington recall from Seoul the U.S. chargé d'affaires ad interim, who had opposed Chinese interference in Korea, and the United States promptly acquiesced. Later that year, however, when the Chinese government sought to prevent the departure of the appointed Korean minister to the United States, Washington did not give in. The minister was received in January 1888 "on a footing of diplomatic equality with the representatives of other States." One year later, Secretary of State James G. Blaine informed the U.S. minister resident in Seoul that the king of Korea remained "under some form of feudal subjection to the Chinese crown" on internal matters, but not with respect to foreign affairs. Washington wanted to bolster U.S. commercial rights in Korea without becoming entangled in regional power plays.

By 1882, when the U.S.-Korean treaty was signed, things had changed in Korea. King Gojong and Queen Min wanted to reform and modernize Korea and sought help, in succession, from Japan, the United States, China, Russia, and then America again. But the royals began to follow the advice given by a Chinese counselor on how to resist Russian expansion: "Be intimate with China, unite with Japan, and ally with the United States," which the adviser depicted as a powerful Christian country with no territorial ambitions abroad.[17] In 1883 Queen Min established English-language schools in Seoul with U.S. instructors. That same year the queen sent a special mission to the United States. The delegation carried the newly created Korean national flag, visited many American historical sites, heard lectures on U.S. history, and attended a gala event for the mission given by the mayor of San Francisco. Later the mission dined with President Chester Arthur and discussed U.S. investment in Korea and the growing threat posed by Japan. The head of the delegation, a relative of the queen, reported to her: "I was born in the dark. I went out into the light, and your Majesty, it is my displeasure to inform you that I have returned to the dark. I envision a Seoul of towering buildings filled with Western establishments that will place [Korea] back above the Japanese barbarians. Great things lay ahead for the Kingdom, great things. We must take action, your Majesty, without hesitation, to further modernize this still ancient kingdom."[18]

In 1885 President Grover Cleveland affirmed U.S. amity toward Korea, "whose entrance into the family of treaty powers the United States were the first to recognize. I regard with favor the application made by the Korean Government to be allowed to employ American officers as military instructors, to which the assent of Congress becomes necessary, and I am happy to say this request has the concurrent sanction of China and Japan."[19] In 1888 Cleveland noted that a "diplomatic mission from Korea has been received, and the formal intercourse between the two countries contemplated by the treaty of 1882 is now established." Cleveland later reported an agreement "between the representatives of certain foreign powers and the Korean Government in 1884 in respect to a foreign settlement at Chemulpo [Inchon]."[20]

Korea's treaty with the United States served as a model for treaties with Britain and Germany in 1883, Italy and Russia in 1884, France in 1886, and Austria-Hungary in 1889. But Cleveland exaggerated U.S. primacy, for Korea had already signed with Japan the Treaty of Ganghwa in 1876.[21] Whereas Korea's rulers had been pressured to accept the unequal treaty with Japan, they sought the pact with the United States.

The relationship with America meant far more to the Korean than to the U.S. government. The 1882 treaty contained a "good offices" clause that both sides came to interpret quite differently. It provided that "if another power deals injustly or oppressively with either Government, the other will exert [its] good offices, on being informed of the case, to bring about an amicable arrangement, thus showing their friendly feelings." Viewing the clause as firm commitment, King Gojong several times invoked it to request America's backing against intimidation by Korea's neighbors. But the U.S. government denied that the clause created any obligation to assist Korea or even to mediate when outside powers intruded.[22]

While Washington kept its distance politically, American businesspeople quickly leapt into the arena. King Gojong saw the United States as a progressive and moral country that could guide Korea's modernization and protect its independent place on the world stage. In 1882 the king dispatched a delegation to inspect American industry. One of its first stops was Boston's Hotel Vendome, recently lit up by the (Thomas) Edison Lamp Company. Soon, Korea permitted Edison to establish a subsidiary in Korea. By 1887 the Edison team had electrified the royal palace in Seoul—a model for illuminating Tokyo's Mikado Palace and Beijing's Forbidden City two years later.[23]

Japan's Ambitions

As we saw in Chapter 1, Japanese could view Korea as a menacing dagger or as a bridge to the riches of Manchuria and Siberia. Just as the United States had done to Japan with visits by Matthew Perry's flotillas in 1853–1854, some Japanese resolved to open Korea to Japan.[24] Both shocked and inspired by Perry and America, young radicals in Japan abolished the shogunate and established the Meiji emperor in 1868. The radicals' slogan was "Enrich the state; strengthen the military." Imposing the Treaty of Ganghwa in 1876, Japan terminated Korea's status as a Chinese tributary. This document required the Kingdom of Chosôn to guarantee Japanese commercial access and other interests.

In 1889 U.S. president Benjamin Harrison noted Japan's "advancement . . . evidenced by the recent promulgation of a new constitution, containing valuable guaranties of liberty and providing for a responsible ministry to conduct the Government." Implicitly recognizing Japan's growing influence in Korea, Harrison's next paragraph dealt with Korea. He "recommended that our judicial rights and processes in Korea be established on a firm basis by providing the machinery necessary to carry out treaty stipulations in that regard."[25] In 1892 he put to Congress "for revision a copy of the regulations for the consular courts of the United States in Korea, as decreed by the minister of this Government at Seoul."[26]

Korea soon became a key target as Japan fought first China and then Russia for hegemony there. Both countries, Japan and Russia, wished to control Korea. Russia in the late nineteenth century became a major player. In 1890 the Russian Ministry of Finance published a virtual encyclopedia about Korea—everything from shamanism to language to trade statistics.[27] Much like the British Isles, the Japanese archipelago sits at a comfortable distance from the mainland—not too close, not too far. Also like Britain, Japan lacks raw materials to feed its industry. Japan's desire to occupy Korea was central to its wars against China in 1894–1895 and Russia in 1904–1905. Dominion over Korea would help Japan to extract its resources and access those of Manchuria, while denying the peninsula to Russia and other competitors.

When other actors—Russia and Great Britain as well as China and Japan—vied for dominance in Korea in the late nineteenth and early twentieth centuries, Washington tried to stand aside. Washington rejected proposals from London for joint action to prevent war between China and Japan. When Japan attacked China in 1894, President Grover Cleveland told Congress that both sides had requested that "agents of the United States should within proper limits afford protection to the subjects of the other during the suspension of diplomatic relations due to a state of war"—a "delicate office" he accepted. The war did not directly threaten the United States, Cleveland said, but raised concern for U.S. commerce in both countries and the safety of U.S. citizens in China. As for Korea, Cleveland wanted "at the beginning of the controversy to tender our good offices to induce an amicable arrangement of the initial difficulty growing out of the Japanese demands for administrative reforms in Korea, but the unhappy precipitation of actual hostilities defeated this kindly purpose."[28]

In November 1894 the United States tendered its good offices to both China and Japan to bring the war to a close. China agreed, but Japan demanded that China approach it through the U.S. legation at Beijing, which it did. The resulting Treaty of Shimonoseki (Chinese, Maguan) in 1895 required China to recognize Korean independence.[29] Soon Korea became subject to "direction" and "assistance" from Japan.

Russia took advantage of the Sino-Japanese War to occupy Port Arthur and limit Japanese expansion into the Liaotung peninsula. In 1900–1903 Russian troops covertly crossed into northern Korea. Russia underestimated Japanese strength, and Japan believed it had an even chance to defeat Russia. Perceiving the Russian position as inflexible, Japan broke off negotiations and two days later attacked Russia, quickly defeating a much larger adversary.[30]

TR, the Treaty of Portsmouth, and the Taft-Katsura Memorandum

In 1903 Theodore Roosevelt endorsed the recent U.S. commercial treaty with China for helping to open "the great Oriental Empire" for U.S. traders, miners, and missionaries. "And, what was an indispensable condition for the advance and development of our commerce in Manchuria, China, by treaty with us, has opened to foreign commerce the cities of Mukden, the capital of the province of Manchuria, and An-tung (Dandong), an important port on the Yalu River, on the road to Korea."[31]

Russia's finance minister convinced Czar Nicholas II to call for disarmament in 1899, because Russia was falling behind Austria-Hungary and other powers militarily. But the czar's minister of war contended that arms—not words—were needed to achieve Russia's aims in the Far East and at the Turkish Straits.[32] Declaring war against Russia in February 10, 1904, Japan asserted that Russia was plotting to annex Manchuria and that if that happened, Korea's independence could not be maintained. Because peace in the Far East was at stake, the Japanese statement alleged, Tokyo had tried for six months to reach a negotiated settlement with St. Petersburg. Russia's diplomats, however, had stalled even as its military prepared for war. One Russian proposal called for "neutralization of the Korean territory" north of the thirty-ninth parallel.[33]

Japan's declaration of war asserted: "The safety of Korea is in danger: the vital interests of our Empire are menaced. The guarantees for the future which we have failed to secure by peaceful negotiations, we can now only seek by an appeal to arms."[34] Two weeks after the Russo-Japanese War began, Japan signed a protocol with the emperor (or king) of Korea guaranteeing the independence of Korea and pledging to defend the country against "aggression of a third power

Box 3.1 Vladivostok—Russia's Power of the East

The port city of Vladivostok, "Power of the East" in Russian, founded in 1860, permitted Russian ships to sail out through the Sea of Japan (Korea's "East Sea") to the East China Sea and the Pacific Ocean. Russia built the port in what had been China's Maritime Provinces, ceded to Russia in 1860. This acquisition gave Russia a short border with Korea—much used (or abused) in 1950–1953. Russia started to build its Trans-Siberian Railway (*magistral'*) in 1891, starting from both the east and west, but northern Manchuria (i.e., China) blocked a direct route to Vladivostok. Russia, however, built and controlled the Chinese Eastern Railway that went south from Chita (Siberia) to Harbin (Manchuria) and continued to Port Arthur (now Lushun), on the Kwantung (now Liaodong) peninsula. China in 1896 ceded to Russia a strip of land to build a rail link from Harbin to Vladivostok. Two years later China leased Port Arthur to Russia, finally giving Russia a year-round, warm water port. These and other rail connections across Manchuria, completed in 1903, looked ominous to Japan and helped goad it to attack Russia at Port Arthur in 1904. After 1905 the southern portion of the Chinese Eastern Railway became part of the Southern Manchurian Railway owned and operated by Japan. A single-track railroad connecting Vladivostok with St. Petersburg across Russian territory was completed only in 1916–1917.

or internal disturbances." To this end, Japan could occupy as needed "such places [in Korea] as may be necessary from strategic points of view."[35]

The United States acquiesced in Japanese hegemony over Korea to check Russian expansion, bolster ties with Japan, and secure Tokyo's assent to American occupation of the Philippines. Some Americans believed that Koreans were not capable of governing themselves and would be better off under Japanese rule.

American officials understood that the protocol established a Japanese protectorate over Korea but did not fret that Korea might become a Japanese colony. The U.S. legate in Tokyo assured Washington in February 1904 that Japan intended to maintain the "Empire of Korea intact, although its administration would continue to be under the close Japanese supervision which has already begun."[36] For his part, the U.S. secretary of state seemed more concerned that Korean soldiers, after an accident in a snowstorm, had damaged an American-built streetcar of the Seoul Electric Company than with Japan's tightening grip on Korea. Anxious to give no offense, the Korean minister of foreign affairs apologized to the U.S. legate in Seoul.[37]

One historian summed up TR's views on Korea: "Japanese control was to be preferred to Korean misgovernment, Chinese interference, or Russian bureaucracy."[38] Roosevelt admired Japanese vigor while disdaining the leaders of Korea, Russia, and Germany. He wanted Japan to contain Russian expansion but not interfere with U.S. commerce in China or with U.S. operations in the Philippines. Japan defeated Russia on land and at sea, but—exhausted and strapped for credit—could not finish the job.

In June 1905 both Tokyo and St. Petersburg accepted Roosevelt's offer to mediate their conflict. As Russian and Japanese delegations prepared to meet in Portsmouth, New Hampshire, U.S. secretary of war William H. Taft reached an understanding in July with Japanese prime minister Taro Katsura. Their agreed memorandum recorded a U.S. pledge to recognize Japanese suzerainty over Korea while Japan disavowed any aggressive designs on the Philippines. A nearly full text of the Taft-Katsura memorandum (omitting Taft's name, to avoid embarrassing him) was not published until 1924—in the magazine *Current History.* Expatriate Korean nationalist Dr. Syngman Rhee, who had studied under Woodrow Wilson at Princeton University, later denounced this "sale" of Korea's right to self-determination.[39]

The imperialist Zeitgeist yielded a deep malaise. In August 1905 Great Britain and Japan reached an accord similar to the Taft-Katsura deal as they renewed their alliance: London recognized Japanese dominance in Korea, while Tokyo pledged not to threaten Singapore. The Treaty of Portsmouth, signed by Japan and Russia in September 1905, placed Korea, the Kwantung peninsula (today's Liaodong), and the Southern Manchurian Railroad under Japanese control. Russia ceded southern Sakhalin and the Kurile Islands to Japan. Both Russia and Japan pledged to evacuate their troops from Manchuria.

In November 1905 Japan imposed the Eulsa (or Ŭlsa) Treaty on Korea. It made Japan responsible for Korea's foreign affairs and its ports. In short, Korea became a Japanese protectorate. King Gojong and several ministers refused to sign, putting its legitimacy in doubt.

For helping to end the Russo-Japanese War, the U.S. president received the Nobel Peace Prize in 1906. Koreans felt victimized by Roosevelt as well as by Japan. Some Russians and many Japanese felt they had been shortchanged. Antipeace groups in Japan denounced the Portsmouth peace as a betrayal. Forty years later, Stalin complained that the United States had helped Japan tear away Russian territory.[40] The longest serving Soviet foreign minister ever, Andrei A. Gromyko, recalled that his own father—having returned from serving in the Russo-Japanese War—termed Roosevelt a "crafty president." Andrei's father added that America became richer than other countries by taking their wealth. A neighbor added, however, that Roosevelt was not only "sly" but also "wise."[41]

As Japan moved to incorporate Korea, Washington ignored or rebuffed numerous appeals by King Gojong for U.S. intervention. Roosevelt in his December 1905 message to Congress did not mention Korea at all, though he spoke in favorable or neutral terms of Japan and China—five or six times each.[42] Amid all this bonhomie, the U.S. and Japanese "legations" were raised to the status of "embassies" in January 1906. The U.S.-Japanese deal resembled the August 1939 Ribbentrop-Molotov Pact partitioning Eastern Europe and securing a temporary peace between Germany and the Soviet Union—a deal warmly greeted by both Adolf Hitler and Stalin.

Having defeated Russia in the Far East, Japan tightened its grip on Korea. In January–February 1906 Japan's imperial government "abandoned" its legation in Seoul and set up a "residency-general" there to handle Korea's foreign affairs. Alleging in June 1906 that Korea had no "judicial system in the sense understood in civilized countries," Japan claimed a duty to reform Korean courts. Tokyo also abolished extraterritorial rights for foreigners in Korea and put them under Japanese jurisdiction. The Japanese press reported how the resident-general in Seoul bullied the Korean emperor, replaced his palace guards with hundreds of Japanese police, and demanded expulsion from the court of "intriguers" whose machinations imperiled the friendship between Japan and Korea. Japanese ordinances placed Kwantung and the South Manchurian Railway under a Japanese general subject to Japan's minister of war.[43] U.S. officials seemed or tried to accept at face value Tokyo's assurances that it would safeguard the independence of the "emperor of Korea" and his country's sovereignty.

Washington acquiesced in Japanese annexation of Korea and penetration into Manchuria in part because U.S. officials felt they lacked any tangible means to contain Japanese expansion. They ignored not only America's moral clout—what we now call "soft power"—but also its economic and financial muscle. Japan, after all, was nearly bankrupted by its war with Russia. Indeed, famine seized Japan's northeastern provinces in early 1906 so severely that U.S. offers of financial assistance were accepted, regardless of "face," and gratefully acknowledged by the emperor himself![44]

The sham ended in 1910 when Tokyo made Korea part of the Japanese empire. Japanese occupation sought to destroy Korean culture—a policy tantamount to "genocide" as defined in a subsequent 1948 convention, that is, actions intended "to destroy, in whole or in part, a national, ethnical, racial or religious group, as such." Koreans could not use their own language in schools or publications—not even in conversations with neighbors. They were required to use "Japanized" names, render obeisance at Shinto shrines, and hail the Japanese emperor as their overlord. The brutality of Japanese occupation, which lasted until 1945, left bitter memories that continued to resonate in the early twenty-first century—in North as well as South Korea.[45] Chang Ki-jin, a resident since 1942 of a leper colony established by Japan on Sorok Island in 1916, recalled in 2007 that the Japanese commander of the leper colony "carried a big bat and would hit us whenever we rested" from carrying bricks. "He was really vicious." When Mr. Chang's legs froze one winter, they were amputated.[46]

President William Howard Taft's message for 1910 noted that Japan had annexed Korea, "the final step in a process of control of the ancient empire by her powerful neighbor that has been in progress for several years past." Taft reported Japanese "assurances of the full protection of the rights of American citizens in Korea under the changed conditions."[47] Taft later spoke of the "satisfactory adjustment ... of the questions growing out of the annexation of Korea by Japan."[48]

"Hear no evil; see no evil"—this became Washington's principle. Thus, Taft in 1910 also welcomed the gradual establishment of "representative government" in China and the conclusion of a Japanese-Russian agreement regarding Manchuria. The U.S. president noted also that his secretary of war had toured the Philippines and then visited Japan and China, accompanied by many U.S. business representatives.

In 1911 Taft reported that the 1894 U.S.-Japanese trade treaty had been renegotiated and all outstanding issues resolved. He recalled that Washington had provided warm receptions to both Chinese and Japanese officials, including Admiral Count Togo (who led the decisive attack on Russia's navy at the Tsushima Strait six years before). Taft said nothing about how U.S. efforts to gain markets and financial influence in China and Manchuria were challenging European and Japanese vested interests and adding to tensions in the region.

For the next thirty-one years—from 1911 until 1942—the word "Korea" did not appear in public statements by U.S. presidents. Korea seemed to disappear not only from maps but also from official American consciousness. Engaged elsewhere—including Mexico, Europe, and Russia—the United States paid little attention to Korea under Japanese rule. When Walter Lippmann led an extensive "inquiry" in 1918–1919 for Woodrow Wilson on how to reorder the world, his experts on the Far East and the Pacific rim considered Japan and China in some detail but failed even to mention Korea. (The documents on their deliberations were not published until 1942—by which time another war had enveloped and changed everything discussed after World War I.[49])

The Japanese stood ready and willing to exploit the opportunities that emerged as its giant neighbor dissolved. China fell into near anarchy after the dowager empress died in 1908 and a republic was formed in 1912. The republic's second president, more dictator than democrat, Yuan Shih-kai (who had also been China's last resident in Korea, 1885–1894), passed on in 1916. Soon China had a warlord government in Beijing and a republican government in Nanjing, headed by the Sun Yat-sen. Later regarded by both Nationalists and communists as the "father of modern China," Sun Yat-sen had been educated in and later financed from Hawaii. He sought to merge Western and Chinese ideals, but got no backing from Washington. When Sun and his compatriots failed to obtain aid and diplomatic recognition from Western governments, they turned to the Soviet Union for assistance. Sun died in 1925, one year after two other giants in their countries' development, Woodrow Wilson and Vladimir Lenin.

Sun Yat-sen's story anticipated that of Syngman Rhee, the father of the Republic of Korea and a Princeton Ph.D., who got more frustration than help from Washington until 1950. The U.S. government refused appeals for aid by Rhee and other leaders of Korea's nationalist movement. The Department of State instructed the U.S. ambassador to Japan in April 1919 that the U.S. consulate at Seoul "should be extremely careful not to encourage any belief that the United States will assist the Korean nationalists in carrying out their plans."[50] When Korean nationalists sought to organize resistance to Japanese rule, Tokyo blamed these actions on Wilson's doctrine of national self-determination.

The United States accepted Japanese restrictions on foreign trade with Korea and the abolition of extraterritoriality and foreign settlements in treaty ports in Korea. Concerned that Washington was giving away too much, the Senate in 1916 adopted a resolution requesting the correspondence between representatives of the U.S. and Korean governments relative to the Japanese occupation of Korea. Secretary of State Robert Lansing made a "judicious selection" of the correspondence for delivery to the Senate.[51]

Japanese imperial policies resembled those of Russian and European imperialists, but proved to be exceptionally brutal in Korea. Looking back after World War II, former U.S. secretary of state Cordell Hull wrote that Japan "warred against China in 1894 in order to get hold of Korea." Hull was basically correct in judging that Japan's "diplomatic record was that of a highway robber."[52] As a result, Korean animosity toward Japan persisted long after Japanese troops withdrew in 1945. Whereas most of the former colonies of Portugal, Spain, France, and Great Britain welcomed close ties with their erstwhile metropoles, both North and South Korea remained bitter toward Japan.

From World War I to World War II

As Europeans waged their own civil war, Japan seized the Shantung peninsula from Germany. Tokyo expected no challenge to its position in Korea but wanted the Paris Peace Conference in 1919 to give a green light to further Japanese expansion. The U.S. ambassador in Tokyo reported in late 1918 that eminent financier Baron Shibusawa demanded recognition of Japan's "absolute superiority in China." The baron cautioned that America, "the Champion of Democracy," might try to check Japan's military expansion. The journal *Chuwo* warned America "that if she becomes conceited and attributes the defeat of the enemy to her own strength ... she will be doomed as Germany is now doomed." Presciently if prematurely, the journal predicted that if America "recklessly attempts to display her strength ... the result will be the unhappiness of mankind."[53] Another periodical called for Vladivostok to be converted into a free port and the Chinese Eastern Railway to be placed under Japanese control. One leading politician wanted only special recognition of Japanese interests in Manchuria and Mongolia.

Although the United States may have displayed and used its strength recklessly in subsequent times, it moved in the opposite direction after World War I. Secretary of State Charles Evans Hughes convened the Washington Naval Conference in 1921 and persuaded the conferees to limit tonnage of capital ships and to recognize the "open door" in China. A leading U.S. historian noted that the Washington treaties signed in 1922 set America's "diplomatic frontier way out into Manchuria. But we did not put our military frontier out there; in fact, we disarmed west of Hawaii. That meant we had an imbalance between what we were promising and what we were capable of achieving. When the Japanese moved back into China in the 1930's we were unable to do anything about it."[54]

Like "Korea," the word "Manchuria" also disappeared from presidential statements from 1911 to 1942—save one mention by Herbert Hoover in 1931 after Japan annexed Manchuria. Even though Hoover rejected calls for sanctions against Japan, Secretary of State Henry Stimson in January 1932 enunciated what became known as the Stimson Doctrine: The United States would not recognize any Japanese-Chinese agreements that "may impair the rights of the United States or its citizens in China, including those which relate to the sovereignty, the independence, or the territorial and administrative integrity of the Republic of China, or to the international policy relative to China, commonly known as the open door policy." The legal basis for this position was the Nine-Power Treaty signed in Washington by Japan and others in 1922. But a broader principle was enunciated in the final sentence of the doctrine: *The United States would not recognize any political or territorial changes accomplished by force.* The legal justification for this position was the 1928 Paris Pact outlawing war, signed by most of the world's governments.[55]

Washington never applied the Stimson Doctrine to Korea, even though its principles had been implicit and sometimes explicit in U.S. policy since the mid-nineteenth century.[56] The Stimson Doctrine did not dislodge Japan from territories it seized in the 1930s. Japan was driven from Korea only in the final days of World War II. Even then, Korea remained under foreign rule. Against the will of most Koreans—for the first time in many centuries—the country was split into two warring fiefdoms.

CHAPTER FOUR

HOW ONE KOREA BECAME TWO

One month after Pearl Harbor, a U.S. president finally spoke truth to power. In February 1942 Franklin D. Roosevelt accurately depicted Japan's occupation of Korea as part of a "scheme of conquest" launched by Tokyo in 1894—a reality that a series of U.S. presidents had heretofore passed over in silence. Roosevelt spoke of Japan's harsh despotism in Manchuria and Korea. Nevertheless, the United States did little to help Korea become an independent and united member of the world community.

Independence in "Due Course"?

Even as the United States waged war across the Pacific, U.S. leaders paid little heed to the demands of Korean expatriates that their homeland be restored to independent statehood and become a member of the United Nations.[1] Roosevelt's only vision for Korea was to place it under an international—that is, alien— trusteeship. The Cairo Conference held by Roosevelt, Winston Churchill, and Chiang Kai-shek in November 1943 endorsed the trusteeship idea but assured the world that the three allies coveted no gain for themselves.[2] Mindful of the enslavement of Korea, they were "determined that *in due course* Korea shall become free and independent" (emphasis added).[3]

These high hopes got nowhere. Within a decade, World War II had ended, but a global cold war had erupted; Chiang Kai-shek had been driven offshore to Taiwan; and a divided Korea had experienced three years of intense warfare.

American insouciance to Korea, as we have seen, began in the nineteenth century. But many factors shaped FDR's policies toward Korea and the entire postwar world. The president wanted to use whatever aid the USSR could muster to defeat Germany and Japan as quickly as possible. Wishing to avoid any discord with "Uncle Joe" Stalin, the U.S. president tended to put off detailed postwar planning—even for Berlin. At Tehran in 1943 and Yalta in 1945, he gave Stalin a virtual free pass to retake the three Baltic republics, even though Washington had refused to recognize their absorption into the USSR in 1940. Roosevelt was equally cavalier toward Soviet claims on Finland, Poland, and the Far East. FDR's generosity with other people's futures was greatly appreciated by Stalin.[4] When Roosevelt approved Russia's retaking Sakhalin and the Kurile Islands, Stalin practically danced with joy—even though (or because?) this implied the USSR would have to join the war against Japan.[5]

Harry S Truman, who succeeded Roosevelt in April 1945, also wanted to draw the USSR into the final battles with Japan. When this happened, as experts knew, the Red Army plus two divisions of Soviet-trained Korean troops would cross into the Korean peninsula before U.S. forces could get there in large numbers. Anticommunist Korean exiles and Nationalist Chinese based in Chungking warned American officials that Korean forces backed by Moscow would try to Sovietize North Korea and conquer the South.[6] U.S. planners were suspicious of Moscow's intentions but gave little thought to how America might cope with Soviet and Soviet-backed Korean forces once they entered Korea.

Syngman Rhee and some other Korean exiles urged Washington to recognize the Korean Provisional Government, based in Chungking as well as in the United States, as Korea's legitimate government. However the U.S. ambassador to the Nationalist Chinese government in Chungking advised Washington not to do so. Recognition of the "Korean Provisional Government composed of professional revolutionaries constantly quarrelling among themselves," he wrote, would not stop communist forces from Sovietizing Korea.[7] A Nationalist Chinese expert put it more bluntly: The Korean exiles in China and the United States, said Dr. Chu, had no roots or support in Korea itself, where the Japanese occupiers and their local puppets had destroyed political life. But those Koreans trained in the USSR who had survived the purges there in 1937–1938 had been fully incorporated into the Soviet administration. Their expertise and the prestige of their backers would help them to dominate Korea when the USSR finally joined the war against Japan. When the Soviets begin to fight Japan, Chu added, they might aid the Chinese communists even though they despised them.[8]

Rhee pressed for Korea to become a founding member of the United Nations. But the United States said no. His Provisional Korean Government did not get even observer status at the April 1945 San Francisco conference that finalized the UN Charter. Washington was equally tough on Italy. Neither in Korea nor in Italy, American officials said, was there an established government that could claim to lead the country.[9]

As President Truman prepared for the Potsdam (Berlin) Conference with Stalin and Churchill in July 1945, an aide summarized for the new president the place of Korea in F. D. Roosevelt's deliberations: "There was no reference to Korea in Map Room messages or documents until the Yalta Conference. On 8 February 1945, during a discussion on the Far East when Churchill was not present, President Roosevelt explained his intentions with regard to Korea." Roosevelt envisioned "for Korea a trusteeship composed of a Soviet, an American and a Chinese representative"—an arrangement that "might last from *20 to 30 years*" (emphasis added). Stalin replied: The shorter the trusteeship period was, the better.[10] When Roosevelt opined that Great Britain should be excluded from the trusteeship, Stalin countered that if excluded, London's "resentment would be strong [so] the British should be invited."[11] Stalin's often liberal internationalist stands on Korea in 1943 and again in the first seven months of 1945 do not fit the image of a greedy imperialist. Were they merely a façade, or were they a sincerely held outlook that changed as new conditions emerged?

By the time that presidential adviser Harry Hopkins met Stalin at the Kremlin on May 28, 1945, Washington had adopted Stalin's view that Britain should take part in a four-power trusteeship for Korea. Its duration, however, had not been fixed. Hopkins said the trusteeship "might be twenty-five years; it might be less, but it would certainly be five or ten." Stalin replied that a trusteeship would be desirable but said nothing about its duration. As to China, Stalin assured Hopkins that the USSR had no territorial designs on Manchuria or elsewhere and would back Nationalist leader Chiang Kai-shek. Stalin saw him as "best of the lot" and more likely than communist leaders to unify China.[12] Two weeks later, Truman informed Chiang Kai-shek that there would be a four-power trusteeship for Korea.[13]

As World War II entered its final months, jockeying for postwar advantage intensified. Harbingers of future conflicts multiplied. Contrary to what Stalin told

Hopkins in late May, in early July the Soviet leader insisted to Nationalist Chinese foreign minister T. V. Soong that the USSR should own and manage both the Chinese Eastern and the South Manchurian railroads, though they could be supervised by a joint Soviet-Chinese board. Soong countered that ownership should be Chinese, though the railroads could be operated by a joint Soviet-Chinese company. Stalin wanted Dairen (Dalny) to be managed by Russians, though half of the port could be Chinese. Soong responded that Dairen should be a "free port" under Chinese administration, with technical assistance from Russia. Stalin proposed that the USSR and China share the use of Port Arthur. Stalin wanted arrangements for the railroads and ports to last for forty-five years.

Discussing Korea with Soong, Stalin reiterated his agreement to a four-power trusteeship. V. M. Molotov interjected that this would be an unusual arrangement for which there was no parallel. Hence, he said, there should be a detailed understanding. Adding a major proviso, Stalin said there should be no foreign troops or police in Korea. As Soong later warned the Americans, even with a four-power trusteeship, the USSR could then dominate Korea by means of Korean troops and police trained in the USSR.[14]

Meanwhile, specialists in the U.S. State Department prepared briefing books for the new U.S. president who would soon meet Stalin and Churchill in Berlin. Still expecting that Japan would fight for a long time, the State Department urged that liberation of Korea take place by joint Allied land and sea operations, conducted under a single Allied command. Given Korean hostility to outsiders, the State Department thought it inadvisable for any one country to invade Korea to drive out the Japanese. State worried that, having occupied Manchuria and North China, an advancing Soviet Union might try by unilateral action to establish a "friendly government" in Korea. State therefore advised Truman to seek confirmation of Moscow's adherence to the Cairo Declaration. This would mean international trusteeship for Korea under the United Nations or by the four Allied powers. If the USSR were to become the main voice in Korea's administration, State wanted the trusteeship to be under the United Nations. Any kind of territorial disposition should be based on prior consultation and agreement.[15]

Truman, Stalin, and two British prime ministers (Churchill followed by Clement Atlee) meet in Berlin from July 17 to August 2, 1945. Henry Stimson, then secretary of war, advised Truman one day before the conference opened that the one or two Soviet-trained divisions of Korean troops would "probably gain control, and influence, the setting up of a Soviet dominated local government [in Korea], rather than an independent one. This is the Polish question transplanted to the Far East." Stimson suggested that Truman press for a trusteeship and that "at least a token force of American soldiers or marines" be stationed in Korea during the trusteeship.[16] The Potsdam Declaration, issued a few days before the conference ended, promised implementation of the 1943 Cairo principles, which included Korean independence "in due course." The Potsdam Declaration was issued on July 26, but the Kremlin did not accede to it until August 9—the same day the USSR declared war on Japan.[17]

Origins of the Thirty-Eighth Parallel

Having suffered two nuclear bombings and facing a Soviet onslaught, Japan accepted the Potsdam Declaration terms and surrendered on August 15, 1945. "The suddenness of the Japanese surrender forced emergency consideration by the Department of State and the armed services of the necessary orders to General MacArthur ... about the Japanese surrender." So began a memorandum written in 1950 by Dean Rusk, a participant in the surrender deliberations of the State-War-Navy Coordinating Committee (SWNCC) that took place from August 10 to 15. The State Department wanted U.S. forces to receive the Japanese surrender "as far north as practicable." Rusk and a military colleague were tasked to "come up with a proposal which would harmonize the political desire to have U.S. forces receive the surrender as far north as possible and the obvious limitations on the ability of the U.S. forces to reach the area." They "recommended the thirty-eighth parallel even though it was further north than could be realistically reached by U.S. forces in the event of Soviet disagreement, but we did so because we felt it important to include the capital of Korea in the area of responsibility of American troops." The SWNCC accepted this recommendation, and it was agreed to "internationally." One historic capital, Pyongyang, lay north of the dividing line, whereas Seoul, the capital just prior to Japanese annexation in 1910, lay a short distance to the south. Rusk was "somewhat surprised that the Soviet [*sic*] accepted the 38th parallel since [he] thought they might insist upon a line further south in view of our respective military positions."[18] Before the Russo-Japanese War, as we saw in the previous chapter, Russia proposed to Japan the neutralization of Korea north of the thirty-ninth parallel.

Surrender arrangements to the north and south of the thirty-eighth parallel were enshrined in General Order No. 1 issued by "The Imperial General

Headquarters of Japan under Order from the Supreme Commander for the Allied Powers [Douglas MacArthur]," dated September 2, 1945. The order directed Japanese forces in Manchuria, Korea north of 38 degrees, Karafuto, and the Kurile Islands to surrender to Soviet forces in the Far East. Commanders of Japanese forces in Japan, Korea south of 38 degrees north latitude, Ryukyus, and the Philippines were to surrender to the commander-in-chief of U.S. forces in the Pacific. Nothing was said of Taiwan.[19] The Department of State regarded the surrender arrangements as a temporary expedient and pressed for the administration of civil affairs to be combined "so that the whole of Korea would constitute a centralized administrative area"—perhaps under a council made up of the commanding officers of the occupying powers.[20]

Instead of plotting in World War II to communize all of Korea, Stalin agreed to a trusteeship and then to a division into north and south. Stalin's main concern was to gain a share in occupying Japan or, at a minimum, to prevent a renewed threat to the USSR from Japan. For a time Stalin worked to preserve good relations with the United States. When that became less likely, he wanted to avoid provoking the United States to attack the USSR.

In 1945 and as late as 1947, there were signs that Stalin wished to preserve the spirit of wartime cooperation with Washington. Despite the Soviet advantage in power on the Korean peninsula, Moscow accepted the U.S. proposal to divide Korea at the thirty-eighth parallel. To be sure, the USSR in 1945 broke its Yalta commitments on Poland and shifted from four-power collaboration in Germany to Sovietization of the Eastern zone.[21] Nevertheless, Stalin also agreed to a proposal from President Truman for a joint withdrawal from Czechoslovakia, even though the Americans were preparing to pull out unilaterally. The cold war intensified in 1946, but in 1947 Stalin could still advise U.S. secretary of state George C. Marshall not to take a "tragic" view of U.S.-Soviet relations but understand that differences would arise and should be negotiated.

But the reality was that after Japan's surrender, the Kremlin's policy hardened in Korea. Soviet representatives spurned appeals for competitive politics and free elections to establish an all-Korean government. We do not know if Stalin had planned all along to use unilateral action to achieve his goals or whether new developments triggered a shift away from wartime unity. Possible triggers for a change included contention over Poland, U.S. refusal to commit to a specific sum of German reparations, America's use of its nuclear weapon monopoly, discord over Turkey and Iran, and Washington's refusal to include the USSR in the occupation of Japan.

Many reports reached U.S. authorities in Seoul in 1945 about Soviet suppression of noncommunist political groups in the north. For example, when Soviet troops entered the city of Syn-wi-ju (at the mouth of the Yalu River) on August 30, their commander replaced a local "Self-Rule Council," organized immediately after Japan's surrender, with a "People's Political Committee" in which two minuscule communist groups were given the dominant position.[22] They were then allowed to form a communist party while the Soviets disbanded an opposition "democratic party." Australian observers reported that Russian excesses in the north managed to unite Koreans and Japanese for the first time in forty years. As in East Germany, the Red Army stripped North Korea of industrial equipment. The Soviets organized sham joint stock companies that took Korean minerals to the USSR. Moscow set the terms of trade to its advantage.

In August 1945 the War Department assigned Lieutenant General John R. Hodge to head the occupation of the U.S. zone south of the thirty-eighth parallel. It instructed him to prepare Koreans for eventual self-determination but did not give him enough troops to run an occupation zone where many people clamored for independence. Hodge distrusted Soviets and Korean leftists and felt he needed conservative Koreans, including some who had earlier collaborated with the Japanese, to stabilize that part of Korea occupied by U.S. forces. With the acquiescence of the U.S. viceroy in Tokyo, General Douglas MacArthur, Hodge undercut the trusteeship idea pushed on him by the State Department.[23] Whereas the North came quickly under tight communist control, U.S. authorities in Seoul permitted communist groups and newspapers to vilify the United States and Syngman Rhee's "provisional government" in Chungking. When Hodge allowed Rhee and two associates to return to Seoul, they returned only "in their individual capacities." They could sit on the Advisory Board to the U.S. occupation but on the same terms as existing members.[24]

As in divided Germany, U.S. and Soviet talks to unify divided Korea broke down. Washington authorized the U.S. commander in Korea to negotiate with his Soviet counterpart "regarding the rationalization of communications, commerce, finance, and other outstanding issues in Korea"—for example, resumption of rail and other traffic between the two zones, establishment of uniform fiscal policies, and policies to deal with displaced persons including Japanese. (More than 1 million refugees from Manchuria and the Soviet zone of Korea had entered the U.S. zone, many claiming to have originated there.[25]) In October and November 1945, however, the Soviet commander refused to negotiate working agreements with the U.S. commander until given authority by Moscow.[26] The

Soviet consul general in Seoul accepted American food and services but rebuffed any effort to solve practical problems. Instead, the Soviets labored behind the scenes to discredit the United States in Korean eyes.[27]

Secretary of State James Byrnes discussed Korea and other issues with V. M. Molotov and British foreign minister Ernest Bevin at the foreign ministers' meeting held in Moscow in December 1945. Molotov several times put off U.S. proposals on Korea for further study, but finally submitted a proposal on December 20 to create a "provisional, democratic Korean government" to develop the economy and "national culture of the Korean people." Molotov proposed a joint commission drawn from the U.S. and Soviet commands to assist the provisional government. Moscow also called for a four-power trusteeship for Korea, to last up to five years (much shorter than FDR had contemplated).

Molotov's proposal looked constructive. Byrnes naively approved it with only minor revisions, even though it contained two potential deal-killers. First, the joint U.S.-Soviet military commission was obliged to "consult with Korean democratic parties and social organizations." The Soviet idea of a democratic party or social organization, of course, was that it be communist oriented—thus barring noncommunist organizations in the north or the south. Second, the commission's decisions had to be approved by the four trustee governments—a formula for infinite delay.[28]

The man who later became North Korea's "great leader" by late 1945 stood at the helm of what later became the government of North Korea. Kim Il Sung in the 1930s had led small units of ethnic Koreans fighting the Japanese in Manchuria and, after 1941, in the USSR. Stalin incorporated Korean guerrillas into the Red Army but used them mainly to gain intelligence about Japanese forces in Korea—not to liberate Korea.[29] The Soviet occupation forces north of the thirty-eighth parallel did not permit Kim Il Sung to enter Korea until mid-September 1950. After the foreign ministers conference in December, Kim became head of the Provisional People's Committee in Pyongyang. He allied himself with ethnic Koreans from the USSR and with representatives of the Korean Workers' Party based in Seoul.

In the 1940s Kim Il Sung respected Stalin and adopted a Soviet model for governing. This included "democratic centralism" (the center gives orders, and everyone else follows them) and an assumption that politics is a question of "*kto kovo*—who will do in whom?" As we shall see, however, Kim Il Sung became disaffected when he perceived that Stalin put the security and economic interests of the Soviet state over communist internationalism and the needs of Korean communists. Perceived grievances came to outweigh Kim Il Sung's respect for Stalin and the USSR. A reluctant pawn of the mighty, however, he could do little without Soviet permission and assistance.

Kim Il Sung also came to resent Chinese policies toward his regime. North Korea provided much help to Chinese communists as they fought Nationalists in Manchuria in the late 1940s. North Korea provided a refuge for wounded Chinese and a conduit for Chinese goods and troops. The Chinese Communist Party had a northeast bureau in Pyongyang that coordinated all this. Chinese in turn sent huge quantities of grain to North Korea and helped Kim Il Sung build an army from ethnic Korans who served in China. But Kim Il Sung thought Mao Zedong owed him a great deal.

Did U.S. Policy Invite Aggression?

Tensions in divided Korea reflected and contributed to the global confrontation between the West and the communist powers. In March 1946, however, the SWNCC recommended that the United States provide only limited military aid to South Korea's "National Civil Police Force"—"equipment adequate for the internal police requirements of that country"—until U.S. and Soviet occupying forces had been withdrawn or a responsible Korean government had been created.[30] As the cold war became more intense, the Joint Strategic Survey Committee in April 1947 advised the Pentagon that it should extend military assistance according to a country's importance to U.S. national security. Eleven of the first twelve listed were in Europe. Korea ranked fifteenth— just below Japan and Nationalist China and just above the last, the Philippines (sixteenth).[31]

A year later, in March 1948 (following the communist coup d'état in Czechoslovakia), Korea's importance rose a little in official Washington. The director of European affairs at the State Department disagreed with the joint chief of staff that priority should be accorded to Italy, Greece, and Turkey for military assistance. He argued the "equally vital importance of the Greek-Turkish, Italian, Iranian, and probably also Korean and Chinese situations"—with each individual program considered in relation to America's limited capabilities.[32] By September 1948 Greece and Korea were the only country concerns covered on the task list for the U.S. delegation to the UN General Assembly—and both were assigned to the future secretary of state, John Foster Dulles.[33]

Meanwhile, negotiations to unify the two Koreas got nowhere. In 1948 the Americans sponsored creation of a "Republic of Korea" (ROK) south of the thirty-eighth parallel. The Soviets, in turn, formalized their client state as the "Democratic People's Republic of Korea" (DPRK). Here was the cold war pattern of divided Central Europe recapitulated in Korea. As in East Germany, the Soviets sponsored and equipped their client with a fighting force far superior to what existed across the dividing line.[34] The USSR withdrew most of its forces from the North in 1948–1949, but provided the DPRK with tanks and other arms far superior to anything possessed by the South. The Americans helped put the South on the road to economic takeoff but left the ROK with an army far smaller and weaker than the DPRK's. So remote was Korea from official U.S. priorities that Washington withdrew most American forces from Korea in 1948–1949. By early 1950 only 500 or so U.S. troops remained in Korea. The United States concluded some military as well as economic assistance accords with the new government in Seoul, but took pains to limit the nature of these commitments.[35]

Whereas the U.S. administration of Japan was well planned and put the country on the road to become a democratic ally of the United States, Washington devoted little attention to Korea. American efforts to form a republican government in South Korea were inept. Dr. Syngman Rhee became president of the ROK in May 1948 and kept the post until 1960. For some years many South Koreans respected Rhee because of his age, status, and nationalist credentials.[36]

Korea lay beyond the U.S. defense perimeter as defined by General Douglas MacArthur on March 2, 1949, and by Secretary of State Dean Acheson on

Box 4.1 Authoritarians and Beyond

Rhee was the first of many strongmen to lead South Korea until 1992, when free and fair elections began. By 1949 he purged from political life many Koreans who had resisted Japanese rule, many of them leftist, and brought into his administration many who had collaborated with the Japanese. They and their offspring dominated South Korean politics until the 1990s. Things changed significantly with the elections of the longtime dissident Kim Dae Jung in 1998 and the self-educated human rights lawyer Rho Moo Hyn in 2003. Roh complained in 2004 that "we are still unable to rid ourselves of the historic aberration that the families of those who fought for the independence of the nation were destined to face impoverishment for three generations, while the families of those who sided with Imperial Japan have enjoyed success for three generations."[37] Another conservative won the presidency in 2008, however, and Roh—indicted for financial crimes—jumped off a cliff in 2009.

January 12, 1950. America's defense line used to run along its West Coast, said MacArthur. "Now the Pacific has become an Anglo-Saxon lake and our line of defense runs through the chain of islands fringing the coast of Asia"—from the Philippines through the Ryukyus to Japan and the Aleutian chain to Alaska.[38] Acheson's line was identical to MacArthur's but started with Alaska and ended with the Philippines. Neither man mentioned Korea—or Taiwan (both of which Truman in June 1950 decided to defend). In regard to "other areas of the Pacific," Acheson declared, "it must be clear that no person can guarantee these areas against military attack.... Should such an attack occur ... the initial reliance must be on the people attacked to resist it and then upon the commitments of the entire civilized world under the Charter of the United Nations." Acheson urged people not to become obsessed with military considerations in the Pacific and Far East. Military means could not solve economic dislocations or susceptibility to communist penetration—a liberal dogma that Kim Il Sung nearly destroyed a half year later.[39]

Acheson distinguished U.S. responsibility and opportunities in the northern part of the Pacific from the southern. "In the north, we *have* direct responsibility in Japan and we *have* direct opportunity to act. The same thing to a lesser degree is true in Korea," he declared. Whereas Acheson used the present tense to describe an ongoing obligation to Japan, he used the past tense to describe U.S. responsibility in Korea and the present tense to picture opportunity. In Korea, he said, "we *had* direct responsibility and there we *did* act, and there we *have* a greater opportunity to be effective than we have in the more southerly part." There "the direct responsibility lies with the peoples concerned." American aid could be effective only when it supported the missing component in a situation that might otherwise be solved. He welcomed the dawn of a new day in Asia when "Asian peoples are on their own" (all emphases added).[40]

Critics said Acheson had flashed a "green light" for the North to invade the South, which happened six months after he spoke. Critics charged that Acheson had conveyed to communists in Pyongyang and elsewhere that if they marched across the thirty-eighth parallel, Washington would do nothing. Acheson replied later that the critique was unjustified—part of a larger "attack of the primitives" on the Truman administration. The attack was "specious, for Australia and New Zealand were not included either, and the first of all our mutual defense arrangements was made with Korea." If the Russians were watching for signs of American intentions, said Acheson, they would have paid little heed to his speech and far more to two years' agitation for withdrawal of U.S. combat troops from Korea, the recent defeat in Congress of a minor aid bill for Korea, and the increasing U.S. focus on concluding a peace treaty with Japan.[41] In truth, Acheson for several years had argued the importance of supporting and funding South Korea, against the prevailing views in Congress and the Pentagon.

Acheson's speech added to all the other signs that Washington had written off Korea as a vital American interest. As in 1904–1905 and again in 1919, there were few strong voices in Washington to support Korea against external threat. Acheson's "perimeter" was identical to MacArthur's. But the world had changed radically in the ten intervening months. In Asia it was moving leftward. By October 1949 communists had won mainland China and driven the Nationalists offshore. The USSR had tested an atomic bomb. Rhee's government was doing little to improve life for its people but wanted to attack the North.[42] Stalin reportedly cited all these factors when he explained in April 1950 why he was giving a go-ahead for the North to invade the South.[43] American looked strong in Europe: The Marshall Plan and the North Atlantic Treaty Organization (NATO) were taking hold. In most of Asia, Washington appeared irresolute. Less-than-benign neglect was costly.

North Korea Plays Its Soviet and Chinese Cards

Neither the United States nor China nor any other great power should assume that it can channel or effectively pressure South or North Korea. Even when they were weak and unsteady, both the ROK and the DPRK often countered such expectations. Each managed usually to go its own way while manipulating the larger states that financed, armed, and supported them economically, militarily, and diplomatically.

North Korea could call on the world's two largest countries for support. The USSR had the largest territory; China, the largest population. Each bordered the other as well as North Korea. The DPRK was one of the first countries to recognize communist rule in China—on October 6, 1949. But relations between Russia and China had been strained for centuries and did not improve when communists rose to power in each country. Starting in the 1920s, Stalin's policy toward China favored Chiang Kai-shek's Nationalists over Mao Zedong's communists. After communist forces drove the Nationalists off the mainland to Taiwan in October 1949, however, the leaders of the world's two largest countries appeared to make a fresh start. Andrei A. Gromyko led a delegation to the PRC to discuss formation of joint Soviet-Chinese oil and metal enterprises in Xinjiang (Sinkiang) province. When Gromyko returned to Moscow and reported how conflicted the talks in China had become, Stalin heatedly told the Politburo the Chinese did not want to collaborate with the USSR. This episode left a mark, according to Gromyko. When Mao Zedong visited Moscow in December 1949, Stalin kept him waiting for long periods. Finally, the two sides signed an alliance on February 14, 1950. By this time the political and personal differences between Mao and Stalin had deepened. They barely talked to each other at the banquet to celebrate the alliance—an oddity noticed by many in the room.[44] Tensions between Stalin and Mao affected their willingness and ability to assist or control Kim Il Sung's North Korea.

Starting in 1949, Kim Il Sung importuned Stalin on several occasions for permission to march North Korean forces across the thirty-eighth parallel and unify all Korea.[45] The DPRK leader assured Stalin that communists in the South would mobilize popular support for unification with the communist North. However, neither Stalin nor Mao Zedong wanted a war on the Korean peninsula that might bring U.S. forces to their doorstep. Stalin twice rejected Kim Il Sung's appeals but in April 1950 gave his consent—warning that if North Korea needed help, it would have to come from China, not from the USSR. Kim Il Sung traveled to China in May and informed Mao of his plan to attack the South. Mao Zedong said he would prefer to take Taiwan before entering other adventures. But when Mao received a telegram from Stalin confirming that he supported the invasion, Mao gave his approval as well. He also offered Chinese assistance, which—for the time being—was rejected. Mao declined to enter an alliance with Pyongyang until Korea was unified. Mao's coolness grated on Kim's sensitivities.

Soviet advisers helped plan and supervise the DPRK attack, but Pyongyang's leader lacked the courtesy even to inform Beijing that war had begun on June 25. Chinese learned of it from foreign news sources.[46]

What started as a civil or local war quickly became a global conflict that could explode into a nuclear war. Recalling the 1938 Munich analogy and following his own instincts, U.S. president Harry S Truman agreed with Acheson that the United States had to fight what they saw as a Soviet-inspired, communist aggression. Accused by Republicans of having "lost China," the White House was determined to avoid any hint that it was soft on communism. Truman did not pass the buck, as did France and Britain in the 1930s. The Truman administration acted unilaterally but also mobilized international support. The UN Security Council, by a vote of 9 to 0, with one abstention (Yugoslavia) and one absent (the USSR), declared that an "armed attack" had taken place in Korea and called for an immediate end to hostilities and withdrawal of North Korean forces from the South. Two days later the Security Council adopted a U.S. resolution calling on all members to furnish such assistance as necessary to repel the armed attack.

The United States led a "United Nations" force consisting of South Korean troops and token forces from more than thirty UN member-states against North Korea and—in effect—its Soviet and Chinese backers. The Soviet Union did not use its veto to stop the Security Council from authorizing collective security actions against North Korea. It did not because, starting in January 1950, the Soviet delegate had absented himself to protest the failure of the United Nations to give the PRC the seat assigned to "China." When asked by Czechoslovak communist leader Klement Gottwald to explain the Soviet absence, Stalin replied on August 27, 1950, that the Kremlin had wanted America to become "entangled in a military intervention in Korea" where it would "squander its military prestige and moral authority." When the United States became "distracted from Europe to the Far East," the "global balance of power" shifted to "us." Stalin expected (months before China joined the war) that America, like any other country, would be unable to "cope with China." Stalin averred that the global shift in power would delay a third world war and give communists time to consolidate their strength in Europe while the "struggle between America and China would revolutionize the entire Far East."[47]

The apostle of Washington's policy of containing the USSR feared the very danger that Stalin welcomed. Two months after the Korean War began, George F. Kennan, counselor to the secretary of state, advised Acheson that America lacked the means to "keep Korea permanently out of the Soviet orbit. The Koreans cannot really maintain their own independence in the face of both Russian and Japanese pressures." Kennan deemed it preferable "that Japan should dominate Korea.... But Japan, at the moment, is too weak to compete [with Russia]." Therefore, he concluded, the United States should acquiesce in gradual Soviet domination of Korea so that the United States could be freed "from involvement in that unhappy area."[48]

Kennan recommended that the United States "terminate our involvements on the mainland of Asia as rapidly as possible, on the best terms we can get." He proposed an accommodation with the USSR that included neutralization and demilitarization of Japan; establishment of UN "control" over Korea for a year or two after withdrawal of North Korean troops from the South and pullout of U.S. troops from Korea, demilitarization of Formosa (Taiwan) under UN control, and a plebiscite to determine Formosa's future.

Kennan's proposal, he wrote, did "not imply any written agreement with the Russians. In fact, to negotiate anything of that sort would probably be disastrous. It implies only a general meeting of the minds." If the Russians became too tactless and reverted to harsh measures, as when North Korea attacked the South, America's "sanction" would be to reintroduce U.S. troops into Japan. Given the American public's mood and complaints (especially by Republicans) about "losing China," Kennan conceded it would be difficult to persuade Americans to adopt his recommendations. Nevertheless, he felt obliged before resigning from government service to present his views to the secretary of state.[49] Acheson rejected Kennan's views, and they did not get a public hearing. Some critics judged Kennan naïve, but his views were no more "far-out" than those of U.S. experts who said China was too weak to enter the Korean War or others who called for nuclear bombs to halt communist advances.[50]

Having invited trouble by appearing weak before June 25, 1950, the United States embraced the opposite course. General Douglas A. MacArthur, named commander of "United Nations" forces, dispatched U.S. forces from Japan to establish a defensive perimeter around the southern port city of Pusan. He then landed an amphibious force of Marines at Inchon on September 15. They were followed by U.S. Army troops, which soon severed the North Korean line of attack and liberated Seoul. On September 23 North Korean troops began to withdraw north of the thirty-eighth parallel. On October 7 the UN General Assembly passed a resolution calling for the unification of Korea.

President Truman and the Joint Chiefs of Staff authorized MacArthur to send UN troops across the thirty-eighth parallel. Interpreting his mandate quite freely, MacArthur appeared determined not only to destroy the North Korean regime but also to invade China.

Like George F. Kennan in August, Stalin was also prepared in October to write off Korea. On Stalin's instructions, the Soviet delegation proposed to the UN General Assembly on October 2, 1950, a cease-fire in Korea, the withdrawal of all foreign troops from the peninsula, and a general election under UN supervision that would produce a united Korea. Flush with recent military successes, the United States persuaded the General Assembly to reject the Soviet proposal.

All members of the Soviet Politburo agreed in October 1950 that the USSR should avoid war with the United States, even if this meant abandoning North

Korea. After the Inchon landing, according to Nikita S. Khrushchev, Stalin told comrades that he was resigned to the annihilation of North Korea. If the American forces stood on the border with the USSR, "so what?" said Stalin. "Let the United States of America be our neighbors in the Far East. They will come there, but we shall not fight them now. We are not ready to fight."[51] The upshot of the Politburo's discussion, however, was a decision to increase pressure on Mao Zedong to have China enter the war. Once the war stabilized into a kind of standoff, Stalin preferred to keep it going indefinitely to tie down and wear down U.S. power.[52] Khrushchev later blamed Stalin for giving insufficient help to Kim Il Sung. The impetuous spirit that conceived the Cuban missile gambit in 1962 also blamed Stalin for failing to invade Hokkaido in 1945.[53]

Had the UN General Assembly passed the Soviet proposal of October 2, 1950, Syngman Rhee might well have become president of a united Korea. If the United States and USSR had agreed in 1950 to stop the fighting, more than 1 million lives and much of Korea's buildings and infrastructure would have been spared destruction. Of course, we cannot know whether the country would have been unified under a communist or an anticommunist regime. Either way, a unified Korea would probably have concentrated on internal development and posed no threat to its neighbors. If communist, it might have resembled Marshall Tito's Yugoslavia; if anticommunist, an expanded South Korea. With no fighting in Korea, Washington might well have come to terms with communist China two decades earlier and avoided the Indochina debacle plus the deficit spending it spawned.

But reality took a different fork. As UN forces drove north, Stalin ordered Kim Il Sung to seek Chinese aid. When nearly two weeks passed with no decision by Mao Zedong, Stalin ordered Kim to withdraw his troops over the border—in effect, surrendering the peninsula to the United States. Alarmed, Mao Zedong sent some 260,000 Chinese "volunteers," who—unknown to the UN command—began crossing the Yalu River on October 19. Some U.S. analysts anticipated this contingency, but their warnings were ignored.[54] When UN forces moved toward the Yalu in November, they encountered the Chinese, who quickly forced the Americans and South Koreans into a desperate retreat.

The USSR supplied both North Korean and Chinese forces but avoided any direct pretext for America to expand the war into Soviet territory. The USSR sent thousands of pilots and ground crews to fly patrols intended to protect bridges linking China with North Korea, but the Soviets did nothing to stop U.S. planes from bombing the North with impunity.

Each of the three communist governments found fault in the other. Pyongyang later criticized China for not joining the war earlier. PRC and Soviet officials, in turn, blamed Kim Il Sung for many bad decisions. Beijing urged Kim Il Sung to accept a unified command under Marshal Peng Dehuai. Kim Il Sung resisted but, pressed by Stalin, finally gave in. Nevertheless, this did not end Chinese–North Korean wrangling. Peng at one point told Kim, "You are gambling with the fate of people"—Chinese as well as Koreans.

In early 1951 UN forces gradually drove back the Chinese and North Koreans. By April, UN forces were again approaching the thirty-eighth parallel. President Truman (in agreement with Prime Minister Clement Attlee) proposed a cease-fire to the communists. This displeased MacArthur, who desired to continue his advance. MacArthur then broadcast an ultimatum to the enemy commander that undermined Truman's plan. Furious that MacArthur had pre-empted a presidential prerogative, Truman sacked him and replaced him with General Matthew Ridgeway.

In May 1951 Chinese forces drove some American forces south of the thirty-eighth parallel but then suffered huge losses when surprised by a U.S. attack to the west and north of Seoul. By late 1951 all parties agreed to begin armistice talks on the demarcation line and demilitarized zone, supervision of the truce, and arrangements for prisoners.

By February 1952 Kim Il Sung wanted to sign an armistice and turn over any unresolved questions to a committee. There was no point arguing about the return of prisoners of war (many of whom, he said, had fought for Chiang Kai-shek's Nationalists) when U.S. bombers were killing more Koreans than those imprisoned by the Americans. Stalin and the Chinese, however, argued for continuing the war, because it distracted and weakened the United States. The North Koreans, Stalin said, had lost nothing except their casualties[!].[55]

All sides practiced "talk-and-fight" until an armistice was signed on July 27, 1953, by the commanders of the UN forces, the Korean People's Army, and the Chinese People's Volunteers. They agreed to establish a demilitarized zone four kilometers wide between North and South. Staring a little southwest of Panmunjom, the partition line slanted to the northeast of the thirty-eighth parallel—adjustments that each side said improved its strategic position.

As ROK president Syngman Rhee had feared, his government was excluded not only from the negotiations but also from the signing ceremony, though the ROK was part of the UN command. Nonetheless, Rhee used the war and the negotiations to enhance his own and South Korea's influence in world affairs.

Many Koreans "admired his manipulation of Americans, such as his unauthorized release of 28,000 prisoners of war in June 1953 to frustrate negotiations for an armistice in the Korean War, and his successful bargaining for massive American economic and military support as his price for acquiescence in the truce."[56]

Some 2 million soldiers died in a war that barely altered the boundary. China lost 900,000; the DPRK, 520,000; the ROK, 415,000; and the United States, 54,000. Civilian deaths were uncounted. Though many North Koreans and Chinese died in the fighting and very few Soviets did, Moscow later demanded that Beijing pay in kind for aid rendered during the Korean War—a debt not paid until 1965.

Eisenhower thought that his brandishing an atomic cannon, the Long Tom, ended the war. But the key was Stalin's demise in March 1953. His successors wanted détente with the West and therefore peace in Korea.

Long-Term Consequences

Though a communist dictatorship remained in Pyongyang, many American strategists saw the Korean War as a victory for the U.S. strategy of containment. North Korea had been contained and South Korea given an opportunity to develop in relative peace. Some U.S. policy-makers in the 1960s saw Vietnam in similar terms. American defense of the South, they reasoned, would check communism and permit South Vietnam to follow South Korea's example. Having learned at least one lesson from the Korea War, they avoided any actions that might provoke China join the Indochina war.

A very different interpretation is that the Korean War set a precedent for U.S. presidents to take the country into undeclared and unwinnable wars. Vietnam and the "war on terror" followed the same pattern. For domestic as much as for foreign political reasons, the president in each case misled Congress and the public, mobilizing and consuming vast resources. For each war, the White House spun a rationale, but political is always personal. President Truman wrestled with private demons—including a decades-long hostility toward MacArthur. When the American public perceived that the Korean and other wars were unwinnable, they became unsustainable.[57]

For North Koreans, the struggle became a war of identity: their nation against America. Though North Koreans and Chinese suffered huge losses, their high birthrates meant that the extensive human losses did not stop population growth.

Mao Zedong could claim that the Korean War put China on the diplomatic map; Stalin, that it trapped America in endless labors; Kim Il Sung, that his regime had fought America to a stalemate and survived.[58] More than half a century later, his family still ruled.

The Korean War intensified the global cold war and served to bolster what Dwight D. Eisenhower in 1961 termed America's "military-industrial complex." Believing that the USSR pulled the strings in North Korea, Washington sharply expanded U.S. military spending, reintroduced conscription, and did what it could to make America's NATO allies a real fighting force. Washington resolved to unleash West Germany's industrial potential. In 1955 the Federal Republic of Germany joined NATO and rearmed. Japan served as a forward base for U.S. forces in Asia. Its industry also gained from and contributed to the Korean War effort.

After Stalin's death in 1953, Moscow and Beijing explored another fresh start. But a troubled honeymoon soon led to altercations and then to a divorce. By the early 1960s, the erstwhile allies were denouncing each other in public. Beijing tested its first nuclear weapon in October 1964—the same month that Khrushchev's opponents ousted him for "hare-brained schemes." Soviet planners considered attacking China and its nuclear facilities in 1970–1971, but took no action. Sino-Soviet relations remained on ice until Mikhail S. Gorbachev initiated a détente in the late 1980s. China and Russia remained at odds in the post-Soviet 1990s but grew closer after Vladimir Putin took the helm in Moscow.

Some months after the Korean armistice, on November 3, 1953, Pyongyang and Beijing signed an agreement on economic and cultural cooperation. As Sino-Soviet tensions mounted, the DPRK signed a mutual assistance treaty with China on July 11, 1961. After it lapsed, however, the two countries signed only a consular treaty on November 26, 1985. All this formed the context for the main topic of this book: North Korea's quest for nuclear weapons.

CHAPTER FIVE

HOW NORTH KOREA
GOT THE BOMB

North Korea tested a nuclear device in 2006 and again in 2009. How did it acquire the necessary materials and technology? The story began more than a half century earlier. Soviet and East European documents show a long-standing drive by the DPRK leadership to obtain nuclear weapons, coupled with a growing reluctance by North Korea's professed allies to assist this effort.[1] They did not wish to serve as Pyongyang's comrades-in-arms. They feared that Pyongyang might use nuclear weapons to blackmail them or to endanger peace and security in some other aggressive way. When aid from the USSR was not forthcoming, the DPRK sought to bypass Moscow and obtain assistance from the Kremlin's East European clients and, when that proved fruitless, from Pakistan. The absence of international support reinforced the logic of self-reliance and "military first," pushing North Korea to pursue an independent line with respect to its nuclear weapons. The collapse of the Soviet Union and the emergence of a new policy toward South Korea in Beijing as well as in Moscow only deepened Pyongyang's determination to acquire a nuclear capability, which it ultimately had to do with only limited foreign aid.

North Korea's Strong Interest in Things Nuclear

Any actor's decision to acquire nuclear weapons is irrational in the sense that the consequences of having and—still more—using them are incalculable. A fusion of two powerful emotions—fear and pride—drives "oppositional nationalists" such as the DPRK leadership to seek nuclear weapons.[2] As early as the mid-1950s Kim Il Sung initiated a quest for nuclear weapons, in part to counter nuclear threats from the United States.[3] In July 1955 members of the DPRK Academy of Sciences attended a nuclear energy conference in Moscow. In 1956 the DPRK signed an agreement on nuclear research with the USSR. Soon, North Korean scientists, along with scientists from China and other communist countries, began arriving at the Joint Institute for Nuclear Research at Dubna in central Russia. The Kremlin's ostensible hospitality may have been a response to President Dwight D. Eisenhower's call in December 1953 to share "atoms for peace," which led to the establishment of the International Atomic Energy Agency (IAEA) in July 1957. The work at Dubna focused on peaceful uses of nuclear power.

The Soviets tried to keep military know-how to themselves. Having "mastered the atom," neither Moscow nor—fifteen years later—Beijing wanted to share its nuclear secrets with others, not even with nominal allies. Whatever nuclear or other assistance the USSR provided the DPRK, it was transmitted grudgingly and with many strings attached—as was the case also with Soviet aid to China. Soviet assistance to China's nuclear *power* program began about the same time as to North Korea—in 1954–1955. But Chinese sources assert that the USSR on October 15, 1957 signed a "New Defense Technology Pact" with China. According to Beijing, this pact committed the USSR to assisting China's nuclear weapon program—even to delivering a "sample atomic bomb." As Marxists might say, it was "not by accident" that the very next month Mao Zedong endorsed Soviet leadership of the communist movement at the Moscow Conference of Communist and Workers' Parties. Having pocketed Mao's support, the Khrushchev regime then stalled on its commitment and finally "suspended" the deal on June 20, 1959, citing prospects for arms limitations with the United States. It appeared that Nikita Khrushchev played a double game—never intending to give real support to China's nuclear weapon program.[4] This interpretation was later confirmed by the memoir of the marshal who supervised China's development of nuclear weapons and missiles.[5] Nevertheless, initial Soviet aid put the Chinese on the road that led to their entering the nuclear weapons club in 1964.

The Kremlin probably resolved not to make the same mistake with North Korea. Nonetheless, the Kremlin in September 1959 agreed to assist in the establishment of a nuclear research center in North Korea, code-named "The Furniture Factory," and located on the bank of the Kuryong River some eight kilometers from the town of Yongbyon. Exploiting the Sino-Soviet rift, the DPRK also persuaded China in 1959 to sign an agreement on nuclear cooperation.

When Moscow suspended the 1957 pact in 1959, this drove a stake into the heart of the Sino-Soviet partnership. Signs of a serious rift emerged in 1960, but Beijing revealed the story of the New Defense Technology affair only in 1963—one element in Beijing's denunciations of the Khrushchev regime for signing a limited nuclear test ban with Washington and London, portrayed by China as a nonproliferation accord.

On August 26, 1963, as Sino-Soviet discord made headlines, the Soviet ambassador in Pyongyang, Vasily Moskovsky, reported to the Kremlin that he had received the East German ambassador, who told him "that the [North] Koreans, apparently on Chinese instructions, are asking whether they could obtain any kind of information about nuclear weapons and the atomic industry from German universities and research institutes" (Document 1).

A month later, Moskovsky talked with three Soviet specialists who were analyzing uranium ore in the DPRK. They reported that "the Korean side insistently tries to obtain information about the deposits and quality of the uranium ore mined in the Soviet Union. But our comrades have been instructed on this account, and know how to evade answering such questions" (Document 2).

"Our specialists reported that the Korean uranium ore is not rich and is very scarce. The mining and processing of such ore will be extremely expensive for the Koreans. But from conversations with the Korean specialists they learned that the Koreans, despite all odds, want to develop the mining of uranium ore on a broad scale." The Soviet specialists thought it probable that "uranium ore mined in the DPRK will be supplied to China" because a small quantity of uranium ore would suffice for a North Korean nuclear reactor. The Soviets were trying to persuade the North Koreans that it "would be much easier for the economy of the DPRK to satisfy all internal needs by means of purchasing a small amount of the necessary processed 'product.'" But the Koreans replied that they needed to extract uranium ore in large quantities. Moskovsky concluded: "*I think that by sending specialists to the DPRK from the Soviet Union we are helping China, and at the time of the current struggle against the Chinese splitters, one should not do this*" (emphasis added; Document 2).

North Koreans were often rude to the very parties on whom they depended for assistance. The Hungarian ambassador to Pyongyang, József Kovács, reported to Budapest on January 11, 1964, that Soviet ambassador Moskovsky told him at dinner the previous evening that in 1963 North Korean "officials had demanded fingerprints from the Soviet technical experts who worked on the construction of a radio station, an experimental nuclear reactor, and a weaving mill (!) that were being built with Soviet assistance and co-operation, and made [the Soviet experts] fill out a form of 72 questions, in which they had to describe their circle of relatives and friends in detail, with addresses! A Korean 'colleague' told one of the technical experts, 'if we cannot get you for some reason, we will get your relatives; this is why [the questionnaire] is needed!'" (Document 3).

1965: A Small Reactor at Yongbyon

Despite the end of Soviet nuclear assistance in June 1959 and the withdrawal from China of thousands of Soviet specialists in 1960, China detonated its first nuclear device in October 1964. Pyongyang then sent a delegation to Beijing to request Chinese assistance in nuclear matters, but Mao Zedong sent the Koreans away empty-handed. One year later, however, the USSR sold the DPRK a small 2- to 4-megawatt research reactor, also built in the vicinity of Yongbyon. It began operation in 1967.

Box 5.1 Safeguard Agreements with the IAEA

At Soviet insistence, Pyongyang in 1977 signed a "Type 66" safeguards agreement with the International Atomic Energy Agency governing two nuclear research facilities—the "IRT" research reactor dating from 1967 and a critical assembly.[6] Officials from the IAEA inspected the plant in 1988 and 1989, but they also helped North Korea with uranium mining.[7] In 1992, as we see in Chapter 8, the DPRK signed a more comprehensive safeguards agreement with the IAEA pursuant to its joining the Nuclear Nonproliferation Treaty (NPT) in 1985.

1966–1967: Ingrates Who Demand Ever More

North Korea pocketed foreign aid and then demanded more. It used its existing debts as a bargaining tool to acquire more assistance. But the Soviets could say *nyet*. The Hungarian ambassador to DPRK, István Kádas, reported to the Hungarian Foreign Ministry on March 13, 1967, that the Soviets had recently "rejected a Korean request for the delivery of a *nuclear power plant.*" The request began with an "incognito visit that Comrade Kim Il Sung made to Moscow" in late 1966. The "delegation was received by the [top Soviet party leader] L. Brezhnev and [Prime Minister] A. Kosygin, while the head of the Soviet delegation was First Deputy Premier K. Mazurov." The Hungarian ambassador gave no specific reason for the Soviet rejection except to note that an "experimental nuclear reactor ... established with Soviet assistance ... opened approximately one and a half years ago, and since then the Soviet comrades hardly have any data about its operation" (Document 4). The Soviets probably disliked the North Korean proclivity to demand much and give little in return.

1967: An End Run Deflected in Berlin

Late in 1967 the DPRK tried to persuade the East Germans to do what the Soviets refused. The delegation from Pyongyang was led by the vice chairman of the DPRK Atomic Energy Commission. It sought to sign an agreement with the German Democratic Republic (GDR) in the field of nuclear research, obtain equipment needed for the construction of a nuclear power plant, purchase equipment needed for producing radioactive isotopes, conduct an exchange of nuclear scientists, send nuclear science trainees to the GDR, purchase certain secret equipment used in nuclear research, and acquire copies of articles on nuclear research in Western scientific journals. The East German reply was a long and diplomatic *nein*—unless the Soviets approved (Document 5).

1968

The year 1968 saw turbulence across the globe. Mao Zedong's Cultural Revolution was reaching fever pitch. Chinese placards screamed, "Fry Brezhnev and skin Kosygin!" In January, while communists in Vietnam launched their Tet Offensive, North Korean forces attacked the ROK president's Blue House in Seoul. When the attackers perished, Pyongyang said they had been "South Korean partisans." Needing to mask North Korea's adventurism, the DPRK protested U.S. aggression and seized an unarmed U.S. spy ship, the *Pueblo*. Faced with a strong response from the Johnson administration that seemed to challenge Moscow's Far Eastern fleet and Soviet interests in Northeast Asia, the Kremlin appeared to support the DPRK. Lyndon Johnson backed down. Behind the scenes, however, the Soviets ordered Kim Il Sung to return the U.S. crew. But he did not. Instead, the DPRK regime began to evacuate its capital and mobilize the entire population. Next, Kim Il Sung called on the Soviet Union to honor its alliance. This Leonid Brezhnev refused to do and instead summoned Kim to Moscow. Kim did not go but eventually canceled the evacuation and returned the U.S. crew.[8]

The Nuclear Nonproliferation Treaty drafted by the USSR and United States and submitted to all UN members for signature in 1968 added to tensions between the DPRK and Soviet leaders. It appeared that the USSR stood ready to provide nuclear power assistance only to clients that were both faithful and sufficiently advanced to deal with nuclear technology— Bulgaria, Czechoslovakia, the GDR, and Hungary. Often defiant Romania and North Korea were excluded, and so was Vietnam—obedient but not ready for high tech. When a Romanian delegation visited Pyongyang in February 1968, both sides agreed that "the big countries that have nuclear capacity should ensure that the small countries would also be able to utilize atomic energy for peaceful purposes. The small countries should not suffer a loss as a consequence of the [nonproliferation] treaty" (Document 5). After raising many objections to the NPT in 1968, however, Bucharest signed the treaty; Pyongyang refused until 1985 and put off a safeguards agreement with the IAEA until 1992.

In summer 1968 the DPRK asked Moscow for a large increase in economic and military aid. Constrained by the Sino-Soviet rift, Moscow complied with some requests. The USSR could not intervene in North Korea's domestic affairs as in 1956, when the Soviet embassy had sheltered anti-Kim communists. Moscow "continued to provide North Korea's essential security while asking little in return." As Weathersby writes, this nexus "made it possible for Kim Il Sung to transform the *juche* idea into a full-blown nationalist ideology."[9]

1969: Tilting toward Beijing on Nuclear Proliferation

The newly appointed Hungarian ambassador to Pyongyang stopped in Moscow on November 10, 1969, and talked with two Soviet experts on North Korea. They told him that "patient and persistent persuasion was needed to get the Korean position closer to our common position on the big issues of international politics." On nonproliferation, the Soviets said that Pyongyang understood the dangers if Japan acquired nuclear arms. But otherwise the North Koreans did not oppose nuclear proliferation—thus giving "veiled support" to the Chinese position (Document 6).

1973–1974

Pyongyang's interest in acquiring nuclear power mounted when the price of oil jumped in the 1970s. When the USSR raised the price of oil to its client states, the DPRK complained of Soviet "exploitation," even though Moscow charged its clients much less than world market prices. Whereas Washington permitted and even helped the ROK develop nuclear power, the Kremlin did little to assist North Korea on this path.

North Korea also took note of India's "peaceful" nuclear explosion in 1974. India's example showed how even poor nations could develop nuclear weapons with materials gathered from far and wide—in India's case, a Canadian reactor using heavy water from the United States. India, like Israel, would be treated as a de facto nuclear weapon state. North Korea tried to followed suit.

1975: Moscow, Beijing, and Budapest See Kim Il Sung as a Military Adventurer

In the mid-1970s both the USSR and China sought détente with the United States and did not want North Korea to rock the boat. Kim Il Sung, however, hoped to emulate Vietnam's communists and unite the divided country under his rule. Many details emerge from a report on July 30, 1975, by Dr. János Taraba, a top Hungarian diplomat in the DPRK, who informed Budapest: "China is wary of a second Korean War, whereas Kim Il Sung makes it clear that military force is an option" (Document 7). The DPRK acquired military technology and equipment when a delegation led by Kim Il Sung traveled in spring 1975 to China, Romania, Algeria, Mauritania, Bulgaria, and Yugoslavia. Kim Il Sung also wanted to visit the Soviet Union and Czechoslovakia, but the dates he proposed did not suit the leaders in Moscow or in Prague. His intention to visit Moscow, in Taraba's opinion, showed that the DPRK was trying to balance "the Chinese party and our parties" (Document 7).

The Vietnamese ambassador in Pyongyang told Taraba that according to Chinese sources the DPRK wanted "to create the kind of military situation in South Korea that came into being in South Vietnam" before the communist North took over the entire country. "Taking advantage of the riots against the dictatorial regime of Park Chung Hee, and invited by certain South Korean [political] forces, the DPRK would have given military assistance if it had not been dissuaded." China held back and opposed "any kind of armed struggle that might shake the position of the USA in Asia. A new Korean War would not be merely a war between North and South [Korea]." The "Chinese side strongly emphasized the importance of the peaceful unification of Korea.... For his part, Kim Il Sung said nothing, or hardly anything, about his own proposals to find a peaceful solution. On the contrary, he declared that if a revolution flared up in South Korea, the DPRK could not remain indifferent; it would give active assistance to the South Korean people. And if the enemy started a war, it would be met with a crushing repulse. In such a war the DPRK could lose only the cease-fire line, but it might achieve the unification of the country, he said" (Document 7).

Taraba believed that "of the six visits, the ones made to China and Yugoslavia were also important in regard to the military equipment and military technology made available to the DPRK. China provides the People's Army of the DPRK with many kinds of military equipment and arms." Taraba's language was opaque, but he seemed to say that North Korea asked China for tactical nuclear weapons to offset U.S. nuclear forces in South Korea. Taraba noted that a deputy minister of the People's Armed Forces in Pyongyang who received Hungarian officers "vacationing [*sic*]" in North Korea alluded on June 11 to the DPRK's hope of obtaining tactical nuclear arms from China. Taraba added that Yugoslavia also helped the DPRK, "primarily in the field of naval forces."

An outsider can only be amazed at the assumption that China, *if* it possessed tactical nuclear weapons in the mid-1970s, might share them with the DPRK—

especially given its worries about Kim Il Sung's bellicosity. As for Yugoslavia, its capacity to help any country's naval forces was surely minimal at that time, even though Belgrade was still engaged in its own clandestine effort to develop nuclear weapons.[10]

Another meeting of socialist countries took place in Minsk on August 26, 1975. The North Koreans asked the Hungarian delegation to mobilize the socialist countries to prevent the IAEA Technical Assistance Program from establishing a reprocessing plant for the Far Eastern region in South Korea. If anywhere, Pyongyang suggested it be built in the Philippines.

1976: Anything Goes: Ultimatums from the Demandeur

Pyongyang's demands on its communist comrades reached a new level of intensity in 1976 against a strong uptick in DPRK belligerent actions. On April 7 two North Korean tanks entered the Demilitarized Zone (DMZ) and remained for four hours. On August 18 DPRK troops killed two U.S. officers in a "tree-cutting" incident within the DMZ. Two days earlier, however, while the non-aligned nations were meeting in Colombo, the DPRK asked the UN General Assembly to put the Korean question on its agenda.

Unfazed by the cool reception received in Beijing and Moscow in 1975, a DPRK delegation visiting Moscow in January–February 1976 again demanded that the USSR build a nuclear power plant for North Korea. The Hungarian Embassy in Pyongyang learned from a Soviet comrade that "for various reasons—primarily military considerations and the amount of investment—the Soviet side declared that this [request for a nuclear plant] was now inopportune and proposed to come back to it only in the course of the next [five-year] plan. The Korean side was very reluctant to accept this Soviet decision and [Moscow's] rejection of a few other investment demands" (Document 10).

The Hungarian Embassy also learned that as the two sides discussed credit, "the head of the Korean delegation—Deputy Premier Kang Chin-t'ae—behaved in an extremely aggressive way, definitely crude and insulting in certain statements vis-à-vis his Soviet counterpart, Deputy Premier Arkhipov. He declared several times that if the Soviet Union was unwilling to make 'appropriate' allowances for the 'front-line situation' of the DPRK, and did not comply entirely with the Korean requests, the DPRK would be compelled to suspend its economic relations with the Soviet Union" (Document 10).

When Kang chin-t'ae visited the Kremlin, Soviet prime minister Aleksei Kosygin rebuked him, saying that the Soviet Union did not accept ultimatums. "It was only after his visit to Comrade Kosygin that Kang Chin-t'ae changed his conduct, and thus it became possible to sign the agreements" (Document 10).

When a DPRK delegation visited the Hungarian Foreign Ministry in early 1976, it exaggerated North Korea's military prowess—telling bald-faced lies even to its nominal partners in the communist realm. The North Koreans told the Hungarians that "Korea cannot be unified in a peaceful way.... If a war occurs in Korea, it will be waged with nuclear weapons, rather than conventional ones. The DPRK is prepared for such a contingency: the country has been turned into a system of fortifications, important factories have been moved underground (for instance, recently they relocated the steel works in Kangson), and airfields, harbors, and other military facilities have been established in the subterranean cave networks. The Pyongyang subway is connected with several branch tunnels, which are currently closed but in case of emergency they are able to place the population of Pyongyang there" (Document 8).

Implying some worry about the possibility of a U.S. nuclear attack, the North Koreans were not above bluffing. The North Koreans assured their Hungarian comrade: *"By now the DPRK also has nuclear warheads and carrier missiles, which are targeted at the big cities of South Korea and Japan, such as Seoul, Tokyo, and Nagasaki, as well as local military bases such as Okinawa"* (emphasis added). When the Hungarian diplomat asked "whether the Korean People's Army had received the nuclear warheads from China, they replied that [North Koreans] had developed them unaided through experimentation, and they had manufactured them by themselves" (Document 8).

A few days after this meeting in Budapest, the Hungarian ambassador in Pyongyang reported details of a study by the Far Eastern Institute in Seoul. South Korean researchers reported that "the DPRK spent 60, 165, 135, and 140 million dollars on the purchase of arms in 1970, 1971, 1972, and 1973 respectively. During this time the manpower of the army underwent the following changes: it was 438,000 in 1970, 450,000 in 1971, 460,000 in 1972, and 470,000 in 1973. That is, military preparations continued in the period of [North-South] dialogue as well. The army of the DPRK has 1,100 T-55 tanks and a substantial number of surface-to-surface missiles. The DPRK ordered a substantial amount of diving suits and facilities in Japan.... The number of MiG fighter planes is 200, but they also have Su-7 [fighter] bombers" (Document 9).

The Hungarian ambassador also asserted that the "the DPRK wants to construct nuclear reactors, and is having talks about this issue *in order to become capable of producing atomic weapons in the future*" (emphasis added). The source for this claim was not clear. But it jibed with the report of a Russian intelligence officer that in the late 1970s Kim Il Sung instructed the Ministry of Public Security to initiate a nuclear weapons program at expanded Yongbyon facilities.[11]

Not inclined to take *nyet* for an answer, DPRK deputy premier Kang Chint'ae again demanded a nuclear power plant when DPRK and Soviet officials met at the thirteenth session of the Intergovernmental Consultative Committee held in Moscow from June 8 to 11, 1976. Hungarian officials reported home that the USSR refused to deliver a nuclear power plant to the DPRK in the current five-year (1976–1980) plan because it had long-term commitments to construct such plants elsewhere. Also, the USSR refused "for the time being" to extend its agreement with the DPRK on lumbering in Siberia by three years, because ecological surveys were taking place there (Document 11).

The Hungarians said that North Korea "attempted to evade the questions related to foreign trade, for that was a thorny issue." The Soviets, however, complained that "in 1976 Korean shipments had substantially decreased in comparison with the same period of earlier years; the [DPRK's] failure to deliver the raw materials that were planned to be imported from Korea caused stoppages in the operation of important Soviet industrial plants, seriously jeopardizing the continuity of production" (Document 12). The North Koreans did not deny that a slowdown had occurred but promised to make up for underfulfillments in the second half of the year. The Soviets believed that scanty rainfall in 1975 and 1976 had severely reduced electricity production in North Korea, where hydroelectric power plants provided half of existing power capacity.

When DPRK officials wished, they could be polite. Their behavior and its motivations were described by the chairman of Hungary's National Commission of Atomic Energy in a report dated August 31, 1976. A few days earlier two North Korean officials had given him some small gifts and thanked him for "the very valuable advice" they had received from the Hungarian delegation at a meeting of socialist countries two years before. As a result of this advice, "the DPRK obtained IAEA membership without any difficulty" (Document 13).

1977: Mutual Concerns about Exploitation to Get Hard Currency

By early 1977 the North Koreans made it clear to the USSR that the DPRK did not intend to fulfill its obligations set down in the long-term trade agreement signed in 1976. A Hungarian report from Moscow on January 20, 1977, said that the Soviets expected to hear soon from a DPRK delegation that the "DPRK intends to relieve its serious economic situation by not fulfilling its obligations ... with regard to the export of goods that are saleable on non-socialist markets as well." At the same time, North Korea "constantly insists on the uninterrupted and punctual fulfillment of Soviet export obligations" (Document 15).

The Soviets claimed that they had fulfilled their obligations under the 1976 accord but that the DPRK had fallen far short—delivering only 90 million rubles worth of provisions instead of the agreed 216 million rubles worth of cement, fire-resistant bricks, and other goods. This shortfall caused "considerable difficulties" in the Soviet Far East, because such goods could not be obtained elsewhere without substantial delays. The Hungarian Embassy believed the North Koreans would "probably attempt to convert the deficit ... into a Soviet credit"—which, a skeptic might infer, would evolve into a gift (Document 15).

Meanwhile, the North Koreans opposed application of price policies used in COMECON (Council for Mutual Economic Assistance, where the DPRK had only observer status) to Soviet transactions with the DPRK. "The Soviet side did not manage to achieve the COMECON price level in its relations with Korea" in 1976 and did not expect to do so in 1977 (Document 15).

The Hungarian Embassy reported Moscow's belief that the DPRK intended to divert some Soviet oil deliveries into hard currency earnings. "The Korean side constantly announces new demands (in addition to the agreements), and impatiently presses for their fulfillment. They repeatedly and very emphatically urge, at every level, that Soviet shipments of crude oil be increased to two million metric tons per annum," which the Soviets expected would be sold as processed petroleum derivatives in capitalist markets (Document 15).

Pyongyang continued to press for a nuclear power plant, citing "reasons of prestige." But the current Soviet five-year plan made no provision for this kind of assistance. North Korea ignored Soviet statements that the USSR could not "deliver loss-making articles over the quantity specified in the plan." Adding insult to injury for the USSR, the Soviets believed that DPRK domestic propaganda blamed North Korea's economic difficulties on Soviet exploitation of the DPRK by raising prices and refusing to deliver goods needed for economic development, preferring to sell them to the capitalists (Document 15).

1977: Diverging Assessments in Eastern Europe

On January 25, 1977, the DPRK issued a four-point declaration in response to a South Korean proposal for a North-South nonaggression pact in tandem with a U.S. troop withdrawal. Pyongyang immediately launched an international campaign to win backing for its declaration and, the Czechoslovak Foreign Ministry worried, would soon ask socialist countries for their official support. Hungarian authorities treated the DPRK declaration as nothing more than another call for the peaceful and democratic unification of Korea. This is how the declaration was portrayed in the Hungarian press. When the DPRK ambassador visited the Hungarian Foreign Ministry, he was satisfied with its assurances and did not ask for a public endorsement of the declaration.

But the Czechoslovak Embassy in Pyongyang perceived an extremely threatening tone in the declaration, for example, its description of the situation on the Korean peninsula as one that might lead to the outbreak of a global nuclear war. The embassy also saw a hint that the DPRK was equipping itself with nuclear weapons. Prague could not support Pyongyang's démarche, apparently fearing it could be a harbinger of DPRK adventurism. Hungarian officials often took note of worrisome developments in North Korea, but disagreed with their Czechoslovak comrades in this case (Document 16).

When Soviet and DPRK delegations met in September 1977 in Pyongyang to discuss economic and scientific matters, they agreed not to mention North Korea's difficulty in repaying its debts to Moscow or Moscow's refusal to supply a nuclear power plant to North Korea. They deferred important decisions to higher levels of authority, but the Soviets were satisfied with the atmospherics. This, at least, is what the Hungarian ambassador to the DPRK, Ference Szabó, relayed to the Hungarian Foreign Ministry in November (Document 17).

In 1979 the DPRK again tried to bypass the Kremlin. The Czechoslovak ambassador to Pyongyang informed Szabó that on February 12, 1979, a North Korean official asked Czechoslovakia to deliver uranium mining equipment to the DPRK and to construct a 440-megawatt nuclear power plant in the DPRK. Szabó also heard from the Soviet ambassador that the DPRK had two uranium quarries—one where the uranium content of the ore was 0.26 percent and another with 0.086 percent (Document 18).

Meanwhile, the Soviet government revealed little to the public about its dealings with the DPRK. Nevertheless, Andrei Lankov recalls, "rumors about North Korea circulated widely among educated Soviet people. They were aware of Kim Il Sung's deification, police omnipresence, and strained relations with Moscow. To a large extent, the North Koreans damaged their own standing by flooding the USSR with exceptionally bad propaganda." The bottom line was that "nobody in Soviet intellectual circles of the 1960s or 1970s felt positive toward either Mao Zedong or Kim Il Sung." Soviet Party leader Leonid Brezhnev and most Soviet diplomats disapproved Pyongyang's "brutal and inefficient Stalinism and they also saw [North Korea] as an unreliable, costly and scheming ally."[12] Officials and the intelligentsia in Czechoslovakia and other East European states probably shared these attitudes.

The 1980s

Displeased with the help received by outsiders, the DPRK in 1979 began what the IAEA termed the "indigenous phase" of its nuclear development. This phase commenced with construction of a 5 MW(e) natural uranium, graphite-moderated reactor in Yongbyong, followed by an ore processing plant and a fuel rod fabrication plant. By the time the 5 MW(e) reactor became operational in 1986, the DPRK had begun construction of the first of two larger gas-graphite reactors, and around 1987 the DPRK began construction of a radiochemical laboratory with a sizable reprocessing capacity.[13]

In March 1981 the Soviet ambassador to Pyongyang told his Hungarian colleague about recent discussions between DPRK and Soviet officials in Moscow. The North Koreans repeated their request for a nuclear power plant, which the Soviets deflected, saying that if the DPRK sought an East European–type arrangement, they would have to contribute to the cost—to which the North Koreans could "give no genuine" reply. The North Koreans also asked for "special technology"—probably for nuclear weapons—which the Soviets said would be considered by "competent authorities." Moscow agreed to extend more credits but insisted the interest rate jump from 2 to 4 percent after 1985. Serious differences emerged over Pyongyang's friendly treatment of Cambodia's Prince Sihanouk—mere "hospitality," said the North Koreans, who professed not to know that a book by Sihanouk with anti-Soviet remarks had been published in various languages and sold in Pyongyang (Document 19).

In 1981 North Korea continued to ask East European governments to accept dozens of North Korean postgraduates to study nuclear energy. Authorities in Budapest, Berlin, and Prague rejected these requests even when Pyongyang offered to pay the students' expenses, because the information sought was "confidential." Indeed, "the Korean side was forced to recall" five graduate students from Czechoslovakia in 1980 because the topics they tried to study were "strictly confidential." The East Germans offered only to send two language instructors to North Korea and to consider some DPRK students in social sciences, to which Pyongyang gave no answer (Document 20).

In 1983 the DPRK asked Hungary to train technicians to operate North Korea's first nuclear power plant, soon to be constructed in North Korea (Document 21). The Hungarian Foreign Ministry on April 6 told the Hungarian Academy of Sciences to say no. Hungary's power plant "is being built on the basis of Soviet documents and with direct Soviet support; its machinery is also largely Soviet made. For some time it will be operated with the support of Soviet experts, as the training of Hungarian experts has just gotten underway." The North Koreans should make their "request directly to the competent Soviet authorities" (Document 22).

Anxious and resentful in the 1980s that its nuclear program lagged behind not only South Korea's but also those in Eastern Europe, the DPRK began work on a 20- to 30-megawatt research reactor in the Yongbyon area not far from the much smaller reactor earlier supplied by the USSR. A U.S. satellite spotted a large hole for the second reactor. The U.S. Central Intelligence Agency could not say in 1982 whether the second reactor at Yongbyon was being built by North Koreans alone or with Soviet help. As of May 1983 the agency had "no basis for believing that the North Koreans have either the facilities or materials necessary to develop and test nuclear weapons."[14]

In 1984 relations between Pyongyang and Moscow improved. The USSR provided North Korea with SAM-5 missiles, plus MiG-29 and Su-25 jet fighters it had denied in 1981. The USSR also agreed in 1984 to build a nuclear power plant in North Korea. Details of this project were discussed by a team from GOSPLAN visiting Pyongyang in February 1985—a month before Mikhail Gorbachev took the helm in Moscow. DPRK authorities said they wanted the plant to offset the reactor already operating in South Korea and to secure economic prestige. North Korea agreed to share the plant's cost and to accept IAEA inspection. The Soviets offered a $2 billion loan at 4 to 6 percent interest, although Pyongyang wanted to pay only 2 percent. The North Koreans wanted the plant to be built in five years, whereas the Soviets said it would take ten to twelve years. They would need two years just to decide on the best of six sites. The Soviets would operate the plant for five years, train DPRK technicians, supply enriched uranium, and help survey for uranium in North Korea (Document 23).

Why, then, did the Soviets change course? Moscow's policy shift could have reflected the Soviet Union's diplomatic isolation in the early 1980s and stepped-up pressures from the Reagan administration. But the Kremlin may also have concluded that the DPRK was going great guns in nuclear affairs and that Moscow should monitor the situation. By the end of 1984 the Yongbyon reactor and adjoining buildings neared completion—more than a year before Soviet assistance began. In 1986 the Yongbyon reactor commenced operations. Even though some facts suggest a DPRK decision to use this reactor to make a bomb, the DPRK did not produce plutonium for long periods and failed to put the facility underground, as it did many other potential targets for U.S. attacks.

Three years later, however, the Soviet-DPRK project was stalled. The North Koreans in April–May 1988 wanted production to begin at the reactor's first block by 1993. But the two sides had still not settled on the construction site. The Soviets said safety had to be the sole standard and blamed North Korea for the delay (Document 24).

Were the Soviets going slower now that Gorbachev was courting not only the West but also South Korea? Or were the North Koreans obdurate on details of their project with the USSR as they had also been with the United States and its partners that pledged to build two light-water reactors in the 1990s? Documentation from Soviet and Hungarian archives stops in 1988.

A Partial Victory for *Juche* and "Military First"

No communist regime has been so reliant on foreign aid as North Korea. Nevertheless, the only way the DPRK could enter the nuclear club was by being self-reliant and putting the military first. The nuclear device tested by the DPRK in 2006 represented more than half a century of determined striving. Like China, the DPRK entered the nuclear weapons club by dint of its own efforts, with only marginal and intermittent foreign assistance. Pakistan probably transferred centrifuge technology to North Korea in the late 1990s in exchange for missiles.

But we do not know precisely what Pakistan's A. Q. Khan turned over to the DPRK or Iran. The reality is that North Korea used the plutonium route for the device exploded in 2006 and that Pyongyang refused to provide any information on its uranium enrichment. Absent more evidence of foreign assistance, we should probably regard the Yongbyon plutonium producing reactor as basically homemade. Yes, the examples of Nicolae Ceauşescu's Romania and Muammar Gaddafi's Libya suggested that a government run as a family business could not organize everything needed to produce nuclear weapons.[15] But North Korea, somewhat like the USSR and China, showed that dictatorships could mobilize resources and press or inspire scientists to perform at a high level. ROK officials estimated that by 2001 the DPRK had 2,500 to 3,000 nuclear experts, many of whom trained at the Dubna facility in Russia (*Korea Times,* March 24, 2001).

Many forces and factors encouraged *juche.* Korea's Confucian heritage fostered risk-taking and hostility to outsiders. Communist ideology viewed politics as a zero-sum struggle. Pyongyang felt betrayed by Moscow and Beijing. Other communist leaders—Vladimir Lenin, Josef Stalin, Marshal Tito, Mao Zedong, Ho Chi Minh, and Fidel Castro—espoused self-reliance, but none (except Albania's Enver Hoxha) made it the cornerstone of state ideology.

After a brief uptick in DPRK-Soviet relations in 1984–1985, tensions again mounted. Gorbachev in 1986 called for "New Thinking" in Asia—to include a collective security system for the region and elimination of nuclear weapons. When Moscow agreed to attend the Olympics to be held in South Korea in 1988, this marked a Rubicon for Pyongyang. Its agents placed a bomb in a South Korean airliner that killed 115 persons in 1987—a warning to anyone wishing to attend the games.[16]

Meanwhile, the DPRK built a reprocessing facility at Yongbyon detected by the CIA in 1989 and observed firsthand by IAEA director Hans Blix in 1992. This facility would permit the North to process the nuclear waste from its reactor and extract the small amounts of plutonium produced in the nuclear reactor, plutonium that could then be used to manufacture nuclear weapons. In the late 1980s U.S. satellites detected at Yongbyon tests with conventional explosions of the kind needed to design a nuclear warhead. The head of the Soviet KGB, Vladimir Kyruchkov, reported in 1990 that North Korea had completed "development of [its] first atomic explosive device." By 1992 U.S. intelligence officials believed that North Korea had conducted as many as seventy explosive tests at Yongbyon.[17]

In need of cash and credits, the Soviet leadership agreed with Seoul to establish diplomatic relations in September 1990. Informed of this, the DPRK threatened retaliation. Pyongyang warned it would feel free to act on its own without consulting Moscow and to build its own nuclear weapons. It might extend diplomatic recognition to breakaway Soviet republics. Seoul insisted on and got a substantial quid pro quo: an end to Soviet military aid to the DPRK. "Consequently, in 1991, Moscow's military support to the DPRK, which had guaranteed the country's security since its inception, abruptly evaporated."[18] The DPRK press howled: "Diplomatic Relations Sold and Bought with Dollars."

In the years 2000–2002 Kim Jong Il and the new Soviet leader, Vladimir V. Putin, met three times and concocted huge plans for Russian military deliveries and for economic cooperation. Putin envisaged an iron silk road that would tie an intra-Korean rail system to the Trans-Siberian. But these plans collapsed when the Russian side again demanded cash up front.[19] This left North Koreans dependent on *juche*, plus donations from China, the ROK, and the United States and whatever they could get for their missiles and military technology from Iran, Syria, and other actors searching for such equipment and know-how.

Given that even Pyongyang's professed allies were subject to continual evasion and subterfuge, the record augured poorly for the success of any arms control regime requiring trust. The record surely suggested reasons for caution by those hoping to engage North Korea in a grand bargain. The North Koreans, no less than their erstwhile Soviet backers, excelled at *maskirovka*—camouflage and other deceptions. The more that Pyongyang sought to hide, the more intrusive inspection Washington demanded—making it harder to reach an agreement.

CHAPTER SIX

HOW KISSINGER AND ZHOU ENLAI GOT TO YES

Three basic approaches to negotiation have shaped North Korea's relations with its neighbors and with the United States. Pyongyang and Washington have negotiated not only with words but also with silences, gestures, threats, and even force. Often they have engaged in political demonstrations rather than in negotiation—a word that derives from the Latin for "do business." In the 1970s Henry Kissinger and Zhou Enlai, however, demonstrated how adversaries could accommodate their differences and build relationships of mutual gain. Negotiators for the United States and DPRK could do worse than to learn from these masters.

The Win-Lose Hard Line

Starting in the late 1940s, all parties to negotiations with North Korea usually followed the zero-sum assumptions about politics set out by Niccolò Machiavelli and other realists: What one side wins, the other must lose. The win-lose, hard-line negotiator seeks to be a lion and a fox, blending force with deception, masking both assets and weaknesses. The only rule is to win. Immediate profits outweigh long-term considerations such as a reputation for honesty.[1]

If a relationship is zero sum, a "lion" will meet brute force with brute force or, better still, sufficient force to overwhelm the antagonist. A "fox" may appear friendly but then bite when the other party relaxes. When the Greeks found they could not break Troy by force, they shifted to cunning and prepared a wooden horse as a gift. When the Trojans took the horse into their city, it erupted with soldiers who slew or enslaved most Trojans.

When hard-liners dominated U.S. foreign policy, they opposed talking to Pyongyang and instead urged that Washington wait and work for regime change. Alternatively, they orchestrated negotiations to expose North Korean perfidy. At times the DPRK also pursued a zero-sum strategy. Either it spurned negotiations or used them to buy time or score propaganda points.

The Win-Win Orientation

The win-win orientation seeks accords virtually for their own sake. This negotiator puts all his or her cards on the table and trusts that generosity will overcome greed and envy. From the late 1990s until 2008, the ROK government pursued a "Sunshine Policy" rooted in a positive-sum outlook. Aiming to build mutual trust and clear away misperceptions, the ruling party and some business leaders trusted that South and North could find win-win solutions. Pyongyang, however, did little to reciprocate. To make matters worse, two nominal allies in the White House and Blue House worked against each other: George W. Bush's hard line contradicted Seoul's unbounded generosity to the North.

Conditional Cooperation

Both the win-lose and win-win orientations usually yield bitter results for all parties. A third approach—conditional cooperation—achieved mutual gain when practiced by U.S. and Soviet negotiators, then by U.S. and Chinese diplomats, and, on several occasions since 1994, by U.S. and DPRK negotiators. One cannot say this approach has failed until it has been fairly tried and tested.

The conditional cooperator tries to advance his or her side's interests by *creating* values with other actors for mutual gain—not *claiming or seizing* values for one side only. If the parties can "grow" the pie, it will be easier to divide and achieve joint benefit. The conditional cooperator sees most relationships as variable sum with many possible outcomes. Yes, one side could win and the other lose. Or both sides could lose, for example, from a nuclear war (a negative-sum result). Alternatively, both sides could win (a positive-sum result), though one might gain more or in different ways from the other.

The conditional cooperator makes cooperation contingent on reciprocal action by the other side, taking precautions lest any party feign goodwill while trying to exploit generous concessions. The conditional cooperator is neither malevolent nor altruistic. He or she employs leverage gracefully—not with a sledgehammer. Though slightly distrustful, this negotiator fosters openness and habits of joint problem-solving. He or she shares information about preferences, beliefs, and even minimum requirements. He or she focuses on absolute gains—not relative benefits

Conditional cooperation paved the road to U.S.-Soviet détentes in 1955, 1963, 1972, and the late 1980s. It also opened the way to normalization and expansion of U.S.-Chinese relations in the 1970s.

Before looking at lessons from the past, let us review the menu from which foreign policy actors may choose in Table 6.1.

Sticks and deception are preferred by hard-line Machiavellians. Carrots and some mixed approaches could appeal to win-win optimists. Conditional cooperators look for the appropriate blend of pressures and positive incentives to achieve deals useful to both sides.

The real world, of course, is often muddier than these models imply. Divided opinions in the capital can yield foreign policies that reflect no clear strategy. Thus, U.S. foreign policy during the George W. Bush years reflected moderate as well as hard-line impulses. Because inputs were contradictory, so were outputs.[2]

Most of the strategies and tactics in Table 6.1 are nearly self-explanatory, but let us examine two that call for reciprocity—tit for tat (TFT) and graduated reciprocity in tension-reduction (GRIT).

TFT or True GRIT?

Actors on the world stage often practice tit for tat—replying in kind to tough or friendly words and deeds. For example, when London in 2009 barred DPRK citizens from entering the United Kingdom, Pyongyang responded by refusing visas to U.K. tourists. This has long been the pattern in Northeast Asia. From the late 1940s until the late 1960s, the United States and communist China became deadlocked in a TFT routine as each side matched or exceeded the harshness of the other's words and deeds. TFT also took hold in negotiations at

Table 6.1 Strategies and Tactics in Negotiation

Sticks
1. Bully and compel while bargaining from strength.
2. Insist on an eye for an eye or more.
3. Bargain from set positions.
4. Tighten the screws.
5. Play cards close to your chest and trick the other side.
6. Gang up with allies.
7. Exhaust the other side.
8. Mount a preventive or preemptive war.

Carrots
1. Deny there is a problem: See no evil; hear no evil.
2. Appease and bribe.
3. Bow to demands and pressures of crisis diplomacy.
4. Cultivate high-context relationships.
5. Open their eyes to New York and Inchon.
6. Buy time and hope for change.
7. Anneal (keep trying until a winning formula is achieved).
8. Legitimate and honor the other side.

Blending Sticks and Carrots
1. Cultivate hard, soft, and smart power.
2. Study the past and shape the structure of the situation.
3. Shape domestic mandate, and address domestic concerns of the other side.
4. Go tit for tat or GRIT to elicit cooperation.
5. Negotiate from principle (an agreed standard).
6. Decide to fractionate and move step-by-step, or try to solve all problems at once.
7. Do mediation or engage a third party.
8. Initiate and sustain momentum.

Panmunjom, where representatives of the United Nations Command sat across the table from those of the DPRK and China in rituals of mutual acrimony.[3] Each blamed the other for violating the armistice. An atmosphere of mutual distrust and disdain reigned. If a North Korean gave an American a piece of paper with his left hand—a sign of contempt—the American usually accepted it with his left. If the ROK built a "peace pagoda," the DPRK erected its own structure—slightly higher than the South's. Hoping to remove any doubt about its superiority, the DPRK eventually erected the highest flagpole in world at the Panmunjom Joint Security Area.

A Chinese interpreter described the strict protocol at Panmunjom in 1952–1953. He could not let a pencil shaving cross the midline of the table or acknowledge a colleague from Harvard University now an interpreter for the

---

Box 6.1 Roots of Reciprocity

Some psychologists describe a "reciprocal altruism" that may arise in the brain from a suite of "moral emotions"—sympathy, anger, gratitude, and guilt. Although this picture may apply to individuals' behavior, it probably fails to account for tit for tat between governments, particularly those in contention. Thus, Stephen Pinker says that reciprocal altruism can evolve so as long as the favor given helps the recipient more than it costs the giver and the recipient returns the favor when fortunes reverse. Individuals often do good deeds without any expectation of repayment down the line.[4]

Nevertheless, the presentation of a gift has long entailed the obligation of a countergift. Analysis of Indo-European roots suggests that the acts of giving and receiving were equivalent. The root *dō* of Latin *dōndāre* means "to give" in most dialects, but in Hittite it meant "to take." "Guest" (*ghos-ti-*) in Indo-European times meant the person with whom one had mutual obligations of hospitality. But he was also the stranger—a potential enemy, as in the Latin *hostis* for "enemy." The importance of ritual giving is underscored by the root *spend-*, which meant "to make an offering or perform a rite," whence, "to engage in a ritual act." Its Latin derivative *spondēre* means "to promise," as reflected in "spouse."[5]

UN (U.S.) team. When a flea bothering the Chinese team crossed the table and flew around an American, it broke the rules. Insults were de rigueur. When the North Koreans or Chinese repeated one of their "principles," Lieutenant General William K. Harrison, the often swaggering American leading the UN team, rolled his eyes—taken as shockingly crude by the Chinese. When the Chinese anticipated that Harrison would pick up his papers and leave peremptorily, they agreed beforehand to laugh loudly to make the general lose face before the waiting journalists. When the better equipped Americans offered to give typed-up transcripts to the Chinese, the interpreter refused and stayed up until all hours pecking on an ancient machine.[6]

We often think of TFT in tough terms—an "eye for an eye, a tooth for a tooth—in Korean, "*noon e-neun noon, e e-neun e.*" But the payback could also be a reward for a positive action. The winning formula in a computerized prisoner's dilemma tournament turned out to be a variant of TFT. "If you move first, be nice and cooperate. Thereafter, match the other player's previous move. Start nice and never initiate toughness, but be 'provokable'—immediately respond to toughness with toughness. However, you should also be 'forgiving'—return to cooperation as soon as the other side cooperates."[7]

> **Box 6.2 The Dangers of TFT at the Joint Security Area**
>
> The South Korean film *Joint Security Area* (JSA) shows how TFT can endanger peace. It portrays a DPRK and a ROK soldier standing opposite each other in the JSA. One mutters, "Watch it. Your shadow is crossing the line." Later, the two get into a spitting match. One spits on the ground near the other's shoe. He replies by spitting on the assailant's shoe. The first soldier then spits on the other's chest. He replies with a large glob on the other's face.
>
> But the film also shows two sets of border guards who befriend each other. An ROK sergeant crosses the bridge at night and enters the other's station. They drink alcohol, show each other pictures of loved ones, and play games with bullets. Each risks the strongest rebuke by his authorities if they are caught fraternizing. Finally, a DPRK officer interrupts the party and pulls a gun on the ROK soldier and his friend. The ROK sergeant shoots the newcomer dead and shoots his North Korean friend in the arm so that he will appear innocent.
>
> Back in the Joint Security Area, the head of the Swiss neutral observer team tells his novice but ambitious assistant investigating the incident: "The way we keep the peace at Panmunjom is to hide the truth."[8]
>
> Produced in 2001, *Joint Security Area* was the most expensive film ever made in the ROK and drew the largest crowds up to that time. Believing that the story dramatized the costs of Korea's tense division, ROK president Roh Moo-Hyun presented a DVD of the film to Kim Jong Il at their summit meeting in October 2007.

This version of TFT sends a clear message that force will be punished with force, whereas cooperation will be rewarded. The downside is that if both sides follow TFT, just one tough move puts them on an endless treadmill of DD—mutual defection. Once DD begins, it persists. This explains why the cold war conflict spiral was so hard to break. Washington and Moscow, as well as Washington and Beijing, usually matched each other's tough deeds and ignored tentative gestures of goodwill. The "security dilemma" aggravated perceptions and realities. Each party's defensive steps looked threatening to the other. TFT logic pressed for "multiple symmetry"—matching or surpassing assets and threatening actions in multiple arenas. Aggravating all this, cold war TFT was self-righteous. Each side reasoned: "They started it. We're just paying them back in kind."

The world got a strong dose of TFT in July 2009 when Secretary of State Hillary Clinton gave vent to what she called her mother's instinct. The North Koreans, she said, were behaving like "unruly children" when they test-fired missiles to get attention. A smart mother, she said, would not cave in to such tactics. A spokesman for the DPRK Foreign Ministry fired back that Secretary

Clinton had "made a spate of vulgar remarks unbecoming for her position." Her words, he said, "suggest that she is by no means intelligent. We cannot but regard Mrs. Clinton as a funny lady as she likes to utter such rhetoric, unaware of the elementary etiquette in the international community. Sometimes she looks like a primary schoolgirl and sometimes a pensioner going shopping." The DPRK missile tests were "necessary measures to protect the nation's sovereignty," he added—not conducted "to attract anyone's attention."[9]

The words and deeds of the United States and DPRK showed that they were impaled on the horns of a "security dilemma." If either perceived a threat but did nothing to counter the threat, its security could be jeopardized. But if either acted to bolster its security, this action could provoke the other to countermeasures that heightened insecurity. This dilemma tended to lock in tit-for-tat behavior.

The security dilemma is an example of prisoner's dilemma. Figure 6.1 shows how this model illustrates the choices for Washington and Pyongyang as they deal with each other on arms and other issues. If both sides cooperate, each gains. If one cooperates and the other defects, the cooperator suffers a serious loss while the other scores big gains (at least in the short run). If both defect, both suffer. If Washington or Pyongyang wishes to avoid big losses and possibly score big gains, each will defect. Their self-seeking, however, leads inexorably to joint losses. The ultimate dilemma is, When can potential rivals trust each other?

How can rivals get off the treadmill of mutual hurt and move toward mutual gain?[10] How, during the cold war, could Americans avoid having to choose between "Red and dead"? Professor Charles E. Osgood, a leading psychologist, proposed a form of conditional cooperation—what he called graduated reciprocity in tension-reduction.[11] Osgood saw that tensions escalate when rivals deal with each other on the basis of an eye for an eye, a slap for a slap, an insult for an insult. Once the first blow has been struck (or imagined), the parties find themselves on a treadmill of perpetual combat. To reverse the spiral of tensions, one side must take the first steps. Either side might start, but the stronger party can more safely accept the risks that often go with taking the first steps. As it begins, the initiator must make clear its intentions and say: "We are embarking on a strategy to reduce tensions. We will make several unilateral initiatives to demonstrate our goodwill. We will give you time to respond in a positive way. If you reciprocate, we will proceed to larger concessions and compromise accords. But unless tension-reducing moves become mutual, we will revert to hard-line TFT."

GRIT may encounter many pitfalls. First, a friendly gesture may be misconstrued. Thus, in 1970 a U.S. Army lieutenant in the UN Command at Panmun-

Figure 6.1 The Prisoner's Dilemma: Comply or Cheat on Arms Accords?

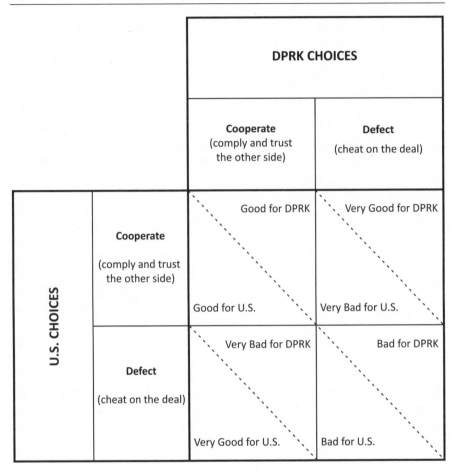

jom decided to improve the climate around the table in the Quonset hut where the two sides negotiated. Instead of glowering when a North Korean soldier indicated that he wanted to pass in a narrow aisle, the U.S. lieutenant smiled and made way for him. Shortly thereafter the American found himself surrounded by several North Koreans who began to jostle him. They interpreted his conciliatory gesture as weakness. "Knuckle practice" nearly ensued.[12] GRIT could not begin with goodwill gestures by a low-level officer. For GRIT to work at Panmunjom, the U.S. president or head of the UN (U.S.) team would have had to announce a new strategy and make sure that North Korean leaders and troops got the message.

Box 6.3 Shakespeare on How to Respond to Provocation

How verbal affronts can escalate and/or be contained was explained by the jester Touchstone in Shakespeare's *As You Like It*. The affronted party can respond with modest rejoinders that may become more intense. First, he makes only "the Retort Courteous"; second, "the Quip Modest"; third, "the Reply Churlish"; fourth, the "Reproof Valiant"; fifth, "the Countercheque Quarrelsome"; sixth, "the Lie with Circumstance"; seventh, "the Lie Direct."

But Touchstone also advised how to stop the escalation. The secret was to make everything conditional. He explained that one could avoid even the Lie Direct "with an If." Even if seven judges or mediators could not take up a quarrel, war could be avoided if the parties inserted an "if" into their dialogue. If,

> when the parties were met themselves, one of them thought but
> of an If, as, 'If you said so, then I said so;' and
> they shook hands and swore brothers. Your If is the
> only peacemaker; much virtue in If.

Such fancy footwork may be difficult in an international arena—especially if the parties speak different languages and must communicate through an interpreter. To reduce tensions, a diplomat should avoid offensive terms such as "unruly children" and use some positive ones (as when President Barack Obama in 2009 began to refer to the "Islamic Republic of Iran" by its preferred name).[13]

Second, small steps may lead nowhere. To be safe, the initiator usually begins with symbolic gestures. The other side may interpret these as cheap tricks and not reciprocate. Utter cynics also do poorly in world affairs, because they are blind to prospects of mutual gain. But suckers and martyrs also fare poorly in power politics. They ignore Laertes's advice to Ophelia: "Best safety lies in fear."

Third, the initiator may give up and renounce GRIT if the other side takes too long to respond. During this interval, the initiator's leaders are exposed to domestic criticism as well as external risk.

Fourth, domestic foes or jealous clients can throw a monkey wrench that disrupts the process of tension-reduction. Détente is a fragile flower, easily crushed.

Fifth, governments are not monolithic. Bureaucratic inertia and vested interests can throttle GRIT. Purveyors of propaganda and "dirty tricks" may continue their standard operating routines—business as usual.

Finally, momentum may be hard to sustain. The first steps toward conciliation may come cheap, whereas further moves encounter profound obstacles at home and abroad.

Without reading professor Osgood, wise leaders and diplomats might intuitively grasp the essentials of GRIT.[14] A series of actions by President John F. Kennedy after the Cuban missile crisis—publicly explained in Kennedy's "Toward a Strategy of Peace" speech on June 10, 1963—accorded perfectly with Osgood's principles. Soviet leader Nikita Khrushchev responded in kind as both men struggled to retreat from the brink of war in 1962 to a stable peace.[15] Despite provocations and foot-dragging by each side, the White House and Kremlin sustained the movement toward détente. By the end of 1963, Khrushchev said that Moscow and Washington were practicing "disarmament by mutual example."[16] Lyndon Johnson succeeded Kennedy in November 1963; in Moscow eleven months later Leonid Brezhnev and Alksei Kosygin replaced Khrushchev. But the White House and the Kremlin continued to grope for détente along the lines proposed by Osgood. The monkey wrench problem, however, repeatedly intruded—in Vietnam, the Middle East, Czechoslovakia, and divided Germany. Between Moscow and Washington, détente remained episodic until 1985–1986 when Mikhail Gorbachev began to implement his "New Thinking" and Washington reciprocated."[17]

The "China Card" and/or the Strategic Arms Limitation Treaty in 1972

The first sustained application of GRIT took place in the early 1970s as two master diplomats, Henry Kissinger, President Richard Nixon's special assistant for national security, and Zhou Enlai, China's premier, sought to normalize relations between their countries. Doing so, they created lessons that could be useful to Pyongyang and its interlocutors in the early twenty-first century.[18]

Even before Nixon's election, the future president signaled his belief that the time had come for the United States to normalize relations with mainland China. Kissinger planned to use a "triangular diplomacy" that played the "China card" to win concessions from Moscow and the "Soviet card" to influence China. History taught Kissinger that "it is usually more advantageous to align ... with the weaker of two antagonistic partners, because this acted as a restraint on the stronger."[19]

Mao Zedong and his number two, Zhou Enlai, decided to partner with the United States against the USSR. China would employ its own version of triangular diplomacy and "use one barbarian against another [*yi yi zhi yi*]." They would have to ignore past American efforts to destabilize their regime and perhaps even to assassinate Zhou.[20]

But how could the Nixon administration explore with Beijing the prospects of a fresh start? Washington had no representatives in mainland China, because it did not recognize the communist government. U.S. ambassadors in Warsaw and Geneva had met with their Chinese counterparts, but their dialogues were usually ad hoc efforts to cope with crises rather than to build a positive relationship.

As Kissinger told the story, Washington began in mid-1969 to use "unilateral steps, intermediaries, and public declarations" to communicate with China. The U.S. government hinted it would accept a Chinese recommendation that the two countries agree to principles of peaceful coexistence. Washington eased restrictions so that a U.S. tourist could buy $100 worth of noncommercial goods made in China. Washington also made it easier for scholars, journalists, and members of Congress to travel to China. Nixon also told leaders of Pakistan and Romania—both close to Beijing—that he wanted better relations with China. Beijing quickly signaled a response. It released two Americans whose boat had drifted into Chinese waters.

Using a Pakistani air marshal as go-between, Kissinger in October 1969 informed Beijing that the United States was withdrawing two destroyers from the Taiwan Strait, the narrow water wall separating "island China" from mainland China, which U.S. ships had patrolled since the Korean War. Other U.S. warships would continue to transit the strait, but Washington meant to remove an "irritant."

As tensions grew along the Soviet-Chinese border, Nixon in November 1969 declared that the United States "shall provide a shield if a nuclear power threatens ... a nation allied with us or ... a nation whose survival we consider vital to our security." In effect, he offered to protect China against Soviet attack! In December China released two other U.S. yachtsmen and invited the U.S. ambassador to visit the Chinese Embassy in Warsaw—not surreptitiously, as in the past, but through the front door.

The steps taken by Nixon and Kissinger harmonized with some but not all the principles of Osgood's GRIT strategy. They initiated small steps that, if reciprocated, could snowball. *Contrary* to Osgood's advice, however, they did *not* begin with an open and clear explanation that the White House was embarking on a new strategy. Instead, they conveyed their orientation to Beijing indirectly and hoped the Chinese would smile back. Both Nixon and Kissinger enjoyed secret diplomacy and later claimed it was necessary to bypass State

Department deadwood and fend off domestic critics in case Beijing spurned U.S. overtures.

Washington entered with Beijing what Kissinger called "an intricate minuet ... so intricately arranged that both sides could always maintain that they were not in contact."[21] Between November 1969 and June 1970, there were at least ten instances when U.S. officials abroad talked to Chinese at diplomatic functions— four times initiated by Chinese.

In December 1970, Pakistan's president sent a message handwritten by Premier Zhou Enlai for Pakistan's ambassador in Washington to read to Kissinger. It invited a special U.S. envoy to Beijing to discuss "the vacation of Chinese territories called Taiwan." The White House sent back an unsigned, typed reply on Xerox paper (not official stationery). It welcomed discussions in Beijing on the "broad range of issues, which lie between the *People's Republic of China* [PRC] and the United States, including the issue of Taiwan" (emphasis added).

Here was another change—cheap but potent: Washington began to speak not of "mainland" or "communist" China but of the "People's Republic of China." Washington had long called the communist Chinese capital by its former name, Peiping; now it used the communists' terminology—Beijing (or Peking), which means "northern capital." (This offended Chiang Kai-shek Nationalists who regarded Nanjing—"southern capital"—as China's true capital.) Zhou Enlai told a Japanese visitor in April 1971 that he "took specific note of the fact that for the first time an American president called China by its official name."[22]

On March 15, 1971, Washington removed all restrictions on travel to China, adding: "We hope for, but will not be deterred by, lack of reciprocity." Two days later Beijing denounced what it called the "renegade" Soviet regime in terms Kissinger interpreted to mean: "The Soviet Union had replaced us as [China's] principal enemy."

Beijing now continued GRIT by other means—what was later dubbed "pingpong diplomacy." On April 6, Chinese officials invited to Beijing a U.S. Ping-Pong team, then in Japan, having been authorized by Mao himself to do so.[23] When the Americans arrived in Beijing, Zhou Enlai hosted a banquet and announced "a new chapter" in Sino-U.S. relations. As Kissinger observed, Zhou "knew how to make gestures that could not be rebuffed." He was preparing the Chinese public and party leaders for a shift. His tactics implied, too, that if official Washington held back, Beijing could appeal directly to the American people.

Kissinger had prepared for this moment a list of "unrejectable steps"—stages of trade relations that could be expanded as Beijing reciprocated. Responding to

Beijing's ping, Nixon ponged: He approved the sale of French trucks to China even though they contained U.S.-made engines.[24]

Nixon and Kissinger, although devoted to realpolitik, were acutely aware that low-level exchanges might evolve into accords of high political significance. On April 14—as the U.S. table tennis players got a warm reception in Beijing—the White House relaxed U.S. restrictions on trade with China. Kissinger informed the Soviet chargé d'affaires of the impending shift and assured him it had no anti-Soviet intent. Kissinger's memoirs explained: "This is the conventional pacifier . . . by which the target . . . is given formal reassurance intended to unnerve as much as to calm, and which would defeat its purpose if it were actually believed."[25] Nixon on April 21 declared that he would cooperate with an invitation for the Chinese table tennis team to visit the United States.

Kissinger later wrote that his secret diplomacy and back channels sought to circumvent normal procedures. But there were heavy costs. For every agency excluded—beginning with the U.S. State Department—Kissinger became dependent upon another agency's facilities, increasingly those of the CIA. Nixon's special assistant for national security blamed the State Department for its tendency to circulate every cable throughout its bureaucracy. But Nixon and Kissinger paid a price for their close-to-the-vest diplomacy. Ignorant of the president's new approach, Secretary of State William Rogers and Vice President Spiro Agnew spoke out like broken records from the past. Rogers even stated in April 1971 that a presidential visit to China could not take place until Beijing complied "with the rules of international law."

Fortunately for détente, Zhou Enlai listened to Kissinger instead of Rogers. On July 9, 1971, after long and secret preparations, Kissinger flew to Beijing from Pakistan. All went well. On July 15, Nixon told the world about Kissinger's trip and announced that he, too, would visit China. In February 1972, the famed anticommunist clinked glasses with the world's leading revolutionist, Chairman Mao Zedong. Meanwhile, Kissinger and Zhou drafted the Shanghai Communiqué, which defined the framework for normalization.[26]

An interpreter for Zhou Enlai, Ji Chaozhu, confirms most of Kissinger's account but also relates many piquant details of failed communications between Washington and Beijing. He adds that Mao Zedong and Zhou Enlai wanted to normalize relations with the United States in 1945. But when they offered to meet President Franklin D. Roosevelt anywhere at any time, the U.S. ambassador to China, Patrick J. Hurley, who favored Chiang Kai-shek's Nationalists, did not deliver the message. Another opportunity evaporated when, after the

Chinese communists won control of the mainland in October 1949, Washington instructed U.S. ambassador Leighton Stuart to tell Mao and Zhou that the United States stood ready to provide a substantial credit to their government. But Stuart relied on a dilatory intermediary who did not deliver the message until the very day that China allied with the USSR.[27] When Mao wished to convey his desire to open the way to rapprochement with the United States, he invited U.S. journalist Edgar Snow to share the reviewing stand at a parade in 1970. Kissinger admitted, however, that Washington did not perceive this gesture as Mao intended.[28] Historians can debate whether these stories are based more on fact or on wishful thinking, but communication failures are surely a familiar fact of life—even when people speak the same language and live next to each other.[29]

Realizing that Secretary of State Rogers was being shut out by Kissinger and Nixon in 1972, Zhou Enlai went out of his way to include Rogers in some of the deliberations. Mao felt he was literally on his last legs in 1972, but he perked up and embraced an exercise regimen so that he would be in better shape to meet the U.S. president. Zhou's interpreter was overjoyed by all this because he had grown up in the United States and loved both countries.

Kissinger and Nixon hoped that their "China card" would buttress U.S. policies toward the USSR and Indochina. Just four months after Nixon's visit to Beijing, he met Soviet leader Leonid Brezhnev in Moscow and signed with him the first Strategic Arms Limitation Treaty (SALT 1), which set ceilings on both offensive and defensive strategic systems. A new détente began between the two superpowers known as "the Spirit of Moscow," which lasted just over one year. But it is doubtful that Washington needed to prod Moscow with its China card, because the Kremlin had many other reasons to welcome SALT 1 and improve ties with Washington. For its part, North Vietnam returned to the negotiating table with Kissinger, where, not much influenced by Beijing or Moscow, it got a deal permitting the North to swallow the South.

GRIT across the DMZ

GRIT can fail—especially sham GRIT when one or more parties fakes its desire for reconciliation or puts deal-killing jokers into its negotiation deck. Both Pyongyang and Seoul took turns in the 1970s proposing steps to foster North-South reunification. Each side was skeptical of the other. South Koreans had not forgotten North Korea's massive attack in 1950 and its many acts of terrorism since. As we saw in the last chapter, even Kim Il Sung's communist allies worried that he wanted war to accomplish reunification. And as the U.S. lieutenant learned at Panmunjom in 1970, a friendly gesture by one side without a high-level explanation could trigger not a reciprocal smile but an attack.

In the early 1980s the South's growing prosperity buoyed ROK diplomacy.[30] Seoul proposed a summit meeting with Pyongyang and twenty pilot projects to help the North and South to cooperate. But North Korea balked. It demanded withdrawal of U.S. troops from Korea as a precondition for high-level dialogue. A pattern emerged: North Korea demanded "all or nothing" while South Korea advocated "step-by-step" reconciliation. This was not true GRIT, but a propaganda war. Each side blamed the other for the ensuing deadlock. The next chapter shows how even if all parties have read and digested *Getting to Yes*, Osgood's theory, and Kissinger's memoirs, cultural differences can still obstruct an accord.

CHAPTER SEVEN

HOW TO GET TO YES ACROSS CULTURES

"For far too long," a veteran observer of North Korea remarked, "American diplomats have treated Kim Jong Il's political culture as his business. It's ours as well."[1]

"The central conservative truth is that it is culture, not politics, that determines the success of a society. The central liberal truth is that politics can change a culture and save it from itself." These realities, as expressed by former U.S. ambassador and senator Daniel Patrick Moynihan, apply not only to domestic affairs but also to international relations.[2] Most societies have their own strategic culture—manifested in consistent and persistent historical patterns in the way they and their leaders think about the use of force for political ends.[3] Attention to the strategic culture or national style or, to use George Kennan's phrase, the "sources of conduct" can "provide a way of distilling and making concrete and relevant the distinctive historical experiences of different nations and elites." In culturally diverse Asia, it is crucial to grasp this essence.[4] As Alexis de Tocqueville observed, "The importance of mores is a universal truth to which study and experience continually brings us back."[5] As Lucian Pye points out, the concept of culture, especially when enriched by depth psychology, is one of the few mega-concepts shared and enriched by several social sciences.[6] Clinching the point, Samuel Huntington's "clash of civilizations" thesis, valid or not, has resonated worldwide—translated in languages from Finnish to Farsi to Chinese.

High-Context and Low-Context Cultures of Diplomacy

The role of culture is minimized or even denied by neorealists who contend that power is the decisive factor shaping international behavior, that diplomacy is window dressing for the bedrock realities of military and economic might. In a different but parallel track, some modernization theorists assert that cultural differences nearly disappear when negotiations are conducted by professional diplomats—cosmopolitans liberated from misunderstandings and quirky behavior rooted in diverse languages and cultures. But is this so? In the era of globalization, do diplomats transcend the biases and habits of their upbringing? One expert replies, "No." Raymond Cohen makes a strong case that culture—a society's basic values and way of life—is a matrix that continues to condition how negotiators perceive the world and respond to signals, what they say, and how they say it. Cohen argues that negotiations are heavily shaped by whether participants embody a "high-" or a "low-context" approach to negotiations.[7] Most Asians, including Koreans, are said to lean toward a high-context style. They place great importance on the overall setting of negotiations. For Asians, a negotiated deal is impossible without personal bonds between the negotiators. Low-context Americans, by contrast, are said to focus on the bottom line and on abstract rules and laws, with little regard for cultural sensitivities and diplomatic niceties.

The Linton Thesis

An American with vast experience in Korea, Stephen W. Linton, has identified the North Korean approach to negotiations as very high context: "From the North Korean perspective, human relations should never be made conditional on something else. Problems should be portrayed as annoying obstacles to what is most important: friendship between the highest levels of leadership.... [An attempt] to meet leadership, resolve sensitive issues, and conclude agreements, all on a three-day trip to Pyongyang, sends the wrong message." Unlike many Westerners, Koreans see the personality behind law, not impersonal law itself, as the framework for action. "Proof of interest at the highest level is paramount for giving the negotiating process legitimacy."[8]

What if Linton is correct that Koreans, unlike Westerners, do not see impersonal law as the framework for action? Personal ties might help negotiators reach a deal, but if law counts for so little, how long will the deal last? Linton replies that "what appears to Westerners as 'the rule of law' can look like the 'misrule of law' to North Koreans. They would rather focus on the 'intention' rather than the wording of agreements.... Legalistic parsing of documents, accepted as a matter of course by Westerners, can look like insincere 'twisting,'" undermining faith in the written word. North Koreans' search for personality behind law is thus a search for constancy—not just emotion."[9]

"More focus on atmospherics and relationships between principals would go a long way," says Linton—but only if U.S. officials take these relationships seriously. "Many Koreans note, however, that while Americans are quick to use first names and slap people on the back in a display of friendship, their 'true intentions' are often 'inscrutable', and they do not seem to take friendship itself that seriously." An apparent "obsession with being 'neutral' and 'fair' ... can translate as a selfish reluctance to 'stand up for your friend' ..."[10]

As we shall see in the next chapter, Linton's thesis helps explain Jimmy Carter's accord with Kim Il Sung in 1994. It also dovetails with the observations of North Korean behavior by former Secretary of State Madeleine Albright in the late 1990s. It is consonant with Pyongyang's apparent rapture at former president Clinton's visit in June 2009. As we saw in Chapter 5, however, North Koreans often appeared callous and grabby when dealing with their ostensible benefactors in the USSR. Even with Western and international donors of humanitarian aid, DPRK officials are often rude and demanding.

Koreans can be abrasive—not only with adversaries but also with ostensible allies and fellow Koreans. Experience shows that when Koreans negotiate, whether from the South or the North, they are often tough with each other and practice all the varieties of *kojip* (stubborn intransigence). Thus, one experienced U.S. diplomat pictured Koreans as "very direct and tough people." When South Koreans tried to open negotiations with PRC representatives in Hong Kong in the early 1980s, "they made quite a hash of this. They tended to demand things up front, and to use very blunt and insulting bargaining techniques, and to misunderstand the difference between things that needed to be done with a wink and a shrug and things that could be done explicitly. And so they were getting nowhere."[11]

At times North Korean negotiators have seemed to play roles in "a theater of the absurd: Pyongyang promises, then procrastinates, then provokes, then pauses. After a long pause come new promises, and the cycle starts anew."[12] An American based in Seoul perceives a "now-familiar cycle of North Korean provocation, American warnings, North Korea follow-through and American calls for more peace talks"—calls mocked by Pyongyang as abject surrender.[13]

Can these contradictory impressions be reconciled? Scott Snyder's 1999 book devotes an entire chapter to what Cohen would call the high-context approach taken by North Koreans in negotiation.[14] North Koreans value *punuigi* (atmosphere) and *kibun* (good feeling). If these are absent, North Koreans practice *kojip*—expressed in brinkmanship, cries of wolf, demands for unilateral concessions, bluffs and threats, manufactured deadlines, and threats to walk away from the negotiations. All this aims to *create leverage out of weakness*. Also, before a deal is possible, the lead DPRK negotiator may need to show *kosaeng* (suffering)— proof for his bosses that he has done everything possible to extract the most possible concessions. Underlying the entire enterprise is "face." An American visitor to Pyongyang was told: "For us, saving face is as important as life itself."[15]

Snyder argues that North Korea's crisis-oriented negotiation style manifests a pattern of drama and catastrophe. Rather than a linear process with a discrete beginning, middle, and end, North Korea's dealings with the United States, according to Snyder, should be seen as a *cycle* in which issues are revisited, points reexamined, and interpretations redefined. Expanded, the process may include new issues and deeper mutual understanding.

Whereas Linton emphasizes face and feeling, and Snyder focuses on drama and catastrophe, each behavior may be part of a larger and quite distinctive "Korean" way of negotiating. Thus, one reviewer of this chapter observed: "One has only to spend time working with a South Korean company to see how similar are these strands, and how they have their own internal logic. It is inordinately frustrating to outsiders to encounter Koreans, because the mixture of bombast, face, stubbornness, and emphasis on context and good relations seems quite illogical. But ... it's all part of a whole that has an internal logic." This logic arises from the fact that "Korean culture is the most hierarchic in East Asia. As a result, when discussions between two 'equals' breaks down, it is a huge break, and also virtually impossible for them to back down or compromise from a stance, no matter how illogical that stance is—to do so is to lose all face and submit to the other side. In this context, a third party, usually of higher 'rank' is necessary to intervene and find a solution. Once relations are restored, great warmth and flexibility is possible by all sides, but approached in the wrong manner, this is impossible." These patterns of conflict and conflict resolution are evident in South Korean television drama. One reason that negotiations with North Korea began to record some progress after 2005 was that, in contrast to previous years, some negotiators were "deeply experienced with Korea itself (not just East Asia or negotiating in general), and the expectations of what to expect from the North Koreans in terms of style were much clearer than before."

Au fond, Confucianism may also shape Koreans' negotiating behavior.[16] Koreans are taught to show respect to elders. They believe that deference to superiors is proper, but they also expect that it may bring rewards—of equal or greater value. Indeed, elders are expected to take care of younger persons. But whereas it may be virtuous for a younger brother to give way to his older brother, or a wife to her husband, it could be wrong for a business or government agent to make a concession to another firm or country, because a concession might imply recognition of the other's superior standing. North Koreans, we shall see, often objected to any sign of unequal treatment in negotiations with the United States. They insisted on the principle *a word for a word, an action for an action.* The South's Sunshine Policy, however, endorsed one-sided concessions in the hope of gradually transforming the relationship.

Business deals may be concluded at a feast that celebrates a relationship rather than in some formal setting. "Good vibes" may set the stage for developing a personal and working relationship. But conviviality can also incubate corruption.

Can Politics Change a Culture and Save It from Itself?

Pyongyang's tough negotiating style probably reflects its dual heritage of Confucianism and communism. North Korea's political culture imbibed a double dose of aggressive authoritarianism as communist ideology and tactics were imposed on a Confucian foundation. At times DPRK diplomacy resembled that of Soviet warhorse Andrei Vyshinsky—known as Mr. *Nyet* at the United Nations during the early cold war—and the tough behavior of Chinese representatives at Panmunjom.

"Culture," however, may be long-lived, but it is not static. The behavior of Soviet negotiators mellowed in the last decades of the cold war, as did that of Chinese representatives when they sought normalized relations with the United States. A survey of Chinese negotiating behavior found that PRC diplomats often utilized ostensible personal bonds in pursuit of their goals.[17] "Friendship," for them, could be real or feigned. Either way, ostensible friendship would be exploited.

Henry Kissinger noted that the Chinese used friendship as a halter in advance of negotiation. By getting the interlocutor to admit at least the appearance of personal intimacy, the Chinese placed a subtle restraint on the claims the other side could advance. Unlike most depictions of DPRK negotiators, Kissinger, however, saw Chinese diplomats as "meticulously reliable." Also, "they never stooped to petty maneuvers; they did not haggle; they reached their bottom line quickly, explained it reasonably, and defended it tenaciously. They stuck to the meaning as well as the spirit of their undertakings." Across ten visits to China, Kissinger felt he was engaged "in one endless conversation with an organism that recalled everything, seemingly motivated by a single intelligence."[18]

Kissinger enjoyed immensely his talks with Zhou Enlai. Far from being a hard bargainer, Zhou asked only that Kissinger explain what he needed and why. China's number two leader practiced the openness valued, for example, by the founders of the Harvard Negotiating Project. To be sure, Zhou got much of what he wanted, but his style could not be classified in any formulaic way. It combined personal rapport with openness in what could be read as a sincere quest for mutual gain.

But we are left with the reality that, for both Koreas, "militaristic language seems to be a cultural preference." Even in South Korea, company statements are full of the words for "stronghold" and "military base." One firm calls its new mobile phone factory in Spain a "bridgehead to attack the European markets."[19]

The leitmotif of domestic propaganda in North Korea is not outrage that U.S. bombers once flattened the country, but pride that the DPRK compelled the United States to back down in the late 1960s over the *Pueblo* seizure and the shooting down of a U.S. reconnaissance aircraft. "Every North Korean school child knows that the United States did a lot of saber-rattling but ended up doing nothing." In recent years North Koreans know that they are poor compared to South Koreans, but are told that this is the price of going nuclear so as to keep America at bay—unlike people in the South, who must live under America's thumb.[20]

And even while Pyongyang's official Korean Central News Agency (KCNA) sometimes asserts the regime's desire for peaceful coexistence and friendship with the United States, audiences within the hermit kingdom are told that the North's "attack diplomacy" is forcing U.S. and other foreign adversaries to their knees. School textbooks, wall posters, and literary works show stammering American and international officials trying to placate the relentless "warriors" of the DPRK Foreign Ministry. The novel *Barrel of a Gun* ends with recognition by a U.S. negotiator that the DPRK is "a mighty superpower." The North agrees to let Americans inspect a cave for nuclear facilities provided they agree to provide 700,000 tons of food as atonement for their "strangulatory" blockade of the North. Posters assure North Koreans that DPRK bombs can reach not only Seoul but even Washington.[21]

"There's a siege mentality" in Pyongyang, said Michael Harrold, author of the book *Comrades and Strangers* about his seven years editing speeches for Kim Il Sung. "They're still on a war footing and one of the great unifiers is the constant threat from America." DPRK commentaries are filled with "burning hatred" for "imperialist aggressors." Because the term "U.S. imperialists" was used so often, the DPRK coined a special word—"*mi-je*," a contraction of "*miguk* [American]" and "*jegukjuija* [imperialist]." If DPRK propaganda did not find new ways to denounce foreign foes, says Harrold, "the outside world might think they're softening their positions."[22]

The diverse tacks taken by the KCNA and domestic media in the North resemble the apparent contradiction between the Soviet Foreign Commissariat's campaign for disarmament and the revolutionary line taken by the Comintern in the 1920s and early 1930s. On occasion, somebody in Moscow would explain how Soviet disarmament diplomacy revealed the impossibility of negotiated disarmament by capitalist regimes and thus the need for revolution. But *if* Western governments had agreed to cut their arms (then far superior to Soviet), the Kremlin would have been faced with a difficult choice between revolutionary purity and practical gain. Similarly, outsiders will never know how North Korea would respond if and when the United States and its negotiating partners make a convincing effort to bridge the gaps across cultural and political systems.

Whatever cynics may say about high-context opportunism, we see in the next chapter that the diplomatic breakthrough in U.S.-DPRK relations in 1994 owed much to personal contacts between Kim Il Sung and individual Americans, especially former president Carter.[23] Ambassador Robert L. Gallucci, who followed up on Carter's understanding with Kim Il Sung, negotiated an Agreed Framework with the North, mindful of the cultural and political differences between the sides. He sought to avoid forcing the DPRK regime to choose between its own collapse and military adventure. We see also that Madeleine Albright, secretary of state in the late 1990s, seemed to establish some personal rapport with North Korean officials and even with Kim Jong Il. Clinton may have done the same in his whirlwind visit in June 2009. All these individuals made progress in some negotiations with the DPRK in part because they showed deference to North Korea's political culture. Their behavior was rooted in American culture and backed by massive hard power. But their diplomatic skills, alert to cultural and political differences, were also critical.

How to Bridge Gaps

The balance sheet is complicated. Americans can rightly be pictured as *comparatively* low context and Koreans as high context in their approach to negotiations. But Koreans (both South and North) as well as Americans can be polite and friendly if they wish—or the opposite. Bad vibes can kill a prospective accord, whereas good vibes can help to foster and maintain one. Cultural differences probably played only a supporting role in the breakdown in U.S.-DPRK contacts after George W. Bush entered the White House. The Bush administration felt little need to negotiate seriously with North Korea. Its lead negotiator from 2005 through 2008, Christopher Hill, managed to find some common language with his DPRK counterparts. But he could not throw off the dead weight of overt and outspoken distrust and disdain toward the Kim Jong Il regime emanating from Washington.

Box 7.1 Does Creative Problem-Solving Benefit from Living Abroad?

Research suggests that experience gained by living abroad and adapting to foreign cultures enhances constructive imagination. Investigators analyzed a simulated negotiation between pairs of MBA students ($n = 108$) that demanded a creative solution to circumvent the nonoverlapping range in price between buyer and seller. It found that when *both* negotiators had lived abroad, 70 percent struck a deal acceptable to each side. Where neither of the negotiators had lived abroad, none found an acceptable solution.[24]

Because most Western negotiators have had more experience living abroad, they might be expected to be better at finding creative solutions to disputed issues than North Koreans, who, even if posted abroad, tend to lead insular lives. But U.S. diplomacy has been no more creative than North Korean. The formula for the 1994 Agreed Framework (discussed in the next chapter) originated in Pyongyang. Many of the trade-offs incorporated in six-party accords in 2005–2008 were first suggested by North Koreans. Why this paradox? Some U.S. diplomats may be creative but hamstrung by their bosses, the White House, or Congress. Thus, Republicans in Congress nearly torpedoed the 1994 Agreed Framework. If an authoritarian regime, though relatively isolated, arrives at an innovative solution, it brooks no opposition.

Also, the MBA students who excelled at problem-solving were younger and probably more open-minded than the American politicians, bankers, and diplomats whose opinions shape decisions on international crises. To challenges such as the 1997–1998 financial meltdown in Asia, authoritative voices in Washington and New York tended to recommend doing things the "American way." Their preference for market-driven solutions led to severe economic difficulties in the United States and globally in 2008.

To save a culture from itself and to bridge differences require a positive constellation of factors on all levels—individual, societal, and international. Included in these are effective negotiators, who possess these qualities:

- Knowledge of the players and the issues
- Management skills to coordinate his/her own team
- Timing—knowing when to wait, pull back, initiate, persist, and follow through
- Empathy with all whose interests are at stake
- Communications skills in speech, writing, and gestures
- Constructive imagination to identify or create mutual gain solutions
- Leverage—carrots and sticks—to motivate an accord
- Toughness—capacity to stand pat, threaten, bluff, or fight
- Flexibility to accommodate when appropriate
- Stamina and patience to endure long hours, frustration, and travel
- Integrity to inspire trust
- A winning personality
- Draftsmanship—ability to produce treaty language that copes with differences either by precision or by creative ambiguity
- Domestic support from his or her own government and society
- Internal drive to succeed
- Emotional intelligence

That Kissinger and Zhou embodied most of these qualities helped them to find ways to advance their overlapping agendas. But their personal rapport would have counted for little unless their governments already perceived reasons to cooperate. In short, a cordial relationship is not sufficient for a deal. Even the most gifted negotiators need a favorable society and state backstop, which includes the following:

- Confidence: can-do, problem-solving orientation
- Capacity to live with and even enjoy divergent viewpoints and cultures
- Acceptance of interdependence
- Checks and balances to promote rational decision making
- Hard, soft, and conversion power
- Societal fitness
- Consensus on foreign policy and willingness to follow smart diplomacy

Except for consensus, all these qualities have usually been abundant in the United States but nearly absent in North Korea. The DPRK regime has made the best of a weak hand.

The Global System

The transnational Edison Company helped modernize Korea in the late nineteenth century. Its business counterparts today, along with international organizations such as the European Union, could do far more to encourage North Korea to emerge from its shell. To make each participant feel more at home in the universe, all actors need to strengthen (1) habits of cooperation and global governance, (2) webs of international law, (3) networks of perceived interdependence, and (4) representation and acceptance of each party, weak and strong, small and large.

None of the foregoing conditions guarantees success in negotiations. A deal may be possible even though some are weak or absent. We see in the next chapters what worked and what failed in negotiations with North Korea in the last decade of the twentieth century and first decade of the twenty-first. From those experiences we can also discern what kinds of strategies and tactics are likely to succeed—or fail.

It is easier to fail than to succeed. Mutual trust is difficult to build but easy to destroy. Neither cynics nor martyrs do well when faced with prisoner's dilemma situations. Machiavellian pursuit of one-sided gains, reliance on deception, and addiction to positional bargaining get nowhere. However, naïve optimists open themselves to abuse.

CHAPTER EIGHT

HOW CARTER AND CLINTON
GOT CLOSER TO YES WITH PYONGYANG

The Clinton administration faced major challenges from North Korea from its first days in office in 1993 until its exit in 2001. Using combinations of military threat, private and public diplomacy, and positive incentives, the Clinton team managed to freeze North Korea's plutonium output and open the way to curbs on DPRK missile programs. In 2001 the stage was set for a grand bargain.

Crises abroad often paired with crises within North Korea. The Soviet Union's collapse in 1991 meant that the DPRK lost its premier patron even as North Korea's economy crumbled. A perfect storm ensued as Pyongyang's second most important backer, China, established diplomatic relations with Seoul in 1992 and profited from an upsurge of trade with and investment by South Koreans. In the midst of all this, North Korea's first and longtime leader, Kim Il Sung, expired in 1994, leaving a callow son, Kim Jong Il, to deal with multiple crises. American diplomacy toward North Korea under presidents Ronald Reagan and George H. W. Bush left a mixed but basically positive legacy on which the Clinton team could build. Nevertheless, there was a disturbing pattern in the 1980s and 1990s: Every one or two steps closer to an accommodation with Pyongyang seemed to be accompanied by one or more steps backward. North Korea joined the NPT in 1985 and the Biological Weapons Convention in 1987, but not the Chemical Weapons Convention or Comprehensive Nuclear Test Ban.

What *should* have contributed to harmony—the DPRK's accession to NPT in 1985—quickly became an international incident. As a non-nuclear state, North Korea pledged to forswear the development and acquisition of nuclear weapons. But then Pyongyang failed to complete a safeguards agreement with the International Atomic Energy Agency within eighteen months, as required by Article III of the NPT. Instead, the DPRK waited six years before meeting this obligation. Pyongyang linked its adherence to the safeguards agreement to the withdrawal of U.S. nuclear weapons from Korea.[1]

As we see from Table 8.1, the sources of conflict between the United States and the DPRK were stronger in 1993 than in other dyads and the bases for accommodation weaker. Whereas the United States had historical affinities and shared interests with China, the USSR, and other potential adversaries, there were virtually no perceived foundations on which to build U.S.-DPRK cooperation.

The trend line for South Korea in the 1990s was up; for North Korea, mostly down. South Koreans became more self-assured. In 1991 an ROK general replaced an American as head of the UN delegation at Panmunjom. In the early 1990s, the ROK had burgeoning ties with China, Japan, and Russia as well as

Table 8.1 Comparing U.S.-DPRK Relations with Other Dyads

Spurs to Conflict

	Resentment over Past Bloodshed or Other	Ongoing Political Territorial Dispute	Personal Animosity Between Leaders	Global Competition for Influence	Opposed Ideologies Institutions
U.S.-PRC in 1972	Yes	Taiwan	Some	Some	Yes
U.S.-USSR in 1983	Little	No	Yes	Yes	Yes
U.S.-Libya in 1983	Yes	No	Yes	No	Yes
U.S.-Iraq in 1993	Yes	Kuwait	Yes	No	Yes
U.S.-Iran in 1993	Yes	Israel	Yes	Little	Yes
U.S.-Cuba in 1993	Yes	Guantánamo	Little	Little	Yes
U.S.-DPRK in 1993	Yes	Korean peninsula	Yes	No	Yes
U.S.-ROK in 1993	Some	No	Little	No	No
ROK-DPRK in 1993	Yes	Yes	Yes	No	Yes

with the United States and Europe. North Korea, in contrast, was more isolated than ever. As if to deny economic reality or make it worse, Kim Jong Il, now known as "Dear Leader," established the principle "military first" (*sŏngun chŏngch'i*) to guide resource allocation for a near failing economy.

In early 1994, the DPRK proclaimed the Military Armistice Commission defunct and withdrew its delegation, replacing it with a military liaison. In September 1994 the Chinese delegation left the Military Armistice Commission at the "request" of the DPRK. Pyongyang also expelled the Czech and Polish delegations to the Neutral Nations Supervisory Commission established after the Korean War. In 1993–1994 Pyongyang revived its 1974 proposal to expand DPRK-U.S. talks into negotiations on a peace treaty—which would have left the ROK on the sidelines, as in 1953.[2] Though increasingly isolated, North Korea had two aces: First, its 1 million plus army, much larger than combined ROK and U.S. forces, was deployed within striking distance of Seoul. Second, many signs suggested that the DPRK was "going nuclear" in spite of its commitments to abjure nuclear weapons.[3]

South Korea's growing clout elicited contradictory responses in the North. The DPRK leadership had to consider whether to continue its quest for nuclear weapons. The likely terms of the debate are suggested in Table 8.2.

Table 8.1 continued

Bases for Conciliation

Positive Cooperation in the Past	Military Parity	Mutual Gain Available from Cooperation in Science and Culture	Economic Interdependencies	Shared Culture	Shared Enemies
Little	No	Yes	Yes	Some	USSR
World War II	Yes	Yes	Some	Some	No
Some	No	Little	Potential	No	No
Some	No	Some	Yes	Little	Iran
Yes	No	Some	Some	Little	No
Some	No	Some	Some	Little	No
No	No	No	No	No	No
Yes	No	Yes	Yes	Little	DPRK
Little	No	Little	Yes	Yes	No

Table 8.2 The Debate in Pyongyang: Should the DPRK Continue to Develop Nuclear Weapons?

Yes	No
We must practice self-help because Moscow and Beijing deserted us for the West and South Korea.	Our economic plight compels us to join the world economy while preserving our system.
Even a few bombs can deter an enemy attack and give us leverage. The U.S. talks big but does little.	If we go nuclear, South Korea and Japan may follow. It is better to strike a deal with the U.S. that isolates South Korea.
Our foes will not dare attack us because they do not want a major war. Besides, we can attack Seoul and blow up the South's reactors.	Hanging tough is pointless. No one will attack us if we renounce nuclear arms. The U.S. promises us energy assistance and normalization.

Events in distant places impinged as North Korea veered toward and away from arms control in the early 1990s.

1991. President George H. W. Bush announced on September 27 the unilateral withdrawal of all naval and land-based tactical nuclear weapons deployed abroad—believed to include some one hundred U.S. nuclear weapons in South Korea. Bush did not aim to please Pyongyang but to encourage Soviet president Mikhail Gorbachev to pull back onto Russian soil the tactical nuclears deployed in other Soviet republics, expected soon to split from the USSR. Eight days after Bush's unilateral action, Gorbachev reciprocated. All this permitted ROK president Roh Tae Woo on November 8, 1991, to issue the Declaration on the Denuclearization of the Korean Peninsula, under which South Korea unilaterally pledged to be nuclear-free. The stage was now set for the South-North Joint Declaration on the Denuclearization of the Korean Peninsula on December 31, by which the ROK and DPRK agreed not to "test, manufacture, produce, receive, possess, store, deploy or use nuclear weapons" or to "possess nuclear reprocessing and uranium enrichment facilities." They also agreed to mutual inspections for verification. Both sides also agreed to hold a summit meeting in Seoul—an encounter that nearly two decades later had still not materialized. North Korea's subsequent actions clearly violated its commitment to denuclearization, but a "declaration" between two entities not recognizing each other's sovereignty falls short of a treaty with legal obligations.

1992. Apparently satisfied that U.S. nuclears were gone, North Korea signed the safeguards agreement with the IAEA in January 1992 and ratified it in April.

In May the DPRK declared to the IAEA that it had seven nuclear sites and some 90 grams of plutonium that could be subject to IAEA inspection—the result of reprocessing eighty-nine defective fuel rods in 1989. Meanwhile, however, tensions were rising on related fronts: The United States imposed sanctions on two North Korean firms for missile proliferation, and IAEA inspectors reported that North Korea had diverted plutonium for a weapons program.

1993. As the recently elected Bill Clinton settled into the White House, the IAEA demanded special inspections in North Korea. Pyongyang's response was defiant. On March 12 the DPRK became the first country to announce plans to withdraw from the NPT and from the nuclear safeguards regime administered by the IAEA. Pyongyang said it would withdraw from the NPT

Box 8.1 The IAEA on DPRK Compliance with Safeguard Obligations

After the DPRK submitted its initial report to the IAEA under its Safeguards Agreement in May 1992, the IAEA began inspections. Inconsistencies soon emerged between the DPRK's initial declaration and the agency's findings. When the IAEA requested access to additional information and to two sites for storing nuclear waste, the DPRK refused access. In February 1993 the IAEA director general invoked the special inspection procedure provided for in the Safeguards Agreement. Rebuffed, the IAEA on April 1, 1993, concluded that the DPRK was in noncompliance with the agreement. The IAEA then referred this noncompliance to the UN Security Council. On 11 May 1993, the council called on the DPRK to comply with the agreement. On March 12, the DPRK announced its decision to withdraw from the NPT, but the DPRK "suspended the effectuation" of its withdrawal in June.

During 1993 and 1994, the DPRK permitted the IAEA to conduct safeguards activities of limited scope—containment, surveillance, and maintenance—to ensure, as the DPRK phrased it, the "continuity of safeguards" versus "full implementation" demanded by the agency. The IAEA reported in December 1993 that the limited safeguards permitted by Pyongyang gave no meaningful assurance of the peaceful use of North Korea's declared nuclear installations. Based on this report, the UN Security Council on March 31, 1994, again called on the DPRK to enable the inspectors to complete their required activities.

The agency needed to ascertain whether the core of North Korea's 5 MW(e) experimental nuclear power reactor was the first core as claimed by the DPRK. In May 1994, however, the DPRK hastily discharged the fuel from the 5 MW(e) reactor in such a way that the IAEA could not verify the core's history and ascertain "whether nuclear material from the reactor had been diverted in past years." On May 30 the president of the Security Council called for immediate consultations between the DPRK and the agency on this matter. On June 10, 1994, the IAEA Board of Governors decided to suspend all nonmedical technical assistance to the DPRK.[4]

in ninety days, citing a provision allowing withdrawal for supreme national security considerations. The DPRK government indicated its intention to remove fuel rods from its nuclear reactor and extract the weapons-grade plutonium. Following talks with the United States in New York, however, North Korea suspended its decision to pull out of the NPT on June 11—just one day before its withdrawal would have become legally effective. For its part, the United States granted assurances to North Korea against the threat or use of force, including nuclear weapons. Washington also promised not to interfere with North Korea's internal affairs. In July the DPRK announced it was "prepared to begin consultations with the IAEA on outstanding safeguards and other issues." Pyongyang also indicated it might consider a deal with Washington to replace its graphite nuclear reactors with light-water reactors (LWRs). This was the germ of the Agreed Framework signed in November 1994. But good news again paired with bad. In late 1993 U.S. intelligence estimated that North Korea had separated about 12 kilograms of plutonium—sufficient to produce one or two nuclear weapons.

The U.S.-DPRK "Agreed Framework"

1994. The second year of Clinton's presidency witnessed powerful displays of how combinations of private and public diplomacy, backed by threats and political-economic carrots, could turn a collision course to a path toward arms control and political détente. Clinton's memoir, *My Life* (2004), detailed how military pressures, material incentives, mediation by Jimmy Carter, and negotiations by Ambassador Robert L. Gallucci combined to move the United States and North Korea away from confrontation and to signing an Agreed Framework limiting the DPRK nuclear program. The year ended, however, with dramatic reminders that domestic politics can subvert an enlightened foreign policy.

North Korea seemed intent on hiding something. Early in 1994 the U.S. intelligence community reported that North Korea might already have produced one or two nuclear weapons. In February the DPRK finalized an agreement with the IAEA to allow inspections of all seven of its declared nuclear facilities, averting sanctions by the UN Security Council. On March 1 inspectors from the IAEA arrived in North Korea for the first inspections since 1993. But when the DPRK refused to allow the IAEA team to inspect its plutonium reprocessing plant at Yongbyon, the IAEA Board of Governors called on North Korea to "immediately allow the IAEA to complete all requested inspection activities and to comply fully with its safeguards agreements." On May 19 the IAEA confirmed that North Korea has begun removing spent fuel from its nuclear research reactor even though international monitors were not present. The United States and the IAEA had insisted that inspectors be present for any such action because spent fuel can potentially be reprocessed for use in nuclear weapons. On June 13 North Korea announced its withdrawal from the IAEA. In theory the DPRK was no longer a member of the IAEA but was still obligated to accept IAEA inspections as a corollary to its participation in the NPT.

The options and restraints facing the Clinton White House were similar to those that challenged the George W. Bush and Barack Obama administrations in later years. Should Washington try to conciliate the North by canceling the maneuvers conducted annually by U.S. and ROK forces? Or should the exercises be conducted again to intimidate the North and please hard-liners in the South? Going further, should U.S. bombers or missiles attempt "surgical strikes" to wipe out DPRK nuclear facilities, as Israel destroyed Iraq's Osiraq reactor in 1981 (and an alleged Syrian nuclear site in 2007)? Even if U.S. bombs hit their targets, radiation might spread. Even without nuclear weapons, North Korea threatened to ignite a "firestorm" in South Korea. Washington reckoned that if war erupted, 1 million South Koreans and 100,000 Americans could die. Despite the risks, the Clinton administration in early 1994 geared up for a surgical strike to knock out the Yongbyon plants.

The "atmosphere" (*punuigi*) in 1994 was extraordinarily complex. Even as the United States was beefing up its military forces in Korea with Patriot missiles and Bradley fighting vehicles, U.S. ambassador Madeleine Albright was trying to mobilize the UN Security Council to demand sanctions against the DPRK. Behind the scenes, Beijing was urging restraint on North Korea.

Meanwhile, several private American visitors met with Kim Il Sung. He talked with the Reverend Billy Graham, "pastor" to U.S. presidents; scholar Selig Harrison; and then former U.S. president Jimmy Carter. These unofficial contacts of "Track 2 diplomacy" laid the groundwork for subsequent "Track 1" negotiations by government officials. Meeting with Carter on June 16–17, Kim Il Sung (just weeks before his death), approved an outline of what became the Agreed Framework.[5] Some of what Carter did and promised exceeded any mandate he carried from Washington. Outflanking hard-liners in Washington and offering some international publicity to Kim Il Sung, Carter brought with him a CNN television crew.

The DPRK leader avoided any sign he was bowing to pressure. Just weeks before Carter's visit, Kim Il Sung had refused to meet with two emissaries chosen by President Clinton, Senators Richard Lugar and Sam Nunn, expected to carry a blunter message than Carter.

How did Carter's intervention defuse the crisis and bring the contending parties to the table? He went to the top (as recommended by Stephen Linton) and created a way for the parties to move beyond the impasse on special inspections. He enabled each side to back away without losing face. Washington could retreat from its commitment to pursue UN sanctions. Washington's counterdemand—not to refuel the shut down reactor—permitted it to declare victory. The North Koreans could say they had simply been seeking a secure source of electricity. Unlike conventional mediators, Carter took actions that effectively committed the Clinton administration to resume negotiations even though he was acting as a nearly free agent.[6]

Neither Washington nor Pyongyang in 1994 followed Charles Osgood's GRIT principles precisely. Neither side issued a public declaration of peaceful intent. Neither promised that small steps would lead to larger ones. But when Kim Il Sung signaled to Carter a willingness to trade the DPRK nuclear weapon program for a package of economic aid and international recognition, the White House responded promptly and positively. U.S.-DPRK negotiations began in July and stopped only briefly after Kim Il Sung's death on July 8, 1994 (at age eighty-two), after which the designated heir, son Kim Jong Il, became the paramount DPRK leader.

Negotiations resumed in August. Following several rounds of talks, the heads of each delegation—Gallucci and Kang Sok-Ju—signed the Agreed Framework in Geneva on October 21, 1994.[7] The pact was neither a treaty nor a legally binding executive agreement;[8] rather, it was a political commitment between the two countries noted by the UN Security Council. A model of diplomatic finesse, it constituted a package of conditional cooperation. The agreement (just a few pages) stipulated that "in accordance with the October 20, 1994 letter from the U.S. President [Clinton]," the United States would lead a consortium "for the provision to the DPRK of a LWR project with a total generating capacity of approximately 2,000 MW(e) by the target date of 2003." For its part, the DPRK would freeze its graphite-moderated reactors and related facilities and dismantle them "when the LWR project is completed." The IAEA would monitor the freeze. The United States and the DPRK would cooperate in finding a method to store the spent fuel from the 5 MW(e) reactor and "dispose of the fuel in a manner that does not involve reprocessing it in the DPRK." To offset the energy lost by the freeze, the United States would every year supply the DPRK with 500,000 tons of heavy oil for heating and electricity production (an amount just half what the Soviets provided annually in the 1990s) until the first LWR unit became operational. The Americans thought that coal-powered energy plants would be more useful to North Korea, but if Pyongyang insisted on LWRs, the Americans would go along.

The framework committed the two sides to "move toward full normalization of political and economic relations." They would "reduce barriers to trade and investment, including restrictions on telecommunications services and financial transactions"; open liaison offices in their respective capitals; and, as progress was "made on issues of concern to each side," "upgrade relations to the Ambassadorial level."

The United States would "provide formal assurances to the DPRK, against the threat or use of nuclear weapons by the U.S." For its part, the DPRK would "consistently take steps to implement the North-South Joint Declaration on the Denuclearization of the Korean Peninsula" and "engage in North-South dialogue." The DPRK would remain a party to the NPT and "allow implementation of its safeguards agreement under the Treaty."

The last paragraph read: "When a significant portion of the LWR project is completed, but before delivery of key nuclear components, the DPRK will come into full compliance with its safeguards agreement with the IAEA." Spelling out this provision, the parties agreed in confidential notes that full-scope IAEA safeguards would be applied when the major non-nuclear components of the first LWR unit were completed but before the delivery of key nuclear components. Here was one way the accord bridged differences. It stretched out the schedule for inspections and linked them to delivery of key reactor components.

Looking back, we see that the DPRK shaped the structure of the negotiations more than the United States did. North Korea managed to exclude the ROK and China from the deliberations. Pyongyang was better organized for the negotiations than Washington was. Gallucci came onto the job full time late in the game. Pyongyang excelled in orchestrating moves at and away from the table—threatening to withdraw from the NPT and to unload the reactor.

Because the winning formula was proposed by Pyongyang in 1993 and revived by Carter in 1994, some observers said that the Agreed Framework could have been concluded a year earlier. One U.S. official replied that political support in Washington would have been too weak then. The 1994 deal won support by compelling "the North Koreans to defuel the reactor [and] to have roughly 30 kilograms of plutonium sitting in this pond of water deteriorating."[9] A more sinister explanation was that some U.S. politicians thought the Kim Jong Il regime would collapse before the LWRs were completed.

Was the Agreed Framework a Mirage?

Critics—right, left, and center—found or invented many reasons to fault the Agreed Framework. Some complained that it gave too much to a bad actor—that Clinton was deceived by signs that North Korea would rein in its WMD programs. Some arms controllers said the framework weakened the nonproliferation regime the IAEA was trying to impose on Iran and Iraq. The accord required the DPRK to "can" and store its spent nuclear fuel, but did not require the North to give up its nuclear components entirely—as Belarus, Ukraine, and Kazakhstan had done following the Soviet Union's breakup. This gave North Koreans easy access to spent nuclear fuel that could be reprocessed—their major lever in the tense times after 2002. Another shortfall was that the 1994 accord permitted North Korea to delay its return to the NPT by more than five years. Finally, the framework focused on a single known plant that could produce *plutonium* for nuclear weapons, but did not cover the rest of the country. What about *other* facilities that might produce plutonium *or* enriched uranium?

Defenders of the Agreed Framework argued that politics is the art of the possible. The 1994 accord was not ideal, but the Clinton team saw it as the least bad option available. It generated value for each side and avoided war. Yes, the Agreed Framework mentioned no facilities other than Yongbyon, but it reaffirmed the 1991 declaration by North and South Korea banning uranium enrichment facilities as well as plutonium reprocessing facilities in the DPRK or ROK.[10]

The benefits of the 1994 Agreed Framework were no mirage. The plutonium production halted in 1994 was a much larger program than the uranium enrichment allegedly activated circa 1998 (discussed in our next chapter). Had the earlier program kept going, it would have yielded sufficient plutonium to make several nuclear weapons a year.

The Agreed Framework promised security on the cheap. The total cost of providing North Korea with heavy oil and two LWRs was expected to be

Box 8.2 The IAEA and DPRK under the Agreed Framework

The IAEA maintained a continuous presence at Yongbyon to verify the freeze until 2002. The agency viewed its activities under the Agreed Framework as a subset of its duties under the earlier Safeguards Agreement. It monitored the 5 MW(e) reactor, the radiochemical laboratory (for reprocessing), the fuel fabrication plant, and the partially built 50 and 200 MW(e) nuclear power plants. The agency and DPRK continued to disagree on the legal status of the Safeguards Agreement, but the two sides held technical meetings, usually twice a year, to deal with outstanding issues. For the agency, the main topic was the preservation of existing information. Despite seventeen rounds of technical consultations, however, the agency reported "no progress" on key issues. In September 2000, just before high-level visits by U.S. and DPRK officials, the agency determined it would need three or four *years* to verify the correctness and completeness of North Korea's initial report. But the DPRK refused even to discuss such a program of work. The last such technical meeting took place in November 2001. IAEA efforts to convene another technical meeting in 2002 were rebuffed.[11]

$5 billion—most of it paid by Japan and South Korea. This was not small change, but it was trivial next to the cost of building defenses against DPRK nuclear-tipped missiles. As of 1994, the United States had already invested more than $50 billion just researching antimissile defense. By 2010 the total bill for developing and deploying rudimentary antimissile defenses would exceed $200 billion.

Implementation: Slow and Not Sure

Like Henry Kissinger and Zhou Enlai in the early 1970s, Washington and Pyongyang seemed quite aware in the mid-1990s that small steps could have large consequences. Both sides began in January 1995 to dismantle the trade embargo each had imposed forty-five years before. Each side would now permit direct phone calls and financial transactions. Washington would permit U.S. steelmakers to buy magnesite from North Korea to line their blast furnaces. DPRK and U.S. journalists could now open news bureaus in each other's country. But the U.S. State Department said that further relaxation of economic sanctions would depend on progress on the "nuclear issue" and on DPRK restraint in exporting missile technology—an issue not mentioned in the Agreed Framework.[12]

The Clinton administration organized the Korean Peninsula Energy Development Organization (KEDO) with Japan and the ROK to build two light-water reactors for the DPRK. But Republicans, who won control of Congress in November 1994, balked at funding the Agreed Framework. Never approved by a Congress short on funds, the Clinton administration went, hat in hand, to the European Union to gain funding for the undertaking. That is how the EU became a member of KEDO alongside the United States, Japan, and South Korea. KEDO's first director, Stephen Bosworth (Barack Obama's choice in 2009 to oversee dealings with the DPRK), later commented that "the Agreed Framework was a political orphan within two weeks after its signature."

Kim Jong Il introduced his "military-first" priority not long after approving the Agreed Framework. Did this mean that Pyongyang ignored and even exploited the Clinton administration's efforts to improve relations? More likely, Kim Jong Il—trying to fill his late father's role—felt that he must appease military elites. Noting Republicans' disdain for the Agreed Framework, Kim may have felt that North Korea must be prepared for all contingencies.

The LWR project moved very slowly.[13] The target date for its completion was 2003, but key contracts were not let until 1997—three years after the framework was signed! In 2002 the first concrete was poured, but KEDO was still soliciting bids for some components. By 2002 it looked as though the reactors could not be completed until 2009 or later.[14] The KEDO Web site in 2002–2003 showed a glorious drawing of the LWR project but not much else.[15]

Responsibility for the delays fell on many shoulders. KEDO members had to resolve who would pay how much and who would build what. North Korea demanded such high wages for its workers that KEDO looked to import labor from other countries. Seoul and Tokyo would pay most of the LWR construction costs, but Pyongyang wanted to deal only with Washington. The North sought to exclude any evidence of South Korean equipment, know-how, or personnel. It wanted not just the reactors but also—gratis—the supporting infrastructure and communications links.

North Korea charged that the United States was not fulfilling its obligations. Work on the LWRs proceeded slowly. Oil shipments were often late. Many economic sanctions remained. Diplomatic relations between the United States and North Korea were not established. The Clinton administration said that it suspected illicit nuclear programs in North Korea, but several on-site visits by U.S. experts, including former defense secretary William Perry, found no evidence for these suspicions.

Famine and *Juche*

In 1997 North Korea faced a severe famine. Harvests slumped thanks to the chronic ailments of communized agriculture aggravated by two years of floods followed by drought. The DPRK regime urged its people to get by on two meals a day—one, if they could manage.

North Korea's rule seemed to be: "Never admit any weakness." Outsiders mobilized to send food, but Pyongyang still balked at direct talks with Seoul. The ROK sent rice, but Pyongyang refused to say thanks. Instead, it arrested some South Korean fishermen on charges of spying. Seoul then blocked outside food aid until Pyongyang changed its tune. Even as North Korea began to receive more food and other assistance from outside, a DPRK submarine crashed onto the South Korean coast, disgorging a dozen commandos, whom the South Koreans hunted down. Even as DPRK diplomats met with U.S., PRC, and ROK representatives at Columbia University, Pyongyang demanded withdrawal of U.S. troops from the peninsula and cancellation of U.S.-ROK maneuvers scheduled for late 1997.

The year 1997 thus marked an intensification of what we might call the *juche* syndrome. The worse North Korea's economic problems became—when the regime might be expected to be most responsive to foreign pressures—the more belligerent were its behavior and ungrateful its words. In August 1997 North Korea announced it was withdrawing from the International Covenant on Civil and Political Rights after it was reprimanded for human rights deficiencies and for failure to report on its implementation of the accord. The covenant obliges each signatory state to uphold for individuals the rights of expression, of peaceful assembly, of association with others in trade unions, and of taking part in public life and elections. The eighteen-member UN human rights committee responded on October 30, 1997, that no signatory can withdraw from the covenant, which—deliberately—has no provision for termination. However, Pyongyang did not withdraw its 1989 accession to the 1948 Genocide Convention, nor did it as yet repudiate the 1994 Agreed Framework.

North Korea's economic problems led to speculation. Might a dying North Korea launch a last-ditch attack on the South? Might North Korea open its borders and deluge the ROK with millions of refugees? Might a "German" solution became more thinkable—collapse of the communist government followed by a merger of noncommunist and communist regions, endorsed by the great powers? If the DPRK collapsed, would a unified Korea inherit its nuclear arms?

Can Sunshine Open All Doors?

In the winter of 1997–1998 the South Korean economy also shuddered, throwing many people out of work and helping to elect a new president, Kim Dae Jung. Devoted to a win-win approach, Kim Dae Jung in 1998 launched his Sunshine Policy toward the DPRK. No longer would the South seek to undermine or absorb the North. Instead, the new ROK government would foster trade, tourism, and investment in special economic zones in the North. Some ROK corporations embraced these ideas, hoping to profit from closer ties with North Korea. Pyongyang responded fitfully—alternating frowns with occasional smiles.

In the slightly mellower climate of 1998–2000, the DPRK government renewed its efforts to normalize relations with the United States and other Western governments. It established diplomatic relations with Australia, the EU, and most EU members.

Kim Jong Il received Kim Dae Jung in Pyongyang in mid-June 2000. The ROK president agreed to a DPRK formulation holding that the North and the South would resolve the "country's reunification independently"—that is, with no role for outsiders. Thus, Kim Jong Il exploited the Sunshine Policy to drive a wedge between the ROK and its major ally.[16]

The ROK president received the Nobel Peace Prize for these efforts. In 2003, however, the world learned that the North's leader had extorted hundreds of millions of dollars for deigning to entertain his ROK counterpart—even delaying the meeting by days until he had cash in hand. Following the bribery revelations, Pyongyang urged Seoul not to prosecute all those indicted for illegal transfers of funds to North Korea. DPRK officials piously hoped that the suicide of Hyundai Asan chairman Chung Mong Hun, a key figure in the bribery scandal, would not affect Hyundai's projects in the North.[17] Apparently without shame, Hyundai Asan continued to funnel millions to the DPRK.[18]

Kim Dae Jung's Sunshine Policy resembled Osgood's GRIT model, described in Chapter 6, but the mutual trust sought by Osgood's strategy could not be purchased by under-the-table bribes. More basically, Kim Dae Jung failed to demand reciprocity. The practitioner of GRIT must strike a balance between conciliatory initiatives to encourage the other side and defensive measures to guard against exploitation by a manipulative foe.

Osgood assumed that the stronger side can afford to be generous and give the weaker party time to respond.[19] South Korea proceeded from relative strength and gave far more to the DPRK than it got. Whereas the North would get immediate benefits, the South hoped for long-term gains. Some South Koreans expected that the ROK would simply inherit the LWRs after the DPRK collapsed, which could be soon. Nevertheless, Seoul's dilemma was how to sustain movement toward cooperation without "giving away the store."[20] Kim Dae Jung's successor, Roh Moo Hyun, elected in 2002, continued this Pollyannaish approach until it was ended by a new president, Lee Myung-bak in 2008.

Toward a Grand Bargain between Washington and Pyongyang?

Prospects for an accommodation with Pyongyang gained from the near absence of brinkmanship in DPRK policy toward South Korea from June 1999 to June 2002. During those three years, spanning the last eighteen months of the Clinton administration and the first eighteen months of the Bush era, the North provoked no major clashes at sea or along its border with the ROK.

Some experts suggested arms control measures to build confidence between Seoul and Pyongyang. Among the suggestions were measures to increase transparency for each side's military forces; constraints on military deployments near the DMZ; a "nonoffensive defense" military posture to replace any capacity for deep penetration across the DMZ, verifed by the United Nations and observers from each side; a direct communications link between the ROK and DPRK defense ministers; reduced military forces (U.S. as well as Korean) on each side of the DMZ; and promises by Washington, Beijing, and Moscow not to circumvent the DPRK-ROK accords.

In October 1999 the Clinton administration unveiled the "Perry Initiative," named for William J. Perry, special adviser to the president and former secretary of defense. Calling for a new round of negotiations, Perry proposed that if the DPRK agreed to a "verifiable cessation" of its missile program, the United States would provide a series of economic and diplomatic benefits to North Korea leading to normalization of relations with the United States.

The point-counterpoint pattern described in Chapter 1 emerged strongly in 2000. At home, the Pyongyang regime proclaimed that the Arduous March had succeeded and allowed that some forms of free enterprise (by other names) could proceed. Having pocketed a few million for his trouble, Kim Jong Il met with ROK president Kim Dae Jung. Newspapers were exchanged with the South, though Pyongyang ended the exchange after a few days. The Dear Leader's great thoughts were being published and promoted from Madagascar and East

Germany to Laos and Ecuador. Kim Jong Il traded visits and pleasantries with Vladimir Putin. The KCNA reported that the Russian and DPRK leaders "forged intimate relations and deepened trust through their Pyongyang meeting in July 2000." A South Korean report stated that Kim Jong Il offered Putin the giving up of the DPRK intercontinental missile development program in exchange for two or three satellite launches a year.[21]

On October 11 the KCNA reported: "With relations between the DPRK and the U.S. dramatically improving in Washington, the [Worker's] Party's 55th birthday celebrations were held nationwide, marked by a grand parade, an evening gala, a gigantic gymnastic display and various kinds of congratulatory meetings. In a mood of reconciliation between north and south Korea after the historic inter-Korean Pyongyang summit in June, forty-two south Korean delegates, including representatives of civic and religious groups, were invited to attend the ceremony for the first time."[22]

More troublesome for the United States and its allies, North Korea in August 2000 began delivery of fifty Nodong missiles and seven launchers to Libya, reportedly procured on behalf of Iraq and Egypt as well as Libya, at a cost of $600 million. Moreover, as we see in the next chapter, the DPRK was continuing a clandestine program, begun in the late 1990s, to produce highly enriched uranium. Meanwhile, Pyongyang stonewalled any effort by the IAEA to check the accuracy of DPRK reports on activities at Yongbyon. A generous interpretation is that Pyongyang wanted to conceal its past but might be willing to abide by the 1994 and subsequent obligations in the future. But a cynic might infer that Pyongyang labored to deceive outsiders and still win outside aid and concessions.

Nevertheless, the summit meeting between the two Kims in 2000 ushered in a renewed effort by Washington and Pyongyang to reach a grand bargain. These efforts were spearheaded by Madeleine Albright, secretary of state since December 1997. Her experiences confirmed Linton's thesis about the importance for Koreans of high-level personal contacts.[23] Meeting the DPRK foreign minister Paek Nam-Sun for the first time in Bangkok in July 2000, she was struck by his "smooth professionalism."[24] Their talk, expected to last fifteen minutes, continued for an hour. She asked her opposite number if Pyongyang would dispatch a high-level emissary to Washington to reciprocate the visit to Pyongyang in 1998 by Perry. Though it took a few months to get a reply, in October 2000 the DPRK sent to Washington Vice Marshal Jo Myong Rok, thought to be the second most powerful figure in Pyongyang. Visiting the State Department, the vice marshal wore a gray suit; half an hour later, he appeared at the White House in a full military uniform adorned with medals. Was his costume change a sign of professionalism or a sign that Pyongyang remained unbowed?[25]

"With a flourish," according to Albright, the vice marshal presented Clinton a letter from Kim Jong Il inviting the U.S. president to Pyongyang. When Clinton hedged, Jo pressed for a definitive reply. When Clinton suggested that Albright go first to prepare the ground, Jo did not give up. He said that if the president and secretary came together, "we will be able to find a solution to all problems." As Albright observed, "North Korea's top-down decision-making style didn't fit well with our practice of trying to 'pre-cook' arrangements . . . before committing the President." Nevertheless, Jo invited Albright to Pyongyang.

Before Jo left Washington, each side pledged "no hostile intent" toward the other. The joint pledge amounted to a constructive compromise between the North's demand for a nonaggression pact and the traditional U.S. position that the UN Charter already bans aggression. The importance of the pledge was underlined in 2002 when the Bush administration refused to reaffirm it.

But both sides pointed to breakthroughs. In the KCNA version, issued on October 12, 2000, both sides "declared that they are ready to take a new orientation in the bilateral relations. As the first important step both sides . . . affirmed the commitment to make all efforts to establish new relations free from past antagonism in the future." The parties aimed to build on "principles stipulated in the June 11, 1993 DPRK-U.S. joint statement and reconfirmed in the October 21, 1994 agreed framework." These principles included "mutual respect for sovereignty and non-interference in each other's internal affairs" and the utility of sustaining "diplomatic contacts on a regular basis through bilateral and multilateral channels." They discussed a "mutual visit of economic and trade experts in the near future to seek trade and commercial possibilities of contributing to the creation of an environment beneficial to the two peoples and favourable for expanding economic cooperation in northeast Asia as a whole."

The parties agreed that "settlement of the missile issue would make an important contribution to the radical improvement of the DPRK-U.S. relations and peace and security in the Asia-Pacific region. The DPRK side informed the U.S. that it will not launch any long-range missile while the talks are going on to discuss the missile issue as an effort to build new relations." The communiqué "took note of the fact that an access [for former defense secretary William Perry] to the underground facility in Kumchang-ri was useful for clearing the U.S. of its worry"—rendered as "concern" in the U.S. text.

"The DPRK side expressed thanks to the USA for its significant contribution to meeting the DPRK's humanitarian needs in food and medicine aid." The United States expressed thanks to the DPRK for cooperating in the excavation of remains of the U.S. soldiers who were reported missing during the Korean War. Both sides agreed to support and encourage international efforts to combat terrorism as pointed out in the October 6, 2000, joint statement.

The KCNA on October 12 published what it claimed was the full text of the joint communiqué issued at the end of Jo's three-day visit to Washington. But the North Korean version as rendered in English differed from the official U.S. text in several ways. It omitted any reference to the desirability of "transparency" in implementing the 1994 Agreed Framework. Instead, it said that "both sides agreed to make clearer the implementation of the commitments made in the agreed framework." Discussing the desirability of converting the 1953 Armistice Agreement into a permanent peace mechanism, the KCNA alluded to "four-power talks"—which implied participation by the ROK as well as China—as an afterthought, rather than early in the sentence, as in the U.S. version. The DPRK version called for "denuclearization" of the Korean peninsula, whereas the American text called for a "nuclear-weapons-free" peninsula. Anxious to push all troubles under the rug, the DPRK text said that Albright would visit Pyongyang to "make arrangements for the President's [Clinton's] visit." The U.S. text said she would "prepare for a possible visit" by the U.S. president.

Accelerating the pace of diplomacy, Albright arrived in Pyongyang in late October 2000. She had been told that to get diplomatic results with North Korea, one had to take time and build a relationship. But she had only two days—not even the three derided by Linton! When she met Kim Jong Il, the Dear Leader promptly expressed admiration for her energy (after a marathon flight) and expressed gratitude for two symbolic acts—Albright's visit to his father's mausoleum and a condolence letter from Clinton after Kim Il Sung's death—as well as for humanitarian assistance in recent years. Again expressing the hope that Clinton would visit, the DPRK leader averred that "if both sides are genuine and serious, there is nothing we will not be able to do."

During her short stay, Albright found Kim Jong Il to be isolated but intelligent, well informed, and able to discuss a wide range of technical problems without consulting his advisers. He seemed amenable to a missiles-for-cash deal and did not object to the continued presence of U.S. troops in Korea, which he now saw as a stabilizing influence. The main event underscoring cultural differences was a demonstration for Albright by more than one hundred thousand people—what she saw as "an Olympic opening ceremony on steroids"—singing and moving to songs such as "Let Us Hold High the Red Flag." Albright reported to Clinton that Kim Jong Il might accept negotiated curbs on North Korea's missile programs as well as its nuclear weapon ambitions.

The president wanted to visit Kim Jong Il in late 2000 and try to bring to fruition the negotiations conducted by Albright and others. Incoming president George W. Bush did not object. But Clinton felt he had to choose in the final weeks of his presidency between Korea and another mediation effort for the Middle East. He chose the latter. The Americans then invited Kim Jong Il to visit what was still the Clinton White House, but he declined—perhaps because the invitation came so late and could be seen as an affront to "face." But the biggest obstacle to a diplomatic breakthrough was not poor communication or cultural differences but time. Clinton had too many items on his platter and too little time to deal with them.

The Clinton team opened the door partway to yes. In 2001 the Bush administration slammed it shut.

CHAPTER NINE

HOW BUSH AND KIM JONG IL GOT TO DEADLOCK

That a so-called rogue nation entered the nuclear weapons club on George W. Bush's watch marked a major failure for his administration.[1] This failure was part of a broad syndrome wherein the Bush administration alienated U.S. partners and inspired adversaries to resist American policies. Failure in Northeast Asia was different from but no less ominous than the debacle in Iraq. Bush committed hard power to Iraq, where it could do little good, while using few sticks or carrots to sway North Korea from its nuclear ambitions.

The 1994 Agreed Framework lasted just eight years. Both Washington and Pyongyang declared it dead in 2002–2003. North Korea then withdrew from the NPT and expelled International Atomic Energy Agency inspectors. Heavy oil deliveries and KEDO's work on the light-water reactors stopped. Using plutonium from Yongbyon, the DPRK tested a nuclear device in 2006 and another in 2009.

During the president's first term, his administration abjured serious negotiations with North Korea. In his second term, however, Bush permitted the State Department to search for a deal. Despite some movement toward a grand bargain, however, Washington and Pyongyang deadlocked in 2008.[2] How did this happen? Let us review the factors that shaped Bush's dealings with North Korea.

Ideology and Domestic Politics

Taking office in 2001, President Bush and his top advisers did not expect or even want a meaningful arms control accord or broader accommodation with North Korea. The president and his vice president showed little interest in Korean issues. As in earlier times, Korea was not a priority. When Bush took office, the U.S. Defense Department could not say whether North Korea's military assets had increased or diminished in recent years. It did not know if North Korea had nuclear weapons and, if so, how many. Its contingency plans for dealing with North Korea had not been updated for years. As Defense Secretary Donald Rumsfeld saw it, the United States had no options except "rhetoric" and "75 sledgehammers to beat that gnat into the ground."[3]

Critics said President Bush did not have a policy to North Korea; he had an attitude. The attitude was summed up in his phrase "We don't negotiate with evil. We defeat it." Bush saw the Kim Jong Il regime in essentialist terms—evil to the core. Bush's perspective resembled Ronald Reagan's 1983 image of the USSR as an "evil empire." By 1985–1986, however, Reagan adopted a more nuanced view. He thought the Kremlin might bargain based on the realities of power. In 1986–1987, after meeting with Soviet leader Mikhail Gorbachev, Reagan appreciated that the two superpowers were engaged in an *interactive* process that reflected not only ideology and power but also perceptions and misperceptions. Reagan's evolving worldview—along with Gorbachev's—set the stage for the 1987 Intermediate-Range Nuclear Forces Treaty and the end of the cold war. In terms of international relations theory, Reagan shifted from neorealism to constructivism. A similar evolution took place the 1990s. When the Clinton administration saw that the DPRK leaders were not robots but human beings ready to bargain, the White House could deliberate what it could offer Pyongyang to freeze its graphite reactor. When Jimmy Carter and, later, Madeleine Albright interacted with top DPRK leaders, they saw how each side's words and actions shaped the other's behavior. How the three alternative outlooks condition negotiation is suggested in Table 9.1.

So long as the White House lived by the essentialist view, meaningful negotiations with North Korea were unlikely. President Bush spurned serious negotiations with Pyongyang until his second term. His negotiators experienced and perceived the interaction process, but hard-liners close to the White House continued to operate from essentialist assumptions.

Table 9.1 Three Ways to Look at U.S.-DPRK Relations

Outlook	Assumptions	Domestic Influences	Expectations	Negotiation Approach	Obstacles to a Deal	Getting to Yes in Korea?
Essentialist	Enmity is inexorable due to clashes of ideology and political systems	Hard-line factions oppose any accommodation with the enemy	Zero-sum exploitation	Ultra hard-line value-claiming	Antagonistic nature of the parties	Is impossible without regime change
Mechanical	Anarchy and balance of power determine state behavior (structural realism)	Domestic divisions and pressures are of secondary or tertiary importance	Variable-sum with tilt toward zero-sum	Positional bargaining with tilt toward hard-line TFT and value-claiming	Imbalances of power and security dilemma	Requires broad deal that balances asymmetrical security and other interests of each side
Interactive	Problems are what we make of them (constructivism)	How each side sees itself and the other is crucial	Variable-sum with hope for mutual gain	GRIT and contingent cooperation	Distrust, and misperception; lack of creative problem-solving	Calls for understanding each side's deep interests to generate mutual gain solutions

The Bush team repeatedly insulted the Dear Leader. Hard-liners repeatedly choked off efforts to build bridges to Pyongyang. To be sure, Bush had solid reasons to find Kim Jong Il's regime repugnant.[4] It was far crueler than the Soviet system faced by President Reagan—yet no worse than that of Mao Zedong, with whom Nixon clinked glasses.

Bush-league diplomacy was also constrained by its ABC complex—"anything but Clinton." The forty-third president steered away from any kind of deal nurtured by his predecessor. Bush's choice for secretary of state, Colin Powell, did not immediately grasp the ABC pathology. Powell assured Madeleine Albright in late 2000 that the Bush team would pick up with North Korea roughly where the Clinton team left off.[5] Indeed, Powell repeated this formulation for reporters on March 6, 2001, as ROK president Kim Dae Jung—architect of South Korea's Sunshine Policy—arrived in Washington. Powell stated that "some promising elements were left on the table, and we'll be examining those elements." But this did not happen. The very next day, as Bush met with Kim Dae Jung, Powell stepped out of the Oval Office to inform the press that North Korea was "a threat.... We have to not be naïve about the threat." He acknowledged that "there are suggestions that there are imminent negotiations [between the United States and DPRK]," but said "this is not the case." Powell underscored that Bush "understands the nature of the regime in Pyongyang and will not be fooled by it." A day later, Powell told the Senate that the DPRK is a "despotic regime" and that the United States might want to revisit the KEDO deal with North Korea. Powell was catching on to the ABC line.[6] Powell would sacrifice his integrity to remain part of the team. Bush did not listen to views that challenged his predispositions and lost the counsel of one of his most experienced officials.

The ROK president hoped for the southern sun to light up North Korea and was aghast at Bush's way of thinking. Top North Korean leaders were also upset. They had hoped for better ties with the United States after visits by a former president and a secretary of state. They knew that the new president's father, George H. W., had cultivated ties with China and heard that the elder Bush urged his son to continue negotiations with the DPRK.

A pall settled over U.S.-DPRK relations in 2001, but 2002 proved to be a watershed. In January the president assigned North Korea, along with Iraq and Iran, to an "axis of evil." The CIA reported that North Korea was completing a uranium enrichment plant, using technology acquired from Pakistan—giving Pyongyang a second route to nuclear weapons.[7] The Clinton administration had earlier detected signs of a uranium enrichment program but had opted to watch and wait, believing it wiser to improve relations and then deal with the problem quietly, when Pyongyang might believe it had more to lose from a confrontation.[8]

As part of a "bold" new approach to North Korea, the White House sent James Kelly, assistant secretary of state for East Asian and Pacific affairs, to Pyongyang on October 3–5, 2002. His two-day meeting led to exchanges that soon killed the Agreed Framework. Following a script and with no authority to maneuver or explore nuances, Kelly told the North Koreans that Washington had evidence of their uranium enrichment plant. His allegation seemed to catch the North Koreans off guard. The following day, Kelly later reported, DPRK diplomats confirmed his accusation and said their country had every right to this facility. Seeking to keep Congress focused on Iraq, the Bush administration did not report these exchanges for eleven days. DPRK representatives, however, denied ever admitting to having a uranium plant. Translation from Korean into English for Kelly may have led to a misunderstanding. Perhaps the DPRK diplomats meant only to tell Kelly that North Korea had every *right* to a uranium enrichment facility. Perhaps they had felt the need for a strong response to bad *kibun*—the insinuation their country had been cheating. But when a French official proposed taking the matter the United Nations, Kelly replied, "The Security Council is for Iraq."[9]

North Korea's uranium enrichment program probably began in 1997–1998—several years *after* the Agreed Framework and *before* Bush entered the White House. A clandestine operation of this kind surely ran contrary to the spirit of the 1994 accord. But one authority noted that the NPT permits signatories to have civilian enrichment operations under IAEA inspection. Pyongyang may have felt no obligation to declare its uranium plant until the United States and its partners had built the two light-water reactors, as promised in 1994.[10]

Had the 1994 accord masked a drive by one or both sides to continue a zero-sum struggle against the other? The evidence is muddy. The United States supplied fuel oil to the North, as promised, but behind schedule. Progress on the two light-water reactors was so slow that Pyongyang may have inferred that the United States and its partners were trying to sabotage North Korea's development.

When Barack Obama took office in 2009, the quiddity of North Korea's uranium processing remained unclear. Pyongyang had tried to buy centrifuges, electrical frequency converters, and high strength aluminum tubes needed to enrich uranium, but France, Germany, Egypt, and Japan blocked such deliveries. The technical difficulties to producing highly enriched uranium are enormous. Pyongyang may have settled for a pilot program. The nuclear devices exploded in 2006 and 2009 used plutonium—not enriched uranium. Though North Korea in 2008 provided much documentation on its plutonium production, it refused information on uranium enrichment. Did Pyongyang mask a strength or a weakness?

Deal-Makers versus Saboteurs

Unilateralist hard-liners controlled U.S. policy toward North Korea and most other foreign issues—at least until 2005. Vice President Dick Cheney argued that regime change in Pyongyang was the only way to stop nuclear proliferation.[11] Colin Powell and others in the State Department favored dialogue with the DPRK, but even Powell's deputy on arms control, John R. Bolton, was an outspoken hawk. Not surprisingly, when Bolton called Kim Jong Il a "tyrannical rogue" in August 2003, Pyongyang branded him "human scum." Never lost in tit for tat, the North got Bolton excluded from six-party talks held later that month in Beijing. Cheney and his staff insisted that North Korea carry out CVID—"complete, verifiable, irreversible dismantlement" of its nuclear program—before the United States made any payments.[12]

When Kelly again met with DPRK and with Chinese diplomats in April 2003, North Korea wanted to deal directly with the world's superpower. On most foreign problems Washington preferred to go it alone, joined only by an "alliance of the willing." With North Korea, however, the Bush administration demanded a multilateral approach that included U.S. allies Japan and the ROK as well as China and Russia. Washington's preference prevailed, and six-party talks began in August 2003, hosted by China. The Bush team may have demanded the six-party venue because the process was "designed to fail."[13] One against five, Pyongyang was defensive—"uptight." Also, the format was cumbersome: The time required for translations meant that delegates rarely got beyond their prearranged talking points.

The European Union did nothing to halt the conflict spiral. It issued restrictions on development assistance to North Korea in November 2002. In Japan conservatives used Kim Jong Il's extraordinary confession on a few abductions and the release of five Japanese citizens for domestic political purposes.[14]

Hostility to Law and Transparency

Believing that might makes right, President Bush and his entourage opposed any curb on U.S. actions. Defying a tradition of U.S. support for international law, the White House renounced the Kyoto Protocol, "unsigned" the Rome Statute of the International Criminal Court, and abrogated the Anti–Ballistic Missile (ABM) Treaty.[15] It contrived legal doctrines to justify torture of alleged enemy combatants and eavesdropping on U.S. citizens.[16]

The North Korean regime was also hostile to law—at home and across borders. Anything "international" or "multilateral" amounted to smoke and mirrors. Like Soviet Russia in the 1920s, the DPRK felt isolated—encircled by hostile powers. For Pyongyang, the United States and the United Nations were one—North Korea's foe in 1950–1953 and ever since at Panmunjom. The DPRK did not trust even Moscow and Beijing. It suspected the Korean Energy and Development Organization to be a Trojan Horse meant to deceive North Korea. Parallel to their antipathy to law, both the Bush team and Pyongyang resisted transparency. Each played its cards close to its vest. Neither communicated fully with its subjects or its potential partners abroad. The United States, of course, remained a far more open society than North Korea. But multiple revelations about the buildup to the Iraq war showed how those in power could manipulate information to deceive the public, Congress, and foreign governments.

Attitudes toward Arms and Arms Control

Both the Bush administration and Kim Jong Il appeared to value WMD as useful instruments of policy. The Pentagon's *Nuclear Posture Review* (*NPR*) submitted to Congress on December 31, 2001, proclaimed a new strategic triad composed of offensive strike systems, active and passive defenses, and a revitalized research and development base to update U.S. forces as needed. The new triad, bound together by enhanced command and control and intelligence, would reduce but not eliminate U.S. dependence on nuclear arms to deter enemy attack.[17]

Against which targets might nuclear weapons be used? *North Korea headed the NPR list.* "North Korea, Iraq, Iran, Syria, and Libya are among the countries that could be involved in immediate, potential, or unexpected contingencies. All have longstanding hostility toward the United States and its security partners; North Korea and Iraq in particular have been chronic military concerns. All sponsor or harbor terrorists, and all have active WMD and missile programs." Given the "ongoing modernization of its nuclear and non nuclear forces, China is [also] a country that could be involved in an immediate or potential contingency."

What would be the role of antimissile systems? According to the *NPR*: "Missile defenses could defeat small-scale missile attacks intended to coerce the United States into abandoning an embattled ally or friend. Defenses that provided protection for strike capabilities of the New Triad and for other power projection forces would improve the ability of the United States and its allies and friends to counterattack an enemy. They may also provide the President with an option to manage a crisis involving one or more missile and WMD-armed opponents."

Meanwhile, the administration embraced a doctrine of first strike. Bush and Condoleezza Rice averred that in an age of WMD and terrorist actions, the United States would not wait while enemy forces prepared to attack. Instead, Americans would pre-empt. This logic helped rationalize the U.S. attack on Iraq. As there was never any sign that Baghdad had ever prepared to attack America, however, the U.S. assault on Iraq should have been defined as a "preventive" war—one meant to neuter a possible future threat, not some imminent attack.[18]

The Bush White House wanted more and better nukes for the United States and did not worry much if other actors obtained nuclear weapons. Although Washington called on others to abjure nuclear weapons, the Pentagon would develop "bunker busters" and what used to be called "battlefield" nuclear weapons.[19] The *Nuclear Posture Review* advised that U.S. weapons laboratories might have to resume nuclear tests, halted since 1992. All such moves were just heavenly for the "rapture" movement among Bush's backers—Christians anticipating an Armageddon from which only they would emerge triumphant.

Thus, the Bush administration pursued its own version of *juche*. Confident of U.S. military superiority, the Bush team took a cavalier approach to arms control, viewing it as undesirable or unnecessary. Accordingly, the Bush team nearly ignored Iran's nuclear weapons capacity as well as North Korea's, while focusing its energies on Iraq. It did so even though the National Intelligence Estimate of October 2002 identified only a *desire* in Baghdad to obtain WMD without much evidence of a restored WMD capability.[20] The Bush team invaded Iraq for reasons other than arms control, while doing very little to thwart WMD production in North Korea or Iran.

Strategic self-reliance, filliped by an allergy to treaties, led Washington to undermine efforts to strengthen the nonproliferation treaty and conventions on chemical and biological weapons. Bush allowed India to buy nuclear fuel and equipment for its civil nuclear program and persuaded the U.S. Congress and Nuclear Suppliers Group to go along. This permitted India to thumb its nose at the NPT even as Washington sanctioned Iran for its civil nuclear program. Pakistan, of course, worried that every pound of uranium India imported for its power reactors freed up a pound for its weapons.

Though the Bush administration shied away from most arms controls, Washington launched the Proliferation Security Initiative (PSI) in 2003 to prevent the transfer of WMD-related materials and contraband originating from, or destined for, countries or nonstate actors of "proliferation concern." By June 2004 the PSI included seventeen countries and many more signaled their support. At that time, however, North Korea had no missiles deployed except surface-to-air defenses and short-range attack missiles. It did possess transport planes and helicopters capable of infiltrating at least two air force sniper brigades and assault forces deep into ROK rear areas. Flying hours for DPRK air forces, however, amounted to under 20 hours, compared to 150 for Japan and more than 200 for the United States.[21]

The Bush administration's indifference to other countries' WMD was manifest in U.S. policies toward the Russian Federation—still a military superpower but also a potential source of "loose nukes." The Bush team ignored Russia until after 9/11/01, after which it sought Moscow's support for America's "war on terror." The *NPR* issued at the end of 2001 declared that a nuclear "contingency involving Russia, while plausible, is not expected." Bush infuriated the Kremlin by withdrawing from the ABM treaty in 2001–2002 and did not want to update U.S.-Russian arms controls with a formal commitment. Finally he agreed to a three-page "Strategic Offensive Reductions Treaty" signed with Vladimir V. Putin in May 2002. Known as "SORT" (even the acronym implied that arms control is a joke), the treaty was just a few pages long—quite unlike its long and detailed predecessors. SORT called for reductions in U.S. and Russian operationally deployed strategic warheads to no more than 2,200 by the end of 2012, but left each side with enormous flexibility as regards its future deployments.[22]

The Bush team's strategic doctrines and the U.S. assault on Iraq probably intensified the DPRK quest for a deterrent. Pyongyang in 2003 claimed that its nuclear policy embodied "the principle of self-reliant defense based on the juche idea" and served to defend sovereignty and cope with the threat of a U.S. preemptive nuclear attack.[23] If Britain and France were unwilling to rely on their U.S. ally and insisted on having their own nuclear deterrent, with what greater cause would a country still at war with the United States insist on a reliable means to keep its longtime foe at bay?

Ulterior Motives

Top leaders in all six capitals had priorities other than arms control. Each used arms control negotiations to promote its agendas in other realms. Kim Jong Il's regime clearly saw its nuclear and missile capabilities as major levers not to be traded away except for substantial rewards. Pyongyang used arms negotiations to buy time. The DPRK leadership could calculate that *if arms control does not lead to a broader breakthrough, our negotiating efforts will have shielded our nuclear buildup from attack. Sooner or later we can present our nuclear weapons capability as an accomplished fact—like China, Israel, India, and Pakistan. We think Iran follows a similar logic.* As in New Delhi and Islamabad, leaders in Pyongyang also wanted to demonstrate that their country excelled in weaponry, if not in other realms.[24]

A dictatorship can guard its secrets and devote huge resources to military R&D. Like North Korea and Iran in the early twenty-first century, Yugoslavia under Marshal Tito showed that "the more isolated the regime and the more hostile the international environment, the less relevant are global norms regarding weapons of mass destruction. Isolated regimes also are inclined to discount the political costs of violating international taboos." One of Tito's most intellectual comrades, Edward Kardelj, advised in 1950 that Yugoslavia must build an atomic bomb "even if it costs us half of our income for years."[25] This advice came at a time when Yugoslavia already enjoyed U.S. support—quite the opposite of North Korea's position.

The U.S.-DPRK standoff recalled the conflicting priorities that had stymied earlier arms negotiations with Moscow. In the interwar years France and its allies demanded "security first" and "moral disarmament" before what the USSR called "material disarmament." The Kremlin, however, wanted France to disarm before it would rein in the Comintern. During the cold war, Washington usually sought "inspection first," while Moscow again wanted real disarmament before inspection. Washington and Moscow finally came to terms in the 1970s and 1980s when they convinced each other that neither sought regime change and that most inspection could be conducted largely by satellites.

In the early twenty-first century it was North Korea that wanted security before it would disarm. For the United States, this was putting the cart before the horse. Yes, Washington promised trade and aid if North Korea disarmed, but said it would withhold full normalization so long as Pyongyang continued its human rights abuses.

Washington also had its unpublicized agendas. The White House seemed not to worry much about nuclear spread so long as the United States could improve its own arsenal. Bush may have even *opposed* an accord with North Korea, because Pyongyang's incipient nuclear missile capability provided the best justification for a national missile defense (NMD). A missile-proof astrodome had been a holy grail for many conservatives ever since President Reagan promoted the Strategic Defense Initiative (SDI) in 1983. Indeed, in late 2000, the outgoing secretary of state saw that "many in Congress and within the punditocracy opposed a [Clinton–Kim Jong Il] summit because they feared a deal with North Korea would weaken the case for national missile defense."[26] So long as North Korea looked ominous, Japan would chip in and take part in missile defense.

If these arguments are correct, the Bush White House did not really want a "Libyan solution" by which Pyongyang would renounce its nuclear ambitions and open the country to IAEA inspectors. The Bush team pressed North Korea to go even further than Tripoli and give up its other illicit activities, transform its economy, end restrictions on food assistance, and become a "normal" state—not an attractive package for Pyongyang.

Bush's tough line won dollars and political support from passionate conservative donors and voters. Business analysts warned that defense spending might plateau in 2005, but the price of shares in Boeing and Raytheon, each a major NMD contractor, soared in the first days after Bush's reelection.

In 2004 the United States withdrew twelve thousand troops—one-third of the existing force—from Korea for duty in Iraq and planned to pull back most of the remaining U.S. troops from positions close to the DMZ to bases south of Seoul.[27] Concerned that Washington might be planning to attack, some DPRK strategists worried that the United States wished to spare its own soldiers and depend more heavily on long-range weapons to harm North Korea.

The Upshot

Secretary of Defense Rumsfeld seemed almost pleased to declare in June 2004: "Needless to say, time favors North Korea." Having done almost nothing constructive for four years to contain the DPRK, the Bush team could hardly have been surprised that time worked for Pyongyang.

The off-and-on again negotiations allowed North Korea to continue development of a nuclear missile capability. Also, the DPRK managed to sell more weapons abroad. North Korea's economic ties with China, South Korea, and Japan helped to cushion political-military tensions. Far from maintaining a cordon sanitaire around the DPRK, Japan in 2004 moved toward investing in North Korea. Meanwhile, South Korean investors as well as tourists continued to expand their activities across the DMZ. Pyongyang stepped up its efforts to woo public opinion on Korean reunification and to strengthen animosity in the South toward the United States. North and South Korea agreed in June 2004 to stop propaganda broadcasts along their border and to take steps to avoid clashes along the DMZ and in disputed areas of the high seas, but they made no moves to reduce arms or troops (1,105,000 in the North versus 687,700 in the South, with some 4.5 million reserves on each side). They did not sign a peace treaty or take any action on the North's WMD. The tank traps, gun emplacements, and minefields remained in place, with no sign of an imminent political solution to the conflict. Indeed, only a few hours after the June 2004 accord, the ROK Defense Ministry reported that two North Korean navy patrol boats crossed into waters controlled by South Korea off the west coast while chasing Chinese fishing boats poaching in the area and then retreated when ROK warships approached. A different version came from North Korea's state-run news agency, which claimed that three South Korean warships had infiltrated its waters and two South Korean jet fighters threatened its fishing boats as part of the South's alleged efforts to exercise jurisdiction in the area. Similar incidents continued to occur, for example, in early November 2004 and November 2009.

A few marginal economic gains did little to improve living standards in the DPRK. Thousands of North Korean refugees crossed into China and hundreds managed to reach South Korea in 2003–2004. The DPRK remained rather isolated and impoverished, with no immediate avenues to enter the global community of modernizing and prosperous nations. South Korea's economic assistance to the North remained quite limited in 2005 and would not be expanded so long as the DPRK retained its nuclear weapon programs.[28]

Security in Northeast Asia became less stable in Bush's first term. Pressures mounted on Japan, South Korea, and Taiwan to go nuclear. Tokyo authorized Japanese military commanders to shoot down incoming missiles without consulting civilian authorities—seen in China as a worrying move toward a revived Japanese militarism.

Neither the Bush nor the Kim Jong Il government handled its relationship with the other in a way that improved the security and well-being of its own citizens. The Bush team should have picked up where Bill Clinton had left off in 2000, but did not—with tragic consequences that could probably have been avoided. Whatever the shortcomings of the 1994 Agreed Framework, it could have been saved. Besides aborting momentum toward arms control, Bush's blend of bombast and malign neglect undercut voices in Pyongyang calling for accommodation with Washington and its partners. The effect resembled the impact of North Atlantic Treaty Organization expansion in the 1990s on liberals in Moscow. It destroyed their credibility and set the stage for a return to hard-line policies at home and abroad. By 2004 authorities in Pyongyang were uprooting the green shoots of a market economy that had emerged in the late 1990s and, we must assume, were accelerating work on the nuclear device tested in 2006.

Bush's Second Four Years

In Bush's second term the six-party talks appeared to reach several accords—in 2005 an agreement on principles and in 2007 a three-stage plan for dismantling the Yongbyon complex in exchange for aid and security assurances. Two of the stages were nearly completed by late 2008, but Pyongyang and Washington deadlocked over inspection issues as the Bush administration made way for a new president. In the interval between the 2005 and 2007 accords, the DPRK tested a long-range missile and a nuclear device. The UN Security Council condemned the tests, but North Korea's actions served to concentrate Washington's attention and add confidence to Pyongyang's quiver.

Let us summarize the factors that facilitated movement toward a grand bargain and those that after every step forward blocked the road. The positives included a change of attitude and top personnel in Washington, coupled with continued Chinese mediation at the six-party talks. The negatives included the persistent influence of hard-liners in Washington and probably in Pyongyang, Pyongyang's refusal to discuss its uranium enrichment and its role in Syria, DPRK rejection of U.S. demands for on-site sampling to verify plutonium production at Yongbyon, and Japan's intransigence on abductees. Some factors were Janus-faced: North Korea's missile and nuclear tests retarded and encouraged the negotiations; so did the U.S. freeze of DPRK bank assets and, starting in 2008, an end to automatic Sunshine in Seoul. Aggravating all differences, deep distrust remained: Both Washington and Pyongyang worried that the other welshed on its commitments.

Beneath the zigs and zags, a pattern emerged. The "agreed" language was ambiguous. When Washington seemed to toughen its terms, Pyongyang pulled away and raised the ante. The North Koreans threatened to expose the irony that Washington and Moscow wanted the DPRK to demolish its nuclear deterrent even as they retained and improved their colossal arsenals and China expanded its own.

The Confidante as Secretary of State

Asked how to sum up U.S. policy to North Korea, a Washington insider replied, "The failure of Condi Rice." Serving Bush in his first term as special assistant for national security, Rice permitted Vice President Dick Cheney and Defense Secretary Donald Rumsfeld to steer the president toward a belligerent unilateralism. She had permitted both moderates and hawks to produce an incoherent strategy.[29]

The Bush administration's approach to foreign affairs shifted after Rice replaced Colin Powell as secretary of state in 2005. In his second term Bush and Rice looked for ways to generate a legacy more positive than the Iraq war. They adapted parts of the Powell orientation earlier quashed by Cheney and Rumsfeld.

Auguries in Pyongyang were not bad. In January 2005 Pyongyang's Korean Central News Agency said the DPRK stood ready to settle the nuclear issue peacefully and even to treat Washington as a "friend."

Rice now wanted a deal with North Korea. She made Christopher Hill the assistant secretary of state for East Asian and Pacific affairs and gave him some authority to conduct give-and-take negotiations with Pyongyang, unlike his hamstrung predecessor, James Kelly. As U.S. ambassador to the ROK, Hill had become popular there. A creative diplomat, he was willing—like his mentor, Richard Holbrooke—to take risks and sometimes exceed his instructions. Hill proposed to Rice that the administration assemble a package of incentives for North Korea and sell it to the Chinese, who would sell it to Pyongyang—replaying a technique used by Holbrooke and Hill in 1995 when they got Serbian leader Slobodan Milošević to sell their ideas to the Bosnian Serbs for the Dayton Agreements.[30]

Having said in January 2005 it was ready to treat the United States as a "friend," the DPRK suddenly reverted to bluster. In February Pyongyang announced that it had actually produced nuclear weapons and was suspending indefinitely its participation in six-party talks. The DPRK accused Washington of "brazen-faced, double-dealing tactics"—combining dialogue with a policy of "regime change." What sparked the tougher inflection? President Bush had made only one, rather innocuous reference to North Korea in his 2005 State of the Union speech. But Dr. Rice in the hearings about her suitability to be secretary of state had listed North Korea with five other "outposts of tyranny" and, twice that week, affirmed that "all options are available" for dealing with North Korea. None of this persuaded Pyongyang that Bush was making a fresh start. One wonders if America's leading diplomat publicly lambasted recalcitrant deans and department heads when she ran Stanford University. Did her experience suggest that dialogue was improved by publicly goring the other side?

In March 2005 the IAEA declared that it remained "committed to securing full safeguards compliance by the DPRK through peaceful means." Unable to verify the completeness and correctness of the initial report of the DPRK under the NPT Safeguards Agreement, however, the agency had concluded since 1993 that the DPRK was not complying with its obligations under the agreement. Between 1994 and 2002, the Agreed Framework had been a tool for "bringing the DPRK into compliance with its safeguards obligations. However, the reports about a clandestine uranium enrichment programme, the end of the 'freeze' pursuant to the Agreed Framework, and the expulsion of the IAEA inspectors ... brought this phase to an end."[31]

Unrepentant, Pyongyang became more defiant. In March 2005 the DPRK said it was no longer bound by its more than five-year-old moratorium on flight-testing longer-range missiles. In April 2005 Kim Gye Gwan told Selig Harrison that Pyongyang might give nuclear weapons to other actors if "the United States drives us into a corner." In May Pyongyang denounced Bush and his entourage in terms that made "axis of evil" look like a compliment. The KCNA said the U.S. president was "the world's worst fascist dictator, a top-notch war maniac and Hitler junior waving hands stained with blood shed by innocent people." It declared that the whole "brutish Bush bellicose group" is a "bunch of hardened thugs losing their grip on the ability to think normally and not the kind of people we should deal with in the first place." Tough actions followed tough words: In June Pyongyang refueled its reactor at Yongbyon and said it was starting to reprocess eight thousand spent fuel rods removed in March.

Washington began to flex its economic muscles. In June 2005 the U.S. Treasury froze the U.S. assets of three North Korean entities "responsible for WMD and missile programs" and barred U.S. citizens and companies from doing business with those firms. Washington also labored to persuade other governments to block DPRK exports of missiles and nuclear materials and to stop Pyongyang's trafficking in narcotics and counterfeit dollars. In 2005 Japan closed its waters to foreign ships lacking liability insurance against spills and other accidents. As almost no North Korean vessels carried such insurance, the new requirement could halt most shipping traffic between the two countries. Seoul and Beijing, however, were loath to take part in any actions that would further isolate the North.

The atmospherics were not helped by U.S. allegations, later proved unfounded, that North Korea had sold partly processed nuclear fuel to Libya and perhaps to other buyers on the black market. Bush's disinformation campaign regarding Saddam Hussein's WMD left the world dubious about anything the White House might say about anything. Washington had dissipated its soft power, and an impression grew that Washington's words were no more reliable than those of its adversaries.

After meeting with Hill in July 2005, however, DPRK vice foreign minister Kim Gye Gwan said Pyongyang would return to the six-party talks. KCNA explained that the "U.S. side clarified its official stand to recognize [North Korea] as a sovereign state, not to invade it, and hold *bilateral* talks within the framework of the six-party talks" (emphasis added). Later that month, Kim Jong Il told a Chinese envoy of his father's (Kim Il Sung's) dying wish for the denuclearization of the Korean peninsula. Given the traditional Korean respect for elders, this was a sign that the Dear Leader truly wanted a deal.

Agreed Principles versus Frozen Assets

Having resumed talks on September 13, the six parties on September 19, 2005, announced agreement on a set of principles to guide future negotiations. North Korea pledged that in return for energy aid and U.S. promises not to invade, the DPRK would abandon its nuclear weapons programs and return to the NPT and to IAEA inspection "at an early date." But Pyongyang also reasserted its right to "peaceful uses of nuclear energy." The joint statement, however, affirmed only that the United States and others would supply electricity to North Korea. Though Washington would not offer Pyongyang a formal nonaggression treaty, the U.S. delegation declared that the United States had no nuclear weapons on the Korean peninsula and had no intention to attack North Korea.

All six parties committed to achieving "the verifiable denuclearization of the Korean Peninsula in a peaceful manner" and agreed "to take coordinated steps to implement" the agreed-upon obligations and rewards "*in a phased manner in line with the principle of 'commitment for commitment, action for action'*" (emphasis added). The statement also called for the 1992 North-South Joint Declaration of the Denuclearization of the Korean Peninsula to be "observed and implemented."

It soon appeared that the six parties had finessed too much. Ambiguity reigned. The joint statement did not specify *how* electricity would be provided to the North. It put off discussion of the DPRK demand for a light-water reactor for an "appropriate time." Though the Clinton administration had pledged to build two LWRs for the DPRK, the Bush White House now argued that North Korea could not be trusted with *any* nuclear capabilities. The statement was silent on whether, as Washington charged and Pyongyang denied, the North was running a clandestine uranium enrichment program. The statement set no date for disarmament and specified no details for inspection.

Less than twenty-four hours after the six-party talks ended, hard-liners in Washington and Pyongyang undercut what diplomats in Beijing had fashioned. The DPRK declared it would not give up its nuclear programs until it received a modern civilian nuclear reactor—a demand that Tokyo as well as Washington refused, though Beijing, Seoul, and Moscow had no objections.

Whereas Christopher Hill's admirers called him energetic and creative, hard-liners disliked his quest to reach a deal. Cheney staffers called him "Kim Jong Hill."[32] Senator Sam Brownback, Republican from Kansas, summed up Hill's record with North Korea as "no progress on human rights, terrible deal, failed diplomacy."[33]

If the State Department had become a conciliatory cop, the U.S. Treasury stepped up its role as tough cop. On September 15—just days before the short-lived joint statement—the Treasury Department designated Banco Delta Asia (BDA) in Macao as a "primary money laundering concern" under the U.S. Patriot Act and managed to freeze some $25 million in North Korean funds. In October the Treasury Department sanctioned eight North Korean entities for their "involvement" in WMD proliferation and froze their U.S. assets. In 2006 the Bank of China froze DPRK accounts containing millions of dollars.

On September 20, 2005, the North accused the United States of using the negotiations to "disarm us and crush us to death with nuclear weapons." The DPRK Foreign Ministry underscored the problem of *sequencing*. It declared that the North would not make the first move. Others "are telling us to give up everything, but there will be no such thing as giving it up first." Pyongyang warned that Washington "should not even dream" that the DPRK would give up its nuclear arsenal until the United States provided it with a LWR. Regardless of these harsh words, a few days later in New York the DPRK deputy foreign minister, Choe Su Hun, told the UN General Assembly that the recent joint statement represented his county's "principled positions." Choe affirmed that the DPRK would not need a "single nuclear weapon" if its relations with the United States were normalized, if bilateral confidence was built, and if the North was no longer exposed to a U.S. nuclear threat. But he reiterated that Washington should give civilian nuclear reactors to the DPRK as part of "simultaneous action" on the North's disarmament. Adding to momentary euphoria, South Korean media reported that the North intended to invite Rice and perhaps even Bush to Pyongyang to elevate the status of the Dear Leader and normalize bilateral ties.

Which side(s) should take the first step? Former ROK prime minister Goh Kun suggested that the United States issue a security guarantee to the North "concurrent" with DPRK denuclearization.[34] But the guarantee could be offered in an instant, whereas denuclearization could take years to complete. However, once the North dismantled its nuclear machinery, a security assurance could be withdrawn overnight.

When six-party talks resumed in November 2005, the ROK and Japan proposed separating the outstanding issues into three categories: dismantlement of Pyongyang's nuclear program, economic and energy assistance to North Korea, and Pyongyang's bilateral issues with Washington and with Tokyo. But U.S.-DPRK disagreements blocked progress. The North Korean delegation demanded unfreezing DPRK funds at the BDA. In December North Korea said it would "pursue" the construction of larger "graphite-moderated reactors"—the kind of reactor the Agreed Framework aimed to supplant. KEDO in 2003 had stopped work on the LWRs pledge in 1994 but did not formally end the project until June 2006.

North Korea Goes Nuclear

When Rice became secretary of state, she intimated to Bush that he could match his father's accomplishment in unifying Germany by a nuclear deal with Pyongyang, a peace agreement to replace the 1953 armistice, and eventual unification of North and South. Bush liked big, game-changing ideas, and this gave Rice some room to maneuver. When China's president Hu Jintao visited the White House in April 2006 and suggested security assurances to the North, Bush asked, "How about I give Kim a peace treaty?" Cheney, also present at the luncheon, was stunned. Hu agreed to inform Pyongyang that Bush wanted a breakthrough, but by that time Pyongyang was preparing to test ballistic missiles and its nuclear device.[35]

Chinese mediation often played a constructive role. When North Korean and U.S. diplomats went their separate ways, Beijing stood ready to host more rounds of negotiations. Sometimes China proposed bridging language that helped the two or the six enter another commitment. Beijing tried to use its material support to restrain DPRK actions, but with little effect. Counting on Beijing's devotion to stability, Pyongyang ignored Chinese admonitions.

Things got worse in 2006 before they got better. On July 4–5 the DPRK test-fired seven ballistic missiles. Six short- and medium-range missiles appeared to function as planned, but the three-stage Taepodong-2 fell apart soon after launch. The State Department called the launches a "provocative act" violating North Korea's voluntary moratorium on flight-testing, observed since September 1999. The UN Security Council unanimously adopted Resolution 1695—a compromise between the strong stance favored by Tokyo and Washington and the milder language favored by Beijing and Moscow. China insisted that the resolution not invoke Chapter VII of the UN Charter (dealing with "threats to the peace"). But the resolution condemned North Korea's missile launches, called on Pyongyang to return to the six-party talks, and demanded that the DPRK suspend its ballistic missile activities and reestablish its flight-testing moratorium. The resolution also required states to prevent missiles and related "items, materials, goods and technology" from being transferred to the DPRK. It also required UN members to prevent the procurement of such items from Pyongyang and the transfer of any "financial resources in relation to" North Korea's weapons programs. The United States, Japan, and Australia took the lead in implementing the resolution; Seoul halted food and fertilizer assistance; but China played the paper tiger. It allowed sanctioned goods to cross into the DPRK and North Korean planes to fly over its territory regardless of their cargo.

Pyongyang responded that it would "not be bound" by the UN resolution. Combining a smile with a growl, the DPRK Foreign Ministry on October 3 stated that Pyongyang "will in the future conduct a nuclear test under the condition where safety is firmly guaranteed." It also said that North Korea would refrain from the first use of nuclear weapons, "strictly prohibit any . . . nuclear transfer," and "do its utmost to realize the denuclearization of the [Korean] peninsula."

On October 9, 2006, the DPRK tested a nuclear device underground, with a yield under 1 kiloton—so small that some analysts said it "fizzled." The DPRK averred that its "nuclear test was entirely attributable to the U.S. nuclear threat, sanctions and pressure." The DPRK had to test in order to protect its "sovereignty." Pyongyang warned it might conduct further nuclear tests if the United States "increases pressure" on the country. The Foreign Ministry added, however, that North Korea remained committed to implementing the September 2005 joint statement. It recalled also that the "denuclearization of the entire peninsula was President Kim Il Sung's last instruction and an ultimate goal" of North Korea.

Responding to North Korea's nuclear explosion, the UN Security Council on October 16 unanimously adopted Resolution 1718—this time acting under Chapter VII, Article 41, authorizing measures *not* involving the use of force to enforce Security Council decisions. The resolution condemned the DPRK test and "demanded" the DPRK not conduct any further nuclear test or launch of a ballistic missile and that it return to the NPT. It ordered the DPRK to suspend all activities related to its ballistic missile program and "abandon all nuclear weapons and existing nuclear programs in a complete, verifiable and irreversible manner"; and "return immediately to the six-party talks without any precondition." The resolution authorized but did not require member states to stop and inspect shipments of cargo for WMD going to or from North Korea. It banned DPRK imports or exports of tanks, armored combat vehicles, heavy artillery, combat aircraft, warships, missiles or missile systems, and related materiel including spare parts. The resolution imposed an asset freeze and travel ban on persons related to the nuclear weapon program.

To monitor and adjust the sanctions, the Security Council established a committee consisting of all its fifteen members. China did not approve the practice of inspecting cargo to and from the DPRK and urged other countries to refrain from provocative steps that could intensify the tension. China still believed that the six-party talks were the realistic means of handling the issue and opposed the use of force.

The DPRK representative "totally rejected" the text, saying that it was "gangster-like" of the Security Council to adopt such a coercive resolution against his country, while neglecting the nuclear threat posed by the United States against the DPRK. This, he said, amounted to a double standard.

When North Korea launched another long-range missile on April 5, 2009, Security Council members debated whether this action "violated" Resolution 1718. Russia and China said no, because Pyongyang claimed merely to have launched a satellite now sending back patriotic songs from outer space (more brazen lies). In a compromise move, the Security Council issued a presidential statement— less than a resolution but more than a declaration—condemning the test and saying it was in "contravention" to Resolution 1718. Meanwhile, *the sanctions committee on North Korea had not met in the previous two years and had failed to designate even a single North Korean company to be added to the UN blacklist of banned entities.* The bite of UN, until then, sanctions proved shallow.

Progress in 2007

Pyongyang's nuclear experiment at first deepened the gulf between North Korea and its negotiating partners. But the test permitted North Korea to negotiate from a new sense of strength and deepened Washington's resolve to defang a would-be nuclear power. In December 2006 Hill and his DPRK counterpart happened to meet at the Beijing airport as they prepared to fly home. In the airport they agreed to hold their first bilateral talks in years without Chinese mediation. Meeting secretly in Berlin on January 16–17, 2007, both sides quickly agreed on terms to be finalized at six-party talks in February. Hill arranged the Berlin meeting without the knowledge of Cheney and other hard-liners. Rice backed the initiative and its outcome, and Bush approved.

True to the Berlin understanding between Hill and his DPRK counterpart, the six parties on February 13, 2007, approved the most substantive accord on North Korea since the 1994 Agreed Framework—an "action plan" to implement the September 19, 2005, joint statement. North Korea would halt operation of its nuclear facilities at Yongbyon during a sixty-day initial phase in return for an initial shipment of 50,000 tons of heavy fuel oil. The sixty-day period represented a neat compromise between the initial U.S. proposal of forty-five days and the North's counter of ninety. Both sides knew how to bargain.

The plan established working groups to formulate plans for economic and energy cooperation, denuclearization, a "Northeast Asia Peace and Security Mechanism," and bilateral DPRK relations with the United States and with Japan. Following the shutdown of facilities at Yongbyon, Pyongyang would provide a complete declaration of all of its nuclear programs and disable all of its existing nuclear facilities in return for an additional 950,000 tons of heavy fuel oil or its equivalent. Besides providing energy aid to North Korea, the United States would begin removing Pyongyang from its list of state sponsors of terrorism and stop the application of the Trading with the Enemy Act toward North Korea.

The United States gave North Korea extra time to fulfill its commitments. Pyongyang refused to act on its February 2007 pledge to shut down the Yongbyon reactor until it received $25 million in funds frozen by the U.S. Treasury in Macao. Soon, Treasury's assistant secretary for terrorist financing and financial crimes said that the two governments had reached an understanding on the frozen funds. Washington insisted, however, that the funds "will be used solely for the betterment of the North Korean people, including for humanitarian and educational purposes." Months passed. Finally, a Russian bank assisted the funds transfer to Pyongyang. On June 25 the DPRK confirmed that it had received the funds, and it began shutting down the Yongbyon nuclear facilities, a process confirmed by the IAEA in July.

A new crisis arose on September 6, 2007, when Israeli bombers destroyed a Syrian facility that, U.S. officials later said, was probably a nearly completed nuclear reactor being built with North Korean assistance on the Yongbyon model. For the next year and more, the DPRK refused to discuss the issue except to deny that it was helping a Syrian nuclear project. Washington had to decide whether to press the issue as an example of nuclear proliferation by Pyongyang or ignore it and focus on Yongbyon.[36]

Notwithstanding the Syrian controversy, the six parties met again in late September 2007 and issued a joint statement on October 3. North Korea pledged by December 31 to provide a "complete and correct declaration of all its nuclear programs—including clarification regarding the uranium issue." Pyongyang also agreed to disable its Yongbyon and other nuclear facilities subject to the September 2005 joint statement and not to transfer nuclear material or technology abroad. In return, North Korea would receive the remaining 900,000 tons of heavy fuel oil or its equivalent pledged in the February 13 agreement. Washington agreed it would begin removing North Korea from its list of state sponsors of terrorism and "advance the process of terminating the application of the Trading with the Enemy Act" toward North Korea "in parallel with" North Korea's denuclearization actions.

Pyongyang ascribed a sacrosanct quality to the October 3 joint statement.[37] The fact that it had no provision for verification led to huge difficulties in 2008. In late 2007, however, both sides seemed determined to execute their commitments.

In November a team of U.S. experts arrived in North Korea and began leading the disablement of the Yongbyon nuclear facilities, trying to make the December 31 deadline stipulated on October 3. Funding for the disablement process was provided by the State Department's Nonproliferation and Disarmament Fund.

Sunshine = Moonshine?

For most of Bush's second term, bilateral relations seemed to improve between South and North Korea. It was unclear, however, whether Seoul's Sunshine Policy served to bring the North in from the cold or reinforce its tendency to hunker down and ask for more. A second ROK-DPRK summit took place on October 2–4, 2007. Not insisting on a reciprocal DPRK visit to the South, ROK president Roh Moo-hyun traveled to Pyongyang to meet with Kim Jong Il. They agreed to take steps toward reunification, ease military tensions, expand meetings of separated families, and engage in social and cultural exchanges. They expressed a "shared understanding . . . on the need for ending the current armistice mechanism and building a permanent peace mechanism."

On December 19, 2007, the Grand National Party candidate Lee Myung-bak was elected ROK president, ushering in the first conservative government in Seoul in ten years. Lee pledged to review the Sunshine Policy of his two predecessors and insist on reciprocity by the North. Once the Lee administration was inaugurated in February 2008, Seoul stopped sending rice and fertilizer to the North. In response, Pyongyang then began to restrict cross-border exchanges with the South. In July 2008 DPRK troops shot and killed a South Korean tourist, a middle-aged woman, as she walked on the beach in the Mount Geumgang resort—after which Pyongyang demanded an apology (!) from Seoul. The DPRK refused to allow South Korean officials to inspect the shooting scene, claiming the woman trespassed into a restricted military zone despite repeated warnings.

Following the killing, the ROK halted subsidies for civic groups committed to North-South cooperation. Hyundai Asan immediately suspended its tours. But Seoul's response to all this was quite restrained. In November 2008, however, one day after the North threatened to close its land border with the South, the ROK Ministry of Unification announced plans to resume subsidizing local civic groups to assist their humanitarian activities in North Korea. The ROK government expressed hope that North Korea would accept an offer to send materials and equipment necessary to improve military communication between the two sides. But a telephone message from the ROK military to the North proposing the two sides discuss details of this plan went unanswered. Pyongyang also closed its Red Cross liaison office at the truce village of Panmunjom and cut off direct telephone links with its South Korean counterpart. The DPRK intensified this kind of behavior in 2009.

Point and Counterpoint

Relations between Washington and Pyongyang were more like a Bach concerto than a Beethoven symphony—not entire movements of adagio and allegro but sharp point and counterpoint. Bush in December 2007 wrote a letter to the DPRK leader addressed as "Dear Mr. Chairman" and had it delivered to Pyongyang by diplomat Christopher Hill.

Two months after Bush's somewhat cordial letter, the New York Philharmonic, with State Department approval, played and gave master classes in Beijing, Pyongyang, and Seoul. The concert in North Korea began with the DPRK and U.S. national anthems, for which the elite audience of twenty-five hundred stood. A symphonic rendition of *Arirang,* a folk song loved by Koreans north and south, brought tears to some eyes. The program included *Lohengrin* but also Americana—the *New World Symphony, An American in Paris,* and *Candide.* "Someday a composer may write a work entitled 'Americans in Pyongyang,'" said conductor Lorin Maazel, drawing warm applause from the audience. This visit marked the first occasion a U.S. cultural organization appeared in North Korea and the largest contingent of Americans since the Korean War. Looking for precedents, historians recalled the triumphant visits of the Boston Symphony and New York Philharmonic to the USSR in the late 1950s and the Philadelphia Orchestra's concerts in China in 1973.

The visit came in response to a North Korean invitation the previous year. The hosts and concertgoers provided a warm and friendly reception. DPRK vice minister of culture Song Sok-hwan called the visit a "big stride in cultural exchange." Conductor Maazel was equally positive. "This might just have pushed us over the top" in finding a way beyond past discord, said former defense secretary William Perry after the concert, adding that Washington should reciprocate by inviting North Korean performers to the United States. But there was no replay of ping-pong diplomacy. A White House spokesman said that a concert is just a concert—

not a diplomatic coup. Indeed, U.S.-DPRK negotiations in 2008 encountered one problem after another, and no high-level invitations went to Pyongyang.

Impasse

How near and yet so far. The United States and North Korea in 2008 nearly got to yes on a wide-ranging agreement, only to have the year end in deadlock. Why? Each side, its supporters said, had been reasonable. Each side, its critics maintained, had been two-faced and scheming. Interpreting what happened was difficult because many exchanges took place behind closed doors and some reported understandings were not put down in writing or published. For Washington, the most important problem was verification; for Pyongyang, delivery on time of promised fuel oil. The "sacrosanct" October 3, 2007, agreement laid out a three-stage program for denuclearization but provided no mechanism for verification until the third phase. State Department officials seemed ready on occasion to cut Pyongyang some slack; the DPRK Foreign Ministry also sought to bridge differences. But hard-liners in Washington (also in Tokyo and Seoul) raised the ante on several occasions, giving Pyongyang cause (and excuse) to pull back.

Though required to provide a complete and correct declaration of its nuclear programs by December 31, 2007, Pyongyang failed to produce the declaration until June 2008. Trying to explain the DPRK delay, a State Department spokesman on January 2, 2008, referred to "some technical questions about the cooling of the fuel rods." But Pyongyang offered a different explanation. Because energy deliveries to North Korea were behind schedule, the DPRK was slowing Yongbyon disablement.

In February 2008 Christopher Hill requested Congress to waive the "Glenn amendment" sanctions imposed on North Korea following its 2006 nuclear test. These sanctions, which banned nonhumanitarian assistance to non-nuclear-weapon states that detonate a nuclear weapon, prevented the National Nuclear Security Administration from carrying out work to dismantle the Yongbyon nuclear facilities. Hill also informed the Senate Foreign Relations Committee that in autumn 2007 North Korea showed U.S. officials two conventional weapons systems it claimed were the recipients of the thousands of aluminum tubes imported years before—the tubes that raised suspicions of a uranium enrichment program. Hill said the tubes were currently being used for a second conventional weapons system.

Two former U.S. officials complained that the State Department was conceding too much by focusing on North Korea's plutonium assets and ignoring its commitments in other arenas. "It is one thing to compromise in order to craft an agreement, keep difficult negotiations going and not let the best be the enemy of the good. It is another thing to let the other side breach compromises already reached."[38]

In June 2008 the DPRK provided its long-awaited declaration—eighteen thousand pages of documentation detailing the operations of its 5-megawatt nuclear reactor and reprocessing facility at Yongbyon, records dating back to 1986. President Bush immediately announced that he would begin the process of removing North Korea from the list of state sponsors of terrorism and lift sanctions on North Korea under the U.S. Trading with the Enemy Act.[39] Justifying Bush's commitment, the State Department said that North Korea had not committed a terrorist act since 1987. The White House stated on June 26 that eight of eleven components of the disablement process had been completed and that close to 50 percent of nuclear fuel rods in the Yongbyon nuclear reactor had been removed. But Washington was already changing the goalposts. On June 18, 2008, Secretary Rice told the Heritage Foundation that Washington would delay removing North Korea from the list of state sponsors of terrorism until it could verify the accuracy and completeness of the declaration. She acknowledged that Washington was moving up verification from the third phase to the second phase of the process.

Nevertheless, critics charged that Bush was giving away the store. John R. Bolton, now a private citizen, asserted that the North's nuclear and ballistic missile programs "materially assisted Syria and Iran, two other states on the terrorism honor roll." Bolton could not see what remained of President Bush's doctrine that those who support terrorists will be treated as terrorists. "Nothing can erase the ineffable sadness of an American presidency, like this one, in total intellectual collapse."[40]

A subsequent report by the Congressional Reference Service cited French, Japanese, South Korean, and Israeli sources describing recent North Korean programs to provide arms and training to Hezbollah in Lebanon and the Tamil Tigers in Sri Lanka—two groups on the U.S. list of international terrorist organizations. Moreover, there was much evidence of a long-standing collaboration between North Korea and the Iranian Revolutionary Guards.[41] Although not denying these concerns, some security analysts advised the United States to focus on the most urgent danger and labor to disable the Yongbyon facility so that it could yield no more plutonium. Everything else was of secondary importance.

The Bush administration had its own questions about the accuracy and completeness of the DPRK declaration. The eighteen thousand pages said nothing about uranium enrichment or North Korea's activities in Syria. Some experts thought the report understated DPRK plutonium production—37 kilograms versus a U.S. estimate of 50 kilograms. Washington wanted on-site sampling to determine the efficiency of Pyongyang's nuclear efforts and the likely quantities already produced.

North Korea maintained that under the October 2007 accord it was not obligated to address verification at this stage. But Pyongyang gave way and on July 18 signed a communiqué providing for a six-party verification mechanism that could visit declared facilities, review documents, and interview personnel. But Tokyo and Seoul wanted a tougher stand. So Washington demanded a more intrusive verification system. In response, Pyongyang on August 14 stopped disabling the plutonium facilities at Yongbyon and began restoring equipment there.

Now Washington backed down. On October 1 Hill brought to Pyongyang a draft protocol stipulating less intrusive inspection procedures. Hill and Kim Gye Gwan seemed to reach an understanding. Soon, the Bush administration announced that North Korea had agreed to all demands for inspection of its nuclear facilities and would be removed from the list of state sponsors of terrorism. The State Department cautioned, however, that the DPRK could be returned to the list if it failed to facilitate inspection. Apparently satisfied, Pyongyang resumed disabling the Yongbyon facilities.

But discord immediately erupted over the ostensible accord between Hill and Kim Gye Gwan. U.S. officials asserted that North Korea had agreed to allow inspectors to collect samples from its nuclear facilities and remove them from the country for analysis. But Pyongyang contradicted these claims and said the two sides had agreed that verification would be confined to "field visits, confirmation of documents, and interviews with technicians"—and would begin only after North Korea received energy assistance promised in 2007. The discrepancy may have arisen from differences between written and more extensive verbal understandings.

Getting tougher, Pyongyang in November 2008 said it was slowing by half the pace at which it unloaded the spent fuel rods from its 5-megawatt reactor, because of "the delayed fulfillment of the economic compensation" by China, Russia, South Korea, and the United States. A Japanese source said North Korea was reducing the rate from thirty rods to fifteen rods per day. By November the DPRK had removed about five thousand of the eight thousand total spent fuel rods.

The removal of the spent fuel rods constituted one of the last of eleven steps North Korea agreed to take in November 2007 to disable the three primary facilities at its Yongbyon nuclear complex. In return, the other parties (except Japan) agreed to supply 1 million tons of heavy fuel oil or its equivalent. The U.S. State Department reported in November 2008 that about 550,000 tons had already been shipped or would soon be delivered. In early December the State Department said that U.S. shipments of heavy fuel oil would not continue without a verification agreement, but that the United States had finished supplying its share (200,000 tons) in December. South Korea indicated that its assistance would be reconsidered. Russia's envoy to the six-party talks, Deputy Foreign Minister Alexei Borodavkin, stated that Russia would complete its delivery of 200,000 tons of heavy fuel oil "in a few months." China said it would continue to implement the agreements made in 2007. Japan remained adamant that it would not supply its share of heavy fuel oil (200,000 tons) until its concerns about abductees were resolved. At Washington's request, Australia and New Zealand offered to make up for Japan's share, but they, too, conditioned their assistance on resolution of the verification impasse.

Given the stakes, arguing about 200,000 tons of oil looked both petty and myopic.[42] Isolated and impoverished, North Korea would not permit its adversaries to welsh on their promises. The parties had earlier seen how the DPRK had refused to act on its February 2007 commitments until $25 million from Macao reached Pyongyang. If Kim Jong Il had suffered a serious medical problem in 2008, as was widely believed, whoever was making decisions in Pyongyang could not afford to look weak.

Some ROK and U.S. authorities said the North Koreans would allow sampling when they judged the "price is right." DPRK statements implied that Pyongyang might be willing to address the question of sampling in the third and ostensibly final phase of the negotiations. As of December 2008, however, the parties remained deadlocked on verification. China generated a single negotiating text based on consultations with each of the parties. The draft did not speak of "sampling" but called for "scientific verification procedures" and "international standards" in order to find consensus. Hill told reporters that "most delegations were prepared to work with the Chinese text," although "that consensus was not shared by" North Korea.

In December 2008 Kim Gye Gwan warned that if the energy assistance did not materialize, "we will adjust the speed of disablement." A few days later, another DPRK source stated that "aid from China and Russia has continued and we do not intend to stop the disablement process yet."

The year 2008 ended with the accommodation cup half full and half empty—no reason for Bush to boast of success and a complicated problem for his successor to address. In February 2009 North Korea began preparations to test launch its three-stage Taepodong-2 missile. The United States and its allies "could have been satisfied with the fact that international aid organizations were allowed unprecedented free movement inside North Korea, that markets were given more influence, that North Koreans were interested in learning from the West." But "demands for more access, more transparency, more information and more concessions" looked to Pyongyang like "blunt attempts at data mining and bringing about regime change. Consequently, international organizations were curtailed in their activities and most of them finally driven out of the country."[43]

CHAPTER TEN

HOW IDEAS AND FREE WILL CAN TRUMP HARD POWER AND *FORTUNA*

Tension and détente in Northeast Asia have been shaped by hard power, fortuna, *and the intangibles of ideas and free will. No single factor explains the ups and downs in North-South relations and in six-party talks. But the record shows that ideas and determined individuals have sometimes overcome the thrust of material forces and neutered the vagaries of time and chance. Smart power can outweigh both hard power and* fortuna. *Where there is a will (on all sides), paths to mutual gain can be developed.*

A Basic Explanation: The Weight of Material Forces

Realists contend that world politics is best understood as a quest for power.[1] Intangibles such as ideals do not drive this quest but rather reflect or mask it.[2] "Communications problems" are byproducts, not root causes, of conflict. Neorealists (structuralists) go further: They maintain that individuals, domestic politics, and culture count for nothing in world affairs. International relations are a mirror of the material structure defined by the hierarchy of military and economic power. The strong do what they will and the weak submit—either following the leader (bandwagoning) or seeking partners to resist (balancing).[3] The former president of the Council on Foreign Relations derides soft power as mere "foreplay" to coercive power. The world, he says, is not flat but pyramidal, with one country on top.[4]

Geopolitics

Geography sometimes looks like destiny. Sited where China, Russia, and Japan face one another, Korea has long been pressed to join with or balance against one or more of its neighbors. This kind of pressure intensified after a distant power, the United States, extended its reach to Northeast Asia in the nineteenth century. Annexed by Japan, Korea disappeared from official U.S. discourse from 1911 until 1942. Given the aftermath of World War II and onset of the cold war, prospects were high that the victorious powers would divide the peninsula in two—a communist and an anticommunist Korea.

When North Korea drove south in 1950, the proximity of Russia and the remoteness of the United States led State Department counselor George F. Kennan to advise Washington to consign the entire peninsula to the Soviet sphere of influence. Had the United States followed Kennan's fatalistic realism, Korea would soon have been united under communist rule and probably would have remained so for many years. But this did not happen. Against big odds, the United States chose to fight and soon reversed the tide. General Douglas MacArthur overcame geography by landing forces at Inchon. He then ignored geopolitics by driving north toward the Yalu, thereby provoking China to enter the fray. In 1953 the peninsula was still divided close to the thirty-eighth parallel, but along more defensible lines than had existed before the fighting began.

Geoeconomics

Material forces—military, economic, geopolitical—set the stage. As one Korea became two in the late 1940s, the North possessed significant advantages over the South. Its industrial base was more developed, its military better equipped, its political administration more cohesive, its major patron far more committed than the South's major backer.

Starting in 1950–1951, however, geopolitics began to favor the South. The United States became far more engaged in Korean affairs than Russia or China was. Most of the fighting in Korea stopped in 1953, but the United States devoted major resources to help South Korea (like Taiwan) reach and go beyond "economic takeoff." More than half a century after the Korean armistice, the United States retained large forces ready to fight in and for South Korea. U.S. and ROK forces conducted maneuvers and operated under a Combined Forces Command headed by a U.S. general. Starting in 2007, however, steps began to transfer to wartime control of South Korean forces to the ROK government.

The ravages of war, 1950–1953, left both North and South prostrate. In the 1960s, economic conditions in the North were probably better than in the South. Starting in the early 1970s, however, South Korea became one of Asia's "Little Tigers." Since that time geoeconomics has also favored the South. Per capita income in the ROK is probably thirty to fifty times higher than in the North.

As the South caught up with and then surpassed the North in material output, this trend exerted contradictory influences on Pyongyang. Confronted with its growing weakness relative to the South, the North sometimes offered grand gestures for a broad accommodation and confederation. At other moments, however, the North seemed to shy away from any deal that would permit its people to see and then compare developments in the DPRK and ROK.

Nevertheless, the worsening economic conditions in the North in the mid- and late 1990s and at times in the early twenty-first century correlated with greater willingness in Pyongyang to take on the risks inherent in détente—greater penetration by ideas and institutions of freedom, an upswelling of demands for change, and a possible challenge from hard-liners within the DPRK leadership. The DPRK leadership, like the Soviet in past decades, probably hoped that arms control would lead to détente and an easing of the economic sanctions that separated the country from Western and East Asian advances in technology. The record suggests that food shortages have often driven the North Korean regime, like that of the erstwhile USSR, to make concessions in arms control negotiations.[5] The Agreed Framework of 1994 and the high-level visits by DPRK and U.S. officials in 2000 coincided with bad harvests and starvation in the North. However, a regime that fed its elites and repressed most of its subjects had little reason to fear a revolution from below.[6]

Contrary to materialist and neorealist doctrine, however, the asymmetries in material power on the Korean peninsula did not push the DPRK leadership to its knees. Yes, the North had long been relatively weak, but it did not bow to superior force. Confronted with challenges on all sides, the DPRK championed self-reliance and either walked away from negotiations or drove very hard bargains. Often it opted to hang tough.

North Korea's incipient nuclear weapon capability could push Pyongyang in opposite directions. Though the North remained weak militarily relative to the South and its superpower ally, even a minuscule nuclear weapon capability helped to level the playing field. Confident since 2006 that it already possessed a minimum deterrent, Pyongyang often defied its five interlocutors. On other occasions, however, believing that it operated from a new strength, the North seemed to inch toward a grand bargain.

The forces of global interdependence also registered contradictory impacts. The ROK tapped into these forces to become more prosperous, while the DPRK shriveled—unable to shape or benefit from the forces sweeping the planet. Isolation hurt the North and militated for joining the world, but it also widened the gaps to be bridged.

A Second Explanation: *Fortuna*

To what extent have the zigs and zags of Korean affairs been shaped by fate or by chance? To answer we must define *fortuna*. Is it a mysterious power behind the scenes that intervenes to shape human affairs? Or is it more like blind chance—coincidence that brings us good or bad "luck"?

Niccolò Machiavelli's writings included both concepts. *Fortuna,* for Machiavelli, could be an angry goddess who lays waste like a flooding river that overflows its banks—a primal source of violence directed against humanity and antithetical to reason. "She shows her power where *virtù* and wisdom do not prepare to resist her, and directs her fury where she knows that no dykes or embankments are ready to hold her." *Fortuna* may be resisted by human beings, but only in circumstances where "*virtù* and wisdom" have already prepared for her inevitable arrival.[7]

Nassim Taleb warns us to expect "black swans"—important events that could not have been expected, events so rare that they would not show up even on the tail end of a bell curve. Yes, Europeans believed all swans are white, but when they reached Australia, they found black swans—an event unprecedented for them. Taleb claims that *almost all consequential events in history come from the unexpected*—even though humans convince themselves that these events are explainable in "hindsight bias."[8] His examples include the personal computer, World War I, and 9/11/01.[9] The list could include the collapse of the U.S. banking system in 2008.

Some individuals and societies seem to lead charmed lives, whereas others encounter one disaster after another. But science denies that *fortuna* is an angry goddess. Floods take place as a result of physical forces combined with human impacts on the environment and poor planning by humans.

Nevertheless, there are limits to what science can anticipate. Today's physical features may serve as preadaptations for new life forms if the environment changes. Darwinian preadaptations can neither be prestated nor foreseen. Their evolution is not deducible from physics. The more diversity there is in the biosphere, the more possibilities there are for unpredictable adaptations.[10]

Even though humans cannot expect and plan for all that comes their way, knowledge and prudence help humans prepare to meet challenges both foreseen and unexpected. Both science and experience explain that "good fortune" often results from good preparation. A Chinese fortune cookie reveals: "Thorough preparation makes its own luck."

Some individuals and groups are better equipped and trained than others to cope with challenges and make the most of opportunity.[11] Those whose eyes and minds are open and searching have proved to be most likely to experience serendipity—finding value in unexpected places. Persistent hard work, combined with courage, often pays off. As Virgil put it, "*Audaces fortuna iuvat, timidosque repellit* [Fortune rewards the bold and repels the meek]."[12]

Fortune is not completely capricious, as suggested by an exiled rival to the Medici family, who wrote to Florence from exile in Naples: "I am laughing at the games of fortune and at how it makes friends become enemies and enemies become friends as it suits it." The Medici patriarch Piero, father of Lorenzo the Magnificent, countered: "Your laughing over there is the cause that I do not weep," because if the plot against Piero had succeeded, Piero would be weeping in exile. Therefore, he told his failed rival, "live there in dishonor, since you did not know how to live here in honor."[13]

When we leave all theory behind, history shows that chance and timing have played gigantic roles in Korean affairs. Let us review a few of the key turning points where a slightly different concatenation of events could have catapulted Korea in a different direction.[14]

- What if, at the turn of the last century, anti-imperialists in the United States had resisted Japan's takeover of Korea? Many Americans working in Korea urged Washington to do so. If Washington demanded an open door in China, why not apply the same logic to Korea? If the United States had allowed self-determination in the Philippines, as anti-imperialists demanded, Washington would have had less incentive to cede Korea to Japan.
- What if Woodrow Wilson in 1919 had extended his support for national self-determination to Korea?
- What if Washington had applied the logic of the 1932 Stimson Doctrine not only to Manchuria but also to Korea?
- What if years or months before the USSR joined the war against Japan and occupied northern Korea, the United States had recognized Syngman Rhee's Provisional Government and made "Korea" a founding member of the United Nations?

Were such moves simply "not in the cards" because they contradicted the premises of Realpolitik?[15] No. They would have enhanced America's interests in the world and conformed to moral and legal principles recognized by the U.S. government. Washington sometimes stood on principle. For example, it refused to recognize the forced incorporation of the three Baltic countries into the USSR even though Franklin Roosevelt valued Josef Stalin as an ally.[16] Even when Washington courted the Gorbachev regime, U.S. diplomat Jack Matlock spoke in Latvia in 1986 reminding people there that the United States had never recognized the Soviet annexation of the three Baltic republics.

- What if Stalin in August 1945 had rejected the U.S. proposal to divide Korea at the thirty-eighth parallel? What if he had ordered the Red Army to occupy the entire peninsula as it did some East European countries? Soon after partition, the USSR resisted U.S. efforts to foster trade and other contacts across the dividing line. Quirks of timing saved the South from communist rule.
- What if Secretary of State Dean Acheson in January 1950 had vetted his remarks on the U.S. defense perimeter with U.S. experts on East Asia? Instead, he spoke without a written script and gave the impression that the United States would let South Korea fend for itself if attacked. Acheson,

however, did not intend to convey this message. And when North Korea attacked, he helped convince President Harry Truman to mobilize U.S. forces and the United Nations to resist.

- What if the Soviet delegate had taken his seat in the UN Security Council when it deliberated a response to the North Korean attack? Washington's ability to activate UN collective security was aided by what looked like a freak incident—the absence of the Soviet delegate from the UN Security Council when it voted to condemn and then resist the North's actions. A Soviet veto would have complicated Washington's decisions and, even if the United States opted to fight, would have deprived U.S. actions of legitimacy. When Czechoslovak communists asked why the USSR was not present to veto the Security Council resolutions, Stalin concocted a not-very-convincing excuse.

We can also wonder what might have happened if certain assassination efforts had failed or succeeded.

- What if assassins had succeeded earlier or failed entirely in three attempts on the life of President Park Chung Hee? The 1974 attempt missed the president but killed his wife, Yook Young-soo, leaving Park gloomy and dispirited.[17] Jimmy Carter's inauguration and shift of U.S. policy toward Korea in 1977 added to Park's difficulties. Park's death by assassination in 1979 probably helped preserve authoritarian rule in the ROK, which continued until the late 1980s.
- What if plots against the life of Kim Dae Jung had succeeded and not merely left him lame? The best known challenger to Park Chung Hee's rule, Kim claimed that Park had tried to have him killed in 1971 and on several subsequent occasions. As history evolved, however, Kim Dae Jung not only survived but—on his third try—won the presidency in 1997. Had he been killed or given up hope, he would not have been able to introduce his Sunshine Policy in 1998.
- What if the Chun Doo Hwan administration, the U.S ambassador to Seoul, and the Jimmy Carter administration had handled the May 1980 Kwangju uprising differently? What if other policies had prevailed and nearly two hundred persons not been killed? The incident heightened provincial hostility within South Korea and helped trigger the rise of anti-American sentiment across the country.

- What if the plot against the life of ROK president Chun Doo Hwan had succeeded when he visited Rangoon in October 1983? Instead, he lived, but the explosion killed at least seventeen Koreans (including some ROK ministers) and four Burmese. The government in Rangoon blamed North Korea for the explosion and severed diplomatic ties.[18] Relations between Seoul and Pyongyang became far more tense. Authoritarian rule tightened its grip in South Korea.

- What if Kim Il Sung had not agreed to meet with Jimmy Carter in June 1994? What if he had died before Carter arrived? The Great Leader expired just weeks after his historic deal with Carter that set the stage for the Agreed Framework signed later that year. The elder Kim's son and successor, Kim Jong Il, seemed to feel obliged to carry on his father's understanding with Carter. Had the father in his last months refused to see Carter (as he did some Bill Clinton stalwarts), his son would have inherited a more confrontational legacy—perhaps even a war.

- What if Democrats had not lost control of Congress in the 1994 elections? This happened shortly after U.S. and DPRK negotiators signed the Agreed Framework. Republican reluctance to fund the deal contributed to the long delays in breaking ground for the two light-water reactors. The Clinton administration felt compelled to seek funding from the European Union as well as from Japan and the ROK. All this took time. Meanwhile, North Korean actions also delayed the whole project. Neither side took account of its own role in the denouement.

- What if President Bill Clinton in late 2000 had accepted Kim Jong Il's invitation to travel to Pyongyang and resolve all issues between the two governments? The groundwork had been laid by Madeleine Albright and others, but Clinton opted to work on another worthy cause: striving to mediate Israeli-Palestinian differences. The prospects for a grand bargain looked good just as Clinton lost his lease on the White House.

- What if newly elected George W. Bush had listened to Colin Powell instead of to hard-liners close to the White House in early 2001? Powell wanted to build on the movement toward a deal with Pyongyang generated by the Clinton administration in 2000. Instead, harsh words from Washington fostered confrontation instead of détente with North Korea. Bush's policies not only aborted movement toward arms control, but they also undermined movement in North Korea toward a market economy. They helped catalyze a hard line in domestic as well as foreign policy.

- What if a U.S. armored car had not killed two high school girls in a narrow lane in South Korea in June 2002? What if the drivers had not been on maneuvers for three days with little sleep? What if villages had been forewarned of the military transit? What if U.S. authorities had responded to Korean grievances in a more humane manner? Would anti-U.S. sentiments in the ROK have risen to such a pitch in the early twenty-first century?

- What if, starting in 2003, the United States had not become bogged down in an elective war in Iraq? Washington might have paid more attention to the DPRK and endeavored with sticks and carrots to stop its nuclear weapons development. Were it not for the war in Iraq, Pyongyang might not have wanted or dared to test a nuclear weapon.

- What if Condoleezza Rice, having left the National Security Council for the State Department in 2005, had not become more committed to traditional diplomacy and put a skillful diplomat such as Christopher Hill in charge of negotiations with the DPRK? What if—undercut by hardliners in Washington and DPRK intransigence—Hill had just bowed to the intransigents? What if Hill had not sometimes stretched his instructions? What if he had not crossed paths with his DPRK counterpart at the Beijing airport in late 2006 and set up their bilateral encounter in Berlin? What if Rice had not given her blessing to that meeting and its product—an outline of the accord signed by all six parties in February 2007?

- What if, instead of waiting for a new U.S. president, Pyongyang had opted to clinch a deal in 2008? As happened in 2000, the brightest prospects for a U.S.-DPRK accord took shape just as the president's term ended.

Each of these "what ifs" was shaped by structure and by agency—by the configuration of forces and actions of individual players. They seem to mock any explanation based on materialistic determinism. Looking back fifty or one hundred years later, however, some future historian might say that none of these small events did much to change the big picture. Perhaps the February 2007 accord will have come to naught. Perhaps the underlying forces much respected by neorealists will have controlled relations between Pyongyang and the other five.

Nevertheless, if things had not jelled as they did—if some events had occurred earlier or later—politics in Korea would have become quite different. As in all human relations, timing and coincidence often triggered both positive and negative developments. America's involvement in Iraq, for example, diverted Washington's attention from North Korea in 2003–2004, even as it probably deepened Pyongyang's determination to acquire a nuclear deterrent. Starting in 2005, however, as the burdens of the Iraq war became heavier, the Bush administration appeared to seek a negotiating breakthrough with the DPRK.

The Third (and Deepest) Explanation: Ideas and Free Will

Under ideas and "free will" we consider the intangibles that shape world affairs—ideas, beliefs, words, feelings, soft power, smart power, and—not least—willpower. These are the domains analyzed by students of ideas and ideals, constructivism, psychology, and diplomatic technique.

Let us acknowledge that material forces provide part of the framework for all human actions and that accidents of timing often seem to block some paths and lead to others. None of us is completely free. We are all bound by "nature and nurture," by life experiences, and by elements of chance and timing. As a result, some organisms are more fit than others—better able to cope with complex challenges and opportunities.

Strong individuals and societies overcome many barriers to put their lives on trajectories of their own choosing. To do so, of course, they must be not only fit but also deeply determined and persistent. Machiavelli warned that *fortuna*, like a rain-driven flood, can lay waste to human enterprise. He also noted, however, that wise politicians can anticipate and plan for floods and other stresses. Skillful policy-makers can mitigate damage and sometimes turn a challenge into an opportunity. Often they can mitigate the limits imposed by material forces and by difficulties that result from a "perfect storm."

Idealism and Neoliberalism

Western idealists contend that self-rule should be the underlying principle of politics and that, where practiced, it gets far better results than top-down, authoritarian rule. Self-rule conduces to prosperity and peace—at home and across borders. Communist theorists, by contrast, have argued that an enlightened vanguard should lead and decide for the masses.[19] Rugged individualism, they have said, leads to chaos and domination by the privileged few. Until communism prevails across borders, the contradictions of free enterprise will cause war.

The postulates of democracy are supported by complexity theory.[20] This theory holds that the key to fitness is self-organization—in all realms, political, social, cultural, and economic. Revising "Social Darwinism," it maintains that the capacity to cooperate is crucial for societal fitness. Liberal peace theory takes praise for democracy one step further: It argues that a liberal consensus makes war very nearly unthinkable among democrats. Experiences around the globe in recent centuries have proved that liberal peace theory is basically correct and that arguments for top-down rule are wrong.[21]

The lessons of global history have been confirmed also on the Korean peninsula.[22] The more that freedom and self-organization took hold in South Korea, the more prosperous it became and the more devoted to a peaceful resolution of issues at home and with the North. Authoritarian rule in the North, by contrast, conduced to immiserization, isolation, and bellicosity.[23] Though one-party rule has remained in China, greater economic freedom there coincided with a more constructive role in world affairs, for example, in hosting the six-party talks. Petro-police state Russia, by comparison, did much less to shape the negotiations, even when it overflowed with petrodollars.

Constructivism

"Reality," according to constructivists, is what we make of it. What appears to be "objective" can be subjective—a function of perception and interpretation.[24] Thus, Americans do not worry much about nuclear weapons in British or French hands, but they worry a great deal about nukes in the hands of North Korea and other actors that sometimes behave (at least in U.S. eyes) like rogue elephants. Similarly, most Europeans have come to assume that Washington will not use nuclear weapons except in self-defense, whereas North Korean leaders recall how U.S. bombers flattened their country in the early 1950s and fear a repeat performance. They take note of signs that Washington has threatened the use of nuclear as well as conventional weapons to achieve its goals in Korea. The

George W. Bush administration's espousal of preventive war helped keep these fears alive.

Small things can become big when perceived in a certain light. Some observers thought that DPRK demands for return of $25 million from its accounts in the Banco Delta Asia as a prerequisite for complying with its February 2007 arms control commitment showed that Pyongyang was insincere or petty. A student of public administration might assume that any delay in transferring funds must be due to "bureaucracy." Given that $25 million is a trivial sum on the world scene, a cynic might say that Pyongyang was just exploiting the issue to delay meeting its obligations. But a constructivist might suggest that Pyongyang saw the delay as another case of American conniving.

Punctilious when it chose to be, Pyongyang later threatened to repudiate its arms control obligations unless Washington fulfilled its pledge to remove the DPRK from its list of states that sponsor terrorism. In this case, as with the frozen funds issue and an end to U.S. sanctions, officials in the United States and North Korea construed reality differently. They also differed on Afghanistan and Iraq. Washington claimed it was fighting terror, whereas Pyongyang accused the United States of "terrorism committed by state armed forces."[25]

The deepest divergence in viewpoints concerned nuclear arms. The United States and other nuclear haves assumed they were entitled to membership in an exclusive club whose doors were shut to North Korea and other have-nots. Many Americans saw their country as a beneficent gendarme to the world, whereas Pyongyang saw the United States as a brazen bully. DPRK leaders thought they had every right to nuclear arms; Washington said they had none. Pyongyang also objected to expanded U.S. arms sales to South Korea, authorized by Congress in September 2008 to acquire the same kinds of weapons sold to NATO members.

Hiking with Uncertainty

None of the three basic explanations—determinism, *fortuna,* voluntarism—provides all the answers. None accounts for the up-and-down patterns in the six-party talks or in North Korea's bilateral dealings with South Korea or the United States. Despite huge asymmetries of power, the DPRK has held its own in all these transactions.

Despite the concerted efforts of five larger and richer states, North Korea has accumulated the knowledge and means to test nuclear devices and the wherewithal to acquire a minimum nuclear deterrent. To limit or surrender this capability, Pyongyang demands a high price. Meanwhile, of course, most North Koreans have paid for their leaders' intransigence. More than 1 million have perished from starvation, and millions of children have grown up without adequate nourishment—physical, intellectual, spiritual. Opposed ideologies and ignorance of each other's culture also obstructed efforts to improve ties between the DPRK and other powers—especially the United States.

The ultimate problem has been the lack of strong determination in Pyongyang and in Washington to develop a broad working relationship that subordinates lesser concerns to larger ones. Distrusting one another for more than six decades, each side has preferred to "keep its powder dry."

How do the three factors studied here interact? They do so like a hiker negotiating a rugged landscape.[26] The actual physical contours—the rivers, mountains, etc.—are like the forces that condition and constrain states. The hiker can go from A to B along several possible routes—with some being safer, quicker, or more scenic than others. *Fortuna* may shape the journey in the form of warm, clear skies or flash floods, rainstorms, lightning bolts, fallen trees, and other hazards. Accidents of timing and coincidence—good and bad "luck"—can be critical. At every juncture the prudent hiker must make choices. He or she evaluates the landscape and calculates the likelihood of *fortuna*'s impacting the journey to make it more difficult or easier. The hiker may decide that the best route is the longest or the most arduous one.

At bottom, of course, all three factors feed on one another. The structure of each society, the region, and the global system give rise to and condition each individual actor. Individuals, in turn, may shape the structure. *Fortuna* may intervene, helping or blocking agents of change or putting them on unexpected and unwanted trajectories.[27]

In Korea, as elsewhere, the thrust of material forces has often been altered by apparent accidents of timing and coincidence. Both hard power and *fortuna* have sometimes been trumped by free will. Individuals have often accomplished "miracles"—overcoming physical, emotional, and intellectual obstacles, even when fortune stacks the odds against them.

Smart, skilled, and determined individuals have sometimes overcome all obstacles to reach a deal. Jimmy Carter did so in 1994; Madeleine Albright came close in 2000; Christopher Hill also came close in the last years of the Bush administration. Some North Korean officials and diplomats performed equally or even more difficult feats, given that suspicions of weakness or betrayal in Pyongyang could be far more lethal than in Washington.

Wise and courageous hikers for peace can blaze an uphill path over stubborn obstacles and a mischievous *fortuna*. Their efforts can help avoid the worst and foster the best futures in Northeast Asia.

CHAPTER ELEVEN

HOW TO AVOID THE WORST
AND FOSTER BETTER FUTURES

The key to a better future may be to transform the game: broaden negotiations from arms control—what North Korea will give up and get in return—to a constructive and secure place for North Korea in the world community.

Focused on day-to-day events, we think: "The more things change, the more they remain the same." Even when someone adds grains of sand to a sand pile, it looks stable. At some critical moment, however, adding just one more grain will trigger an avalanche. It is nearly impossible to know when that critical threshold will be crossed and when the structure will collapse. Looking back, we see that the only certainty is change itself.

Prediction is not feasible, but we can outline some alternative futures for North Korea. Taking a time frame from 2010 to 2025, we can ask what combinations of circumstances make each of these scenarios more likely. Finally, we can ask what the United States and other external actors could do to avoid the worst and make better futures more likely.

Even though we attempt to consider all the relevant variables, our horizon may be too narrow. First, the future of North Korea is shaped by more variables than grains added to a sand pile. How these variables interact and change over time is nearly impossible to foretell. Second, rare events—and even black swans with no known precedent—may upset all the existing patterns. Third, what we see today may be just a phase in a punctuated equilibrium—a long plateau that will be followed by a sharp move up or down. Stasis dominates evolution.[1] But the equivalent of a destructive meteor spewing dust storms and blocking the sun could obliterate all our estimates. Allowing for events that break with the past and exceed our powers of imagination, let us outline the main alternatives as they appeared early in the twenty-first century.

1. *Within the DPRK,* there could be
   - more of the same
   - a catalytic collapse of the regime, along East German or Romanian lines
   - a gradual transformation toward a Chinese, Singaporean, or Taiwanese model
   - confederation with the Republic of Korea
   - transformation into a unified Korea
2. *In regard to nuclear issues,* there could be
   - more of the same—a negotiating stalemate
   - a negotiating breakthrough: no nuclear power or weapons
   - nuclear power but no nuclear weapons
   - nuclear power and a small nuclear arsenal
   - an expanding nuclear and missile arsenal
3. *As to the outside world,* North Korea could be
   - more of the same—a rogue state, a proliferator of advanced military technology and weaponry, a fomenter of regional chaos, a challenger to U.S hegemony, a catalyst for global war
   - a satellite for Beijing in a Chinese strategy of trade and economic development or expansion by force
   - a partner in a Northeast Asian zone of peace

Within the DPRK

More of the Same

Top-down rule as in *Brave New World* comforts a narrow elite but deprives most North Koreans not only of freedom but also of the material conditions needed for human development. Poor nutrition leaves most North Koreans much shorter than their cousins in the South. Their brains as well as their bodies have been starved. As in Enver Hoxha's Albania, isolation has cost North Korea dearly. Nevertheless, the DPRK regime has been one of the most stable in the world since World War II—ruled by a virtual dynasty facing only weak and sporadic challenges from other elites and only passive unrest among the broader population, despite or due to repression and privation.

Could cooperative engagement save the regime? What if the six-party talks succeed, economic reform takes off, and North Korea joins the international community and begins to receive massive outside financial support? "Under this scenario," two experts write, "the likelihood of regime change falls to less than 1 percent." But what if instead the "neocon's dream" scenario emerges—an end to outside support, further declines in the DPRK economy, and inflation? Then, the likelihood of regime changes rise to one in seven. But if an "international embargo" cuts off trade and remittances entirely and the economy falls below its mid-1990s level, the probability of regime change rises to 40 percent the first year and to 100 percent in the medium run.[2]

The two authors grant that these forecasts should be taken with "the appropriate grain of salt." Their point is to show the relatively limited impact of economic pressure, because the DPRK has already endured the worst of times—the mid-1990s. These experts then go on to consider political variables.

In my view, however, the cooperative engagement scenario is unlikely to save North Korea's regime for long because the existing system, like that of the former USSR, is so unfit—so wasteful of the country's human and material resources. Conversely, an international embargo would not necessarily terminate the regime. The communist regime in Cuba survived half a century of U.S. embargo and the demise of Cuba's main patron, the USSR.

My own view is that North Korea's existing system is unlikely to endure beyond a few years. As Andrei Lankov once put it, Stalinism may already be suffering a natural death. Centralized dictatorship and isolation are not viable—especially given the vibrant dynamism of South Korea and the increasing permeability of the North. Most communist tyrannies have vanished or mellowed. Sooner or later, the DPRK will change—gradually or quickly. *How—and how soon—are unknown.* Many communist and other authoritarian regimes lived on for decades after experts predicted their demise—from the USSR to North Korea to Cuba.

Catalytic Collapse

Neither *juche* nor *songun* policies sustain the DPRK and its regime. North Korea's Stalinist system might not change gradually. Rather, it might implode or explode.

It could suffer an economic breakdown and intense civil strife. Societal fitness would decline even further as North Koreans shifted from rigid order to anarchy.

Hunger stalks the land. Knowledge of the outside world erodes support for the ruling dynasty. Border controls break down. Huge numbers of North Koreans cross into China or flee to South Korea (by sea or via corridors in the DMZ). Neither the United States nor any of the major powers in the region wish another to take control of the North and its nuclear arsenal. China and South Korea vie for hegemony in the former DPRK.

The DPRK tyranny could collapse with barely a whimper, as in East Germany, or with violence and bloodshed, as in Romania. Serious weaknesses existed in East Germany for decades but offered few signs that the end was nigh. The catalyst was a small event: When the Hungarian government cut the barbed-wire fencing off its western border, thousands of East German "tourists" crossed over into Austria. Soon, other Germans began to pull apart the Wall in Berlin. Soon, the "German Democratic Republic" was absorbed into a united Germany. The nuclear superpower that had long backed the GDR and other communist regimes in Eastern Europe did nothing to prevent these moves. Indeed, it agreed with the other superpower that a united Germany could be part of the Western alliance. Imperial will had collapsed in Moscow.[3] East Europe's communist leaders lost their determination to hold on. Many ditched their ties to the USSR and joined their countrymen—and women—in embracing the West.

Whereas East Germans inflicted little damage on their former rulers, Romanians rose up in large numbers against the regime and soon executed the longtime dynasts man and wife—an event said to weigh on the mind of Kim Jong Il.

Box 11.1 Russian Images of a North Korean Collapse

In the early 1990s Russian writers speculated about North Korea's future. *Endgame*, a novel by Lev Vershinin, described a violent collapse of an imaginary communist dictatorship. The country of the novel blended features of North Korea, Romania, and Cuba. Vershinin mixed geographic names so that the capital of this imaginary country had the Korean-sounding name of T'aedongan and the place of the Stalinists' last stand was called Munch'on.

Along similar lines, the satirical poet Igor Irteniev mockingly wrote: "I still cannot sleep without a sedative / in the darkness of the night / when I imagine what happens to Kim Il Sung / in the blood-stained hands of the executioners."[4]

The prospects of regime collapse in North Korea are unclear. Repression is far more extensive and intensive than, say, in Soviet Estonia, where anticommunists and nationalistic communists in 1988 could form a popular front that challenged the Soviet-backed leadership in Tallinn and soon pressed for national self-determination.

If there was a power struggle in Pyongyang, it would probably take place among factions of the existing ruling circles. If Kim Jong Il was incapacitated, we might see a contest as occurred in the USSR after Josef Stalin's death. Stalin's would-be successors eliminated the chief of internal security, a power seeker in his own right, who possessed the documentation to expose his rivals and the military might to destroy them. Having disposed of Lavrentii Beria, the remaining triumvirs formed a collective leadership. Between 1954 and 1958, however, First Secretary of the Communist Party Nikita Khrushchev pushed his rivals aside or into acceptance of his role as something more than first among equals.

Gradual Transformation

Stephan Haggard and Marcus Noland say that "no communist regime has ever undergone an evolutionary transition to democratic rule."[5] But they ignore the peaceful transitions that took place in most of Eastern Europe, the Baltic republics, and even in Russia in the late 1980s, where multiple parties vied in elections and Boris Yeltsin became Russia's first freely elected president in June 1991 even while the Communist Party occupied the Kremlin. What brought on the demise of communist rule in the USSR was its inherent inefficiency—manifested in rising infant mortality after 1971.

Dictatorships are not efficient. Harsh rule generates opposition. Pressures beneath the surface push for change. Thus, the death of the Soviet dictator in 1953 led to a gradual liberation of the USSR. Even Lavrentii Beria wanted to relax controls at home and in Eastern Europe, because he understood the deep resentments and inefficiencies generated by repression. Nikita Khrushchev quickly sponsored a "thaw" and a turn toward "peaceful coexistence" with the noncommunist world. With many retreats and zigzags, the USSR gradually moved toward greater economic and political freedom—culminating in Mikhail Gorbachev's support for "all-human interests" over those of class or nation. Nearly a decade of chaos under Yeltsin in the 1990s, however, was followed by a strong swing back toward rule by Vladimir Putin's iron fist.

A similar pattern took place in China after Mao Zedong's demise in 1976: first, a power struggle lasting three years, then a loosening of domestic controls and moves to joining the "international community." As in Russia, political power remained concentrated in the hands of an oligarchy, but a species of Leninist capitalism flourished.

Analogous transformations took place in most of Eastern Europe, Mongolia, and Vietnam. The incapacity of Fidel Castro also led his brother to encourage more economic freedom and to loosen some political controls in Cuba. Outside the communist world, the deaths of Francisco Franco and António de Oliveira Salazar quickly led to the political and economic liberalization of Spain and Portugal. If North Korea follows this pattern, the incapacity of Kim Jong Il would lead to a power struggle and then to a gradual relaxation of economic and perhaps political controls.

China's Leninist Capitalism. China offers one model for North Korea's future evolution. Starting in the late 1970s, China's leaders kept centralized political control but relaxed barriers to market economic activity. Unleashing the dragons of materialism produced the world's most rapid GDP growth for several decades. Democrats and some ethnic minorities in China are frustrated and resentful, but most Chinese—at least until 2009—have been content with growing opportunities for material advancement. Few heed the warnings that environmental catastrophes are imminent.

For the long term, however, the communist oligarchy's monopoly of power in China may not be sustainable. Centralized decision making without popular input leaves the system prone to costly and counterproductive undertakings such as the Three Gorges Dam. China's economic gains have fostered environmental dangers that jeopardize the entire system. Some freedom whets appetites for greater freedom. The growing numbers of well-educated, traveled, and prosperous Chinese chafe at the restrictions that remain and even intensify. Nearly one-fourth of China's population accessed the Internet in 2009—a 42 percent increase over 2008. As these numbers increase, top-down controls wage a losing battle as many users find ways to forbidden sites and use Aesopian language to criticize their rulers.

Regardless of China's future, the model it has followed since the 1990s may not be very relevant to North Korea. China, like Vietnam, had a large and inefficient agricultural sector. China improved agriculture by lifting price controls and allowing surplus labor to migrate to the cities and enter light industry.

China financed its industrial expansion by new profits in agriculture, by cutting of outlays for the military, and by investment by overseas Chinese and other foreigners.

None of these avenues is bright for North Korea. The DPRK agricultural sector is relatively small and already somewhat industrialized. There is little surplus labor. The military hogs resources. Foreign investors will be diffident until a new dawn emerges.[6]

Singapore's Authoritarian Capitalism. This model resembles Leninist capitalism but is different in some respects. One party dominates politics, but economic and educational activities are freer than in China. Having risen from a malarial swamp to become a mighty city-state, Singapore ranks twenty-fifth in the world on the Human Development Index—just ahead of the ROK at twenty-sixth but behind Hong Kong at twenty-first and way ahead of Russia at sixty-seventh and China at eighty-first.[7] Singapore, however, labors under some of the same burdens imposed by top-down rule in China. The country is rich but not very creative. In any case, a small city-state cannot be a very useful model for a North Korea many times the size of Singapore and with a very different geographical setting.

Taiwan's Democratic Capitalism. Taiwan is a more appropriate model than Singapore for two reasons. First, its population is roughly the same size as North Korea's. Second, both Taiwan and North Korea face pressures to unite with or stand apart from their ethnic and cultural cousins. Like Taiwan, North Korea was supported for many years by a powerful patron (really, two patrons). The great power protectors of Taiwan and North Korea have tried to reduce their commitments, but remain entangled. Of course, there are also important differences: Taiwan is minuscule next to China and is separated from China by a wide strait. North Korea's population is less than one-half that of South Korea, but the two are separated only by a few miles of DMZ as well as half a century of divergent development.

Taiwan liberalized in the last one or two decades of the twentieth century. Although China is little changed politically, Taiwan has become a multiparty democracy with very high living standards and educational excellence. Many Taiwanese want to declare their country an independent member of the international community. Few wish to live under communist rule. But most want closer trade and cultural ties with mainland China.

Confederation with the South

The most appropriate model for North Korea is South Korea. But if the DPRK will not accept the political and other freedoms extant in the ROK, it is conceivable that the two Koreas could form a confederation in which each side retained its own system—somewhat like Hong Kong and Macao within the PRC. Governments in Seoul and in Pyongyang have sometimes called for such an arrangement—how earnestly is unsure.

A real confederation, however, is not efficient because it lacks a central decision-making body (witness the U.S. Articles of Confederation and today's European Union; even the Swiss "confederation" became a federation in the nineteenth century). A lopsided confederation would probably not long endure—especially if the governing ideologies in each part are quite different. The South, more numerous and more affluent, would overwhelm and then absorb the North.

Transformation into a Unified Korea

If North Koreans fully understood how their country compares with South Korea, most would probably opt for a unified country ruled from Seoul. Reunification could come about gradually, perhaps starting from a confederation, or rapidly, as happened in Germany. The result would be a state larger than most European countries. Convergence of South and North would take decades, because the two Koreas have moved in very different directions since 1945—economically, politically, and culturally. What would happen to the North's plutonium and nuclear devices is unclear. The other parties to the six-party talks would press for their destruction.

Nuclear Issues

More of the Same: A Negotiating Stalemate

Words and deeds like those made since the early 1990s could continue for a long time. The United States and its partners offer carrots and sticks to Pyongyang to induce it to forgo nuclear weapons. For its part, the DPRK makes far-reaching arms control commitments, but then makes their implementation contingent on economic assistance and security guarantees. Pyongyang then reneges, saying that Washington did not make good on its promises. Outsiders suspect that the DPRK is merely playing for time while it labors to develop a more credible arsenal. Meanwhile, the other five negotiating parties are not on the same page. Each wants and offers something different. Negotiations halt from time to time and then resume, but without finality.

A Negotiating Breakthrough: No Nuclear Power or Weapons

Under this scenario, North Korea agrees to forgo nuclear power and nuclear weapons. Washington fears that any kind of nuclear power can be diverted to weapons use and argues that North Korea should meet its power needs by conventional sources. The United States and some of its partners offer to help build electric power stations and a wide grid in North Korea. They offer credible security assurances and other carrots to induce Pyongyang to disable its plutonium and uranium processing facilities and do away with all nuclear weapons and fissionable materials in the DPRK inventory.

Nuclear Power but No Nuclear Weapons

Alternatively, the parties resurrect the 1994 Agreed Framework. North Korea agrees to freeze and later eliminate its nuclear weapon development in exchange for assistance in building nuclear power stations and normalized ties with the United States. If international observers monitor the power stations and North Korea joins the international community, worries about dual-use nuclear power recede.

Nuclear Power and a Small Nuclear Arsenal

This scenario adapts the 1994 Agreed Framework to contemporary realities. The United States and its partners again agree to supply light-water power reactors to the North, but they also agree to let the DPRK keep its existing nuclear arsenal—judged too small and fragile to generate danger to regional or world peace.

An Expanding Nuclear and Missile Arsenal

Negotiations break down, and the DPRK continues to test, develop, and deploy two- and even three-stage missiles and nuclear warheads. Some neorealists welcome the DPRK arsenal because a credible deterrent will make Pyongyang feel more secure and act more responsibly. Other observers worry that these developments menace global security. If the DPRK has even a small nuclear arsenal, it could provoke Japan, the ROK, and Taiwan to acquire nuclear arms—thereby goading China and then India and then Pakistan to take compensatory actions. Rising tensions could stimulate capital flight from South Korea, Japan, and even China.

North Korea and the World

More of the Same: The Rogues' Rogue

The DPRK stirs unrest and chaos in Northeast Asia and around the world. Desperate for cash, Pyongyang sells advanced military technology and weapons. It spawns or joins a bandwagon of revisionist actors, state and nonstate, aiming to destroy U.S. hegemony. If these trends continue, North Korea's words and deeds can spark a regional or even a global war. Pyongyang could strike first against its neighbors. Or Washington mounts a preventive "surgical strike" to disarm the DPRK. This action incites the DPRK to attack South Korea and pushes China, Russia, and Japan to put their forces on alert. The ensuing chaos could spawn war between the United States and China or Russia.

If the DPRK or any other actor exploded just one or two nuclear bombs over the United States, the electromagnetic pulses could severely damage the country's electric grid, transportation networks, and computer systems, with horrific consequences for human life and the economy.[8]

A Chinese Satellite

The PRC increases investment in North Korea and controls the DPRK leadership by manipulating in-flows of oil and food aid. Saved by but chained to Beijing, the DPRK does not act like a rogue or a failed state. If China behaves as a have nation, content with the status quo, North Korea serves merely as an appendage to an empire rooted in economic might. If China turns expansionist and seeks a place in the sun, North Korea becomes a useful tool in its armorarium.

China does not want chaos on the Korean peninsula but would be loath to intervene militarily to save a fraternal regime or establish a client state. Apart from Tibet, China has not used its army to compel regime change. Beijing wants good ties with Seoul and may see Korean unification as inevitable. Against this

Box 11.2 Pariahs May Find Common Ground

Secretary of State Hillary Clinton told an audience in Thailand in July 2009 that the United States worried about growing military cooperation between North Korea and Burma—including the possible "transfer of nuclear weapon technology and other dangerous weapons." Reports were surfacing that DPRK engineers helped to build a maze of tunnels in Burma and that Burma (Myanmar) was providing yellowcake—partially refined uranium—to North Korea and Iran in exchange for nuclear technology. If these trends continued, some experts said, Burma might be able by 2014 to build one nuclear weapon every year. Burma still lacked a plutonium reprocessing plant, but defectors reported that one was planned for northern Burma, parallel to a civilian reactor being constructed with help from Russians (again, myopic).

But external constraints began to bite. In 2009 a U.S. Navy vessel followed a North Korean ship suspected of carrying arms to Burma, in breach of UN Resolution 1874 banning all exports of weapons from the DPRK. The North Korean ship was sailing toward Burma but then turned away. Concurrently, authorities in Japan arrested a Korean businessman and two Japanese suspected of trying illegally to send equipment from North Korea to Burma for use in missile development. India, for its part, compelled a North Korean freighter to dock and be inspected, suspicious that it might have been delivering arms to Pakistan. Though the ship's captain said that mechanical troubles had led him to anchor in Indian waters, other evidence suggested that the ship's charter ordered him to divert a load of sugar intended for Iraq to India, where import duties had been dropped and prices were soaring. Nevertheless, the ship's log did not explain why it had earlier stopped in Singapore or, on previous journeys, in China.

Reporting on a far more imminent danger than Burma, Japanese sources asserted in August 2009 that for two years DPRK technicians had been helping Iran acquire reprocessing technologies required to extract plutonium and that Iran had purchased machinery and parts needed for nuclear reprocessing through a business front, thereby circumventing UN Security Council sanctions.

prognosis, Beijing could not be indifferent to a loss of a deep buffer zone and a potential advance of hostile forces to the PRC border. China has stationed regular People's Liberation Army (PLA) units and exercised elite PLA units close to its border with North Korea.[9]

Participant in a Northeast Asia Zone of Peace and Prosperity

Keeping its present regime or joining South Korea in some manner, Pyongyang joins its neighbors and the United States in a zone of regional harmony. Peace and prosperity nourish each other. Crisis and confrontation give way to cooperation, investment, and trade—probably the best of possible worlds. Notwithstanding heightened tensions between the DPRK and the ROK in 2009, U.S. and other foreign investors snapped up South Korean bonds, thanks in part to improving prospects for economic expansion.[10] If peace instead of fear enveloped the North, economic hopes would be still brighter. In the week following Pyongyang's second nuclear explosion, life in Seoul did not miss a beat, "with residents still chilling at Starbucks or filling their cubicles in the city's modern office towers."[11]

Underlying Factors and Triggers

Alternative futures depend on what happens on every level—individual, state and society, regional, international, transnational—and how they interact.

Individual Agents

A single father and his son were the paramount decision makers in North Korea for more than half a century. The individual or group that succeeds them will be critical. Experiences in the USSR and China were encouraging. The deaths of Stalin in 1953 and Mao in 1976 triggered succession struggles that lasted several years, after which a less repressive and more open-to-the-world set of leaders took over.

The individuals at the helm in Beijing, Washington, Seoul, Tokyo, and Moscow will also play weighty roles in Northeast Asia. Private citizens such as Lorin Maazel and John Bolton may foster or sabotage cooperation across borders. A U.S. president determined to explore and negotiate with adversaries could make a difference, but will face hard-line opposition.

State and Society

Bad government makes for bad economics. North Korea in the early twenty-first century was one of the few countries in the world experiencing negative growth—the others included Zimbabwe, Somalia, and Fiji. All suffered from a dysfunctional political system. But bad economics is not fatal for bad government. Since 1960 more than forty other countries have suffered a decline in GDP of at least 25 percent over a twelve-year period, as North Korea did in 1990–2002, without changing their political system.[12]

Here we see a paradox. If living standards in North Korea improve, its leaders may feel secure in isolation. Alternatively, if they aspire to greater improvement, they could open North Korea to the world. If living conditions worsen, North Korea could still take either fork: The regime could intensify the country's isolation or hope for salvation through openness. If things become too bad, however, the regime may have no choice but to take refuge abroad or beg for assistance. What if energy shortages bring even more factories to a standstill?

If all sides play their cards well, however, a variety of not-so-bad alternatives are attainable. Despite North Korea's many structural differences, the regime in Pyongyang might emulate China and keep a monopoly of political power while fostering a market economy. It might engineer a "bold switchover" of resources away from the military and toward a broad development orientation.

Regionalism

Regional cooperation in Northeast Asia, according to Gilbert Rozman, remains weak. "Unbalanced development dating back many decades has left domestic interests in each county unusually resistant to important manifestations of openness and trust to the outside."[13] All this spawned a set of worldviews fixated on symbols of supposed unfairness or humiliation. The narrow preoccupations of each actor with its short-term economic or political objectives, rooted in how each country rushed ahead in modernization, obstruct effective regional cooperation in the globalized world. In this age of globalization, traditions tend to defend and protect narrow interests. As the most Confucian society, Korea could lead in helping Confucianism become a force for regional cooperation with China and Japan. Unless that occurs, suspicious and jealous neighbors will continue to block regional cooperation. A stronger tide of regionalism could also facilitate integration of North Korea and encourage a compromise to allow both Japan and China to share leadership.[14]

International Coordination

The carrots and occasional scoldings of the UN Security Council, the World Food Program, and the IAEA may push North Korea to join the global community or bolster Pyongyang's *juche* and *songun* mentality. The weightiest external factors are probably the policies of the five states negotiating with Pyongyang—what they do or fail to do, alone and together.

A necessary if not sufficient condition for an accommodation in Northeast Asia is a coordinated approach by Beijing and Washington. The risk is that

North Korea could exacerbate the other strains in Sino-U.S. relations. In the early twenty-first century, however, concerns about North Korea nudged China and the United States closer together. Long gone were the times when Mao's China endorsed nuclear spread to all counties. Instead, twenty-first-century China worried that its neighbor could destabilize the region and beyond. Beijing took the lead in organizing six-party talks in China's capital. It approved UN resolutions condemning DPRK tests of missiles and nuclear weapons, though it held back on sanctions.

Transnational Support

Many forces leaping national borders are beyond the reach of governments. They include not only jihads and pop culture but also business decisions. Potential investors such as the Chosun Fund (Hong Kong and London) may decide to engage North Korea energetically—or hold back. The Internet and foreign radio broadcasts may penetrate widely—or not. North Koreans returning from China and other foreign lands may talk about life abroad—or stay silent. Humanitarian agencies such as the Eugene Bell Foundation may contribute to social and economic development—or merely address emergency needs.

How to Transform the Game

If these are the underlying conditions helpful to reaching an accord, what are the strategies and tactics that can facilitate or break a deal? The future of each society depends mainly on its own people. Nevertheless, outsiders can help at the margins—especially when a country depends heavily on outside economic aid. When we consider the examples set by Henry Kissinger and Zhou Enlai and other cases discussed in this book, what are the strategies and tactics that can make or break a deal? The broad guidelines outlined in this book's first chapter are basic. They are summarized here along with other, more specific recommendations on how to foster a more secure and prosperous world.[15]

- Recognize global interdependence and use smart diplomacy, drawing on hard and soft power assets, to cope with dangers and make the most of opportunities.

- Replace vituperation and confrontation with a strategy to reduce tensions and manage differences.
- Pursue conditional cooperation and value-creation rather than value-claiming.
- Move toward arms control in tandem with security assurances, closer economic ties, and diplomatic recognition.
- Focus on interests. Do not bargain over positions. Invent options for mutual gain.
- Accent the positive—carrots—while using every means to prevent nuclear and missile proliferation, counterfeiting, and drug trade.
- Minimize security dilemmas. Commit to nonaggression and no backing for revolution or regime change. Resolve the North-South boundary dispute in the Yellow Sea. Relax the confrontation along the DMZ, and if negotiations proceed in a promising way, suspend or halt annual U.S.-ROK maneuvers.
- Cultivate open discussion of goals, issues, and assets at home and with negotiating partners
- Generate initiatives for peace—graduated reciprocity in tension-reduction Let stronger actors take the initiative with small steps and, as the other side signals its willingness to cooperate, then with larger measures.
- Respect and bridge cultural differences.
- Use windows of opportunity.
- Convert zero-sum relationships to mutual gain.
- Identify negotiation opportunities where others see no room for discussion.
- Use objective criteria and consensus on standards for a fair deal.
- Avoid prisoner's dilemma and freeloading with structures that encourage cooperation rather than cheating.
- Develop action-for-action sequencing and safeguards.
- Develop a single negotiating text showing agreed language on some issues and divergent views on still-contested issues.
- Decide wisely whether to deal with issues one at a time or as a package.
- Sup with perceived devils. Limit emotions and focus on the problem to be solved.
- Defuse threats, ultimatums, lies, and other hardball tactics.
- Negotiate ethically and foster trust.

- Analyze the best alternative to a negotiated agreement, and decide when the best move is to walk away.
- Demonstrate the value of openness over autarky.
- Ease North Korea's entry into global trade and communication with low-cost computers, Internet infrastructure, scholarships, and other learning opportunities abroad.
- Consider mediation by a third party, as Mongolia offered in June 2009.
- Set up a U.S. embassy in Pyongyang and a DPRK counterpart in Washington.

An easing of tensions along these lines could set the stage for a more constructive relationship between the two Koreas—perhaps a confederation, if not federation or union. These actions, in turn, would help East Asia become a stable zone of peace and prosperity. Surely five of the richest societies on earth can find ways to encourage one of the poorest to turn from swords to plowshares— as in the South Korean effort in 2009 to organize a $40 billion package of incentives, combined with security guarantees, to persuade the North to give up nuclear weapons. Assistance would focus on exports, education, fiscal support, infrastructure and welfare. The fund would include contributions by the Asian Development Bank and World Bank as well as by governments. South Korea aimed to foster one hundred export companies in North Korea each with annual sales exceeding $3 million and create five free-trade zones, according to the plan. It would help build railways, motorways, and telecommunications networks and train a modern industrial workforce of three hundred thousand. Welfare assistance would comprise food aid, tree planting, hospital refurbishment, housing, sewage and water projects. Infrastructure development would include an expressway linking Seoul to North Korea's border with China.

Granted that the plan was wide-ranging, but the problem remained: Who would take the first steps? Kurt Campbell, the U.S. assistant secretary of state for East Asian and Pacific Affairs, said that the five governments negotiating with North Korea would offer a "comprehensive package" but that Pyongyang would have to take the first "irreversible" steps to disarmament.[15] The planned $40 billion was eight times what the United States and its partners planned to spend under the Agreed Framework to freeze DPRK nuclear facilities, but equaled exactly what the ROK hoped to earn from construction projects abroad in 2009.[17]

CHAPTER TWELVE

HOW SHOULD OBAMA DEAL
WITH AUTHORITARIANS?

American experiences in negotiating with authoritarians in Moscow and Tripoli may shed light on how to deal with those in Pyongyang. "The real issue is not whether to talk to the bad guys but how—under which conditions, with which mix of pressures and conciliation, and with what degree of expectations that the bad guys will keep their word."[1]

Emerging Challenges

Following another rebuke by the UN Security Council and new sanctions for an April 13, 2009, missile test, the DPRK declared that it was quitting the six-party talks and was again reprocessing plutonium. In reply, Secretary of State Hillary Clinton told the House Foreign Affairs Committee on April 30, 2009, that the United States had to be "strong, patient, persistent and not give in to the kind of back-and-forth, the unpredictable behavior of the North Korean regime." She was defending a budget request for nearly $100 million for future U.S. economic aid to North Korea if its leaders returned to the six-party talks and began again to disable their nuclear capacity. China and Russia also advised patience, but Seoul and Tokyo worried that the Washington might cut a deal with Pyongyang that bypassed them and their interests.[2] North Korea's second nuclear explosion, in May 2009, pushed even China and Russia to endorse stronger UN sanctions. Even as ROK authorities proposed a $40 billion prize for DPRK nuclear disarmament, Secretary Clinton likened North Koreans to "unruly children," to which Pyongyang's Foreign Ministry returned the insult in spades. Pyongyang's Foreign Ministry returned the insult in spades. In June 2009, however, Hillary's husband, the former U.S. president, paid a whirlwind visit to Pyongyang and talked with the Dear Leader, raising hopes for a return to serious negotiations.

Crucial Questions

Is it possible, useful, and perhaps even necessary for democratic polities to negotiate with authoritarian regimes? If so, should democratic leaders meet and even negotiate with their opposite numbers? Can such negotiations usefully go beyond technical security arrangements to farther-reaching accommodations? Is it wise for a democracy to try to engage, rather than merely contain, an authoritarian-—sometimes aggressive—regime?

To most of these questions, skeptics answer "no." They contend that most dictators proceed from a zero-sum orientation and sense no pressure from voters for peace. Skeptics warn that even if authoritarians do sign an accord, they will feel free to break it if circumstances permit.

Other analysts, cautious but more hopeful, reply with a qualified "yes." They do not assume that all relationships are "win-win." But when survival and other security issues are at stake, proponents of negotiation reckon that authoritarian regimes—no less than democratic governments—may find it necessary and useful to enter into and abide by arms and other agreements. Trying to minimize self-righteousness, these analysts recall that democratic as well as authoritarian regimes may have violated previous commitments. To be sure, any forms of cooperation should be conditioned on reciprocity and on monitoring. Conditional cooperators, as described in Chapter 6, agree with President Ronald Reagan's admonition in 1987: "*Doveryai no proveryai*"—"trust but verify." In fact, most U.S. presidents do talk to "bad guys." George W. Bush in his first term was the exception. He virtually foreclosed negotiations when he demanded regime change in Baghdad, Tehran, and Pyongyang.

Unlike U.S. policies toward Moscow, Beijing, and Tripoli, Washington did very little to seek out and bolster those in Pyongyang willing to break with the past and get to yes with the outside world. Whatever voices for accommodation existed among DPRK elites, they were surely embarrassed, if not silenced, by the words and deeds of the Bush administration. The words and deeds of the Obama administration in 2009 probably looked to Pyongyang like *plus ça change, plus c'est la même chose*. Their first exchanges continued tit for tat.

Three Sets of Accords with Authoritarian Regimes

U.S. negotiations with Moscow on arms control and other security issues began in the 1940s and continued into the twenty-first century. After many dead ends, these interactions began to show promise in the late 1950s. They led to several limited accords in 1963–1964; the NPT signed in 1968; the ABM and other strategic arms treaties in the 1970s; the far-reaching INF Treaty in 1987; the Conventional Forces in Europe Treaty in 1990; and the strategic arms reduction treaties signed in 1991 and 1993. All U.S. presidents save George W. Bush believed it worthwhile to negotiate and sign these accords.

More than a decade of bluster, fighting, and negotiation between Washington and Tripoli produced a deal in 2003 by which Libya forswore any WMD. Inspectors from the United States, the United Kingdom, and international organizations proceeded to dismantle Libya's chemical and nuclear weapons programs, as well as its long-range ballistic missiles. Assistant Secretary of State for Arms Control Stephen Rademaker on May 2, 2005, told the NPT Review Conference that Libya's choice "demonstrates that, in a world of strong nonproliferation norms, it is never too late to make the decision to become a fully compliant NPT state." He added that Tripoli's decision was "amply rewarded." U.S.-Libyan diplomatic relations, severed since 1981, were reestablished in 2006.

Even though most Republican and Democrat leaders endorsed most of the arms treaties with the USSR, many highly placed Republicans challenged the value of any deals with North Korea. When the 1994 agreement fell apart in 2002, some cheered and said: "We warned you."

Underlying Factors for Conflict and for Accommodation

What factors worked for or against these accords? Table 12.1 summarizes the main factors. For the USSR and Libya, most of these factors proved conducive to

Table 12.1 Factors Shaping U.S. Negotiations on Arms Control with Three Authoritarian Regimes

	USSR	Libya	DPRK
Military Balance	Rough parity with USA: nuclear deterrence after 1955 and, by 1972, mutual overkill	Profound asymmetry and no deterrent	Inferiority but with conventional deterrence and prospect of a minimum nuclear deterrent
Economic Incentives	Strong incentives to reduce military expenditures and end sanctions; poor harvests and pressures to import food	Strong incentives to end sanctions and break from isolation	Heavy burden of military expenditures; frequent need to import food; pressure to end isolation
Technological Base	Competitive with the U.S. but usually in catch-up position	Not competitive	Not competitive but with a core of dedicated scientists
Domestic Politics	Little effective opposition to détente within Politburo, but much grousing in the military-industrial complex	Elite support for accommodation with West and progressive reforms	Unknown
Potential Criticism from Partners	Irrelevant after 1959–1963 break with China	Not relevant	Irrelevant after fall of communism in USSR and China's establishment of relations with ROK
Territorial Disputes	Control over GDR and Eastern Europe—less relevant as East Europeans did their own thing	No	Domination of Korean peninsula— an increasingly remote and receding goal for Pyongyang and for Seoul
Previous Bloodshed with USA	Very little	Very little	Huge

Table 12.1 continued

	USSR	Libya	DPRK
Mutual Understanding	Much mutual understanding thanks to cultural overlap and sometime cooperation	Limited	Very little
Verification Techniques	Measures found to be acceptable	Acceptable	Not yet fully acceptable
Diplomacy	Constructive blend of secret and public	Blend	Blend
Attitude Toward Cooperation with the Adversary	Gradual mellowing of zero-sum outlook	Unknown	Zero-sum roots

arms control or at least neutral. Many of these same factors made North Korea far more reluctant than the USSR or Libya to reduce its military assets.

Dealing with the USSR: Containment and Engagement

From about 1947 until 1954, the United States sought to contain, rather than to engage, the USSR. But the Kremlin and Western leaders began efforts to reduce cold war tensions after Josef Stalin's demise in 1953. Trade and cultural exchange were on the table along with security issues. Starting in 1958, the United States and the USSR embarked on a wide range of cultural and scientific exchanges. America added engagement to containment in a grand strategy to moderate and perhaps transform an authoritarian and often dangerous regime.

Critics said that engagement would prolong the Soviet dictatorship. Proponents of engagement replied that Washington could not overthrow the communist regime but that closer interaction with the West would promote system change. Looking back, we see that détente made it easier for Soviet dissidents such as Andrei D. Sakharov to speak out. Greater openness meant that Western TV crews were present in Estonia, Latvia, and Lithuania in the late 1980s–early 1990s, inhibiting Soviet use of force to crush independence movements in the Baltic republics. Fewer than fifty persons were killed as the three Baltic republics regained their independence.

Closer ties also meant greater mutual vulnerability. President George H. W. Bush warned Mikhail Gorbachev that Soviet repression of Lithuanian's independence movement would compel the United States to freeze "many elements of our economic relationship, including Export-Import credit guarantees, Commodity Credit Cooperation credit guarantees, support for 'Special Associate Status' for the Soviet Union in the International Monetary Fund and World Bank; and most of our technical assistance programs."[3]

America's experiences with the Soviet realm during its final decade are relevant to U.S. and ROK dealings with North Korea. During the first half of the 1980s, the Kremlin was headed by three elderly and ailing party leaders with whom President Reagan made little effort to negotiate.[4] Things changed after Gorbachev took the helm in 1985. Reagan and Gorbachev met several times and arrived at far-reaching agreements—an orientation continued in 1988–1991 by George H. W. Bush. The Berlin Wall fell in 1989 and the USSR disintegrated in late 1991.

Self-proclaimed realists and neorealists contend that Reagan and his Strategic Defense Initiative beat the USSR into submission and collapse. If their analysis is correct, it might follow that the United States should also use hard power to compel Pyongyang into submission. But the facts do not support the realist/neorealist interpretation of history. The SDI impeded détente. Had there been no promises of a missile-proof astrodome over America, Soviet proponents of détente would have had greater voice. When Soviet leaders perceived how remote was the threat to their deterrent from Star Wars, Gorbachev entered the INF and other arms controls.[5]

What did help to end the cold war was the chemistry between Gorbachev and Reagan. Each convinced the other that he wanted peace and large-scale arms reductions. Had either refused dialogue, both countries might have continued on the collision course of the early 1980s. The Soviet empire might not have ended with little violence.

Apart from formal exchanges, Western governments and private parties also provided a "Marshall Plan for the mind" to Soviet bloc intellectuals and professionals. One of its architects, George C. Minden, opined that the West did not face "Marxist obstacles, but a vacuum," and that the West should do "something against frustration and stultification, against a life full of omissions. " In some thirty-seven years, Minden's International Literary Centre delivered 10 million Western books and magazines to Eastern Europe and the USSR—300,000 in 1991. Fully one-third of the recipients in later years wrote thank-you letters.[6]

Trying to foster better understanding, the Asia Foundation has sent 120,000 books to North Korea—some 9,000 a year. Authorities there prefer books on science and the teaching of English, but the foundation includes books in humanities, social science, and law as well. A visitor to Pyongyang witnessed a student simulation of a U.S. banker talking to a small-businessman seeking a loan. The visitor found many well-thumbed books donated by the foundation at the Foreign Studies University. But most books go to the Grand People's Study House, a sort of national library; some go to other institutions. Faculty have easy access to these books; availability to students is less certain. In earlier decades, the foundation delivered 2 million books to South Korea.[7]

North Korea invited and hosted the New York Philharmonic in February 2008, but Washington provided no tit for tat. However, DPRK diplomats at the United Nations have sometimes turned down invitations to discussions with American students and academics. The DPRK Mission to the United Nations did not reply to one letter from me proposing a visit to Pyongyang to exchange views with academics there.

Insights from Libya

Washington's experiences with Libya as well as with communist regimes suggest lessons for dealing with America's perceived adversaries on the world stage. Bush administration officials sometimes suggested that North Korea should emulate Libya by dismantling its nuclear facilities and renouncing terrorism. President George W. Bush and Vice President Dick Cheney credited the changes in Libya to the (initial) successes of the U.S. invasion of Iraq. But Washington treated Tripoli much differently than the forty-third president did Pyongyang. Different inputs yielded different results.

U.S. policy toward Libya went through three phases: First, the Reagan administration relied on hard-line pressures—including bombing—to intimidate the Libyan government and perhaps kill its leader, Mu'ammar Gaddafi. Second, the George H. W. Bush and Bill Clinton administrations mixed coercion with multilateral diplomacy. This blend helped initiate secret U.S.-U.K. negotiations with Tripoli that produced positive outcomes in 1999 and, continued under the George W. Bush administration, in 2003.[8]

Third, the winning approach balanced credible force (economic sanctions as well as military threat) with deft diplomacy—and did so consistent with three criteria: proportionality, reciprocity, and coercive capability.[9] Washington demanded *major policy changes* in Libya *but not regime change*. It exploited the willingness of domestic elites in Libya to act as a "transmission belt" pressing the top leader to move the country into the international community.[10] Indeed, the Libyan case even suggested that rogue nations can be reformed when the top leader believes his regime can be better preserved by integration than by isolation. Taking on the mantle of peacemaker, Gaddafi penned his "One-State Solution" for Israeli-Palestinian differences in a *New York Times* op-ed dated January 21, 2009. The *Financial Times* in March 2009 carried stories headlined "Libya Eyes More Property in West" and "Private Equity Firms Beat Path to Tripoli." In July 2009 Gaddafi, once denounced by former president Ronald Reagan as a "mad dog," supped on pasta just two seats away from President Barack Obama at the Group of Eight summit in Italy and even secured a handshake with the U.S. president. Gaddafi attended the summit as president of the African Union. In August, however, when Libyans gave a hero's welcome to the convicted Lockerbie bomber, released from a Scottish jail on humanitarian grounds, Gaddafi again looked like a rogue's rogue to many Westerners.

U.S. attempts over many decades to isolate politically and economically the USSR and other targeted countries—communist China, Cuba, Libya, Iran—failed to alter significantly the policies or character of their regimes. When Washington shifted to an engagement strategy, however, it normalized relations with Moscow, Beijing, and Tripoli—setting the stage for broader accords useful to each party. Only when Washington offered positive incentives as well as threats to employ U.S. economic and military hard power did it enhance American objectives. By contrast, nearly half a century of unremitting pressure against Fidel Castro's Cuba deprived U.S. as well as Cuban citizens of many potential benefits.

Why North Korea Proved More Difficult Than the USSR or Libya

When we review the factors outlined in Table 12.1, we can understand better why it has been much more difficult to reach an accord with Pyongyang than with Moscow or Tripoli.

Military Balance

Moscow has possessed a credible deterrent since the mid-1950s and a strategic redundancy—overkill—since the late 1960s. The Kremlin could (and still can) give up a lot and still retain a deterrent. At the opposite extreme, Libya had few military assets to surrender. With hardly any hope of developing or assembling its own WMD, Libya has almost no coercive leverage except more terrorist acts.

North Korea, though much poorer than Libya, has possessed a relatively strong military—its ace in bargaining. The regime relies on military assets for defense, for deterrence, for intimidation, for bargaining, and for prestige. North Korea has deployed conventional forces able to maim the South in a first-strike or a retaliatory blow. It has had large fleets of transport planes and helicopters capable of infiltrating at least two air force sniper brigades and assault forces deep into ROK rear areas.[11] For nearly two decades it has been close to having the materials and know-how to make nuclear weapons. It tested a nuclear device in 2006 and another in 2009 and claimed to have "weaponized" some of its plutonium. Whether the tests fizzled or not, whether or not the DPRK had any deliverable nuclear weapons, the regime claimed to have entered the nuclear weapons club. To surrender North Korea's nuclear and missile capabilities without major compensation could undermine the regime's legitimacy and spur dissent within the ruling elite.[12]

Past Bloodshed and Destruction

The USSR and Libya lost very few lives fighting the United States, but North Korea lost more than 1 million civilians and soldiers. Memories of the Korean War—reinforced by intermittent U.S. threats to employ nuclear weapons or mount preventive war—make the DPRK reluctant to disarm and trust Americans. Real hurts in the past have been magnified and kept alive by propaganda that emphasized U.S. rapaciousness. The North Korean public knows almost nothing about the real origins of the Korean War, its aftermath, or its legacy.

Economic Pressures

The USSR and today's Russia could and can bargain not only with military overkill but also with material resources needed by the West—oil, gas, precious metals. American oil production began to fall in the 1970s at the same time that European demands for imported gas became more urgent. The Reagan administration tried to impede construction of gas lines from Russia to Europe, but Reagan failed, and today Europe shivers when Russia closes the spigot.

Libya also possesses oil and gas needed by the West. Of course, dependency cuts both ways; there is vulnerability on both sides. Russia and Libya have raw materials needed by the West, but Moscow and Tripoli also need income from selling their commodities. Vendors and buyers need each other.

North Korea, by contrast, has had very little economic leverage. It has minerals, but most can be obtained from other suppliers. For several decades, North Korea obtained hard currency by counterfeiting U.S. dollars and engaging in the drug trade. If peace prevailed, North Korea's space could be used to pipe oil and gas from Siberia to South Korea and China. But this would be a prolonged and expensive undertaking. For now, North Korea could open more special economic zones where South Koreans and other foreigners exploited the skills and low wages of North Korean workers. Even though the DPRK derived hard currency from such projects in the early twenty-first century, it has often treated them with casual disdain. In 2008 it expelled many South Koreans and limited tourism from the ROK. Though faced with much worse economic straits than the USSR or Libya, the Pyongyang leadership often defied conventional economic logic.

All three countries—the USSR, Libya, and North Korea—suffered from economic sanctions imposed by the United States and backed by some U.S. allies. Having much larger cash reserves than Pyongyang, both the USSR and Libya could endure or circumvent these sanctions more readily than the DPRK. In this sense, Pyongyang had a greater incentive to reach an accommodation with Washington so as to reduce barriers to trade and technology transfer. This incentive deepened in the 1990s when North Korea's longtime benefactors in Moscow and Beijing withdrew or reduced their subsidies. As Russia and China became more businesslike, they multiplied trade ties with South Korea.

Apart from technology, the USSR often needed food from the West. As we saw earlier, the first nuclear arms control took place in 1963 when the USSR imported wheat from the United States. The Kennedy administration treated it as a concession to permit wheat exports to the Soviet Union. Many subsequent arms control deals between Moscow and Washington coincided with poor Soviet harvests—an intriguing correlation, if not causation. American farmers came to depend on Soviet purchases and Russia on U.S. exports.

North Korea has been even more dependent on food imports than the USSR or, since late 1991, the Russian Federation. A large fraction of North Koreans has been chronically undernourished since the 1950s. Acute hunger known as "wasting"—starvation and near-starvation—was widespread for several years in the 1990s and again in the early twenty-first century. Oil to heat buildings and power factories and vehicles has also been in short supply. Just as a bad harvest reinforced Moscow's willingness to sign a nuclear test ban in 1963, a poor harvest in North Korea coincided with its signing the Agreed Framework with Washington in 1994.

Considering how desperate are North Korea's economic problems, however, outsiders may marvel at Pyongyang's intransigence in the six-party talks. Pyongyang has made concessions, but it has also held out for better terms and sometimes backtracked.

The DPRK leadership did not buckle under economic pressure. Committed to *juche,* it praised and prized self-reliance.[13] The regime demanded priority in resource allocation for the military and allowed the public to scrounge and even starve, even though the top elite lived in comfort. Thought control and the police made active dissent nearly impossible. Propaganda blamed shortfalls on American imperialism.[14]

The more authoritarian the regime is, the less is any prospect of visible public demand for higher living standards or freedom. Democracies, by contrast, take steps to make sure their people do not starve.[15] As dictatorship weakened in the USSR and Eastern Europe, the greater became the pressures for change. Such pressures are barely felt in North Korea—permitting DPRK rulers to put off whatever concessions might be needed to purchase greater economic ties with the outside world.

Domestic Politics

Some authoritarians are more authoritarian than others. Stalin's dictatorship was totalitarian and cruel, but the Kremlin leadership became more collective, less total, and less cruel. Following Lavrentii Beria's execution in 1953, no leaders were killed in succession struggles.[16] There was opposition within the party to arms control concessions by Nikita Khrushchev and later by Mikhail Gorbachev, but the top party leader usually got his way. Public yearning for peace and higher living standards permitted the top leader to claim victory when he signed arms controls with the United States. Stalin ruled for some thirty years; Khrushchev, for ten; Leonid Brezhnev, for eighteen; Yuri Andropov and Konstantin Chernenko, each for less than two; Gorbachev, for six. Boris Yeltsin held sway (or swayed) for nearly a decade, and Vladimir Putin ruled (without swaying) for more than a decade. In recent decades the ups and downs of the oil industry have shaped politics in the USSR/Russia and in Libya. When petrodollars flow, the regime can purchase popularity; when they ebb, dissidence rises.[17]

In Libya, domestic politics is also complicated by differences among tribes, between town and country, between secular modernists and traditionalists, and between a wealthy few and the poor multitude. There is also a widening generation gap, complicated by rifts between educated pragmatists and religious zealots.

Withal, Gaddafi has ruled for some forty years, having seized power in a 1969 military coup. His sons appear to have encouraged his westward orientation—dramatically signaled by his cautious support for the U.S. coalition against Iraq in 1991. Regardless of some pressures from Washington, however, the Libyan regime continued to crush dissidence from within.[18]

Like Gaddafi, Kim Il Sung had to fight off and purge rivals. But he and his son ruled North Korea for more than half a century. One of Kim Jong Il's sons or another relative may continue the dynasty. The dynasts' dictatorship has been nearly total, though modern technology can weaken as well as buttress central controls. The patriarchs must contend with interest groups that oppose or support some forms of liberalization. Comparing North Korea's top leaders with those in other authoritarian regimes, as in Table 12.2, we see that they have more reasons to resist arms control and détente than past leaders in the USSR or China.

Table 12.2 Why Some Communist Leaders Would Be Reluctant to Negotiate with the West

	Vladimir Lenin 1918 (Brest-Litvosk negotiations and emerging civil war)*	Josef Stalin 1946 (Pre-election speech and incipient cold war)	Mao Zedong 1970 (Cultural Revolution and Soviet threat)	Kim Jong Il 2009
Personality				
Insecure	L	M	L	?
Rigid, inflexible	L	M	M	?
Personality cult	L	H	H	H
Deified	L	H	H	H
Social History				
Remote from Western culture	L	M	H	H
Perceived abuse by the West	M	M	M	H

Table 12.2 continued

	Vladimir Lenin 1918 (Brest-Litvosk negotiations and emerging civil war)*	Josef Stalin 1946 (Pre-election speech and incipient cold war)	Mao Zedong 1970 (Cultural Revolution and Soviet threat)	Kim Jong Il 2009
Political System				
One-party rule	M	H	H	H
Totalitarian	L	H	H	H
Factions opposed to détente	H	M	M	?
Dependency on military elites	L	L	M	?
Zero-sum worldview	H	M	M	H
Expansionist ideology	H	M	L	H
Ethnic-nationalist centrifugal forces	H	M	L	L
Nationalist ideology	L	H	M	H
Commitment to economic self-reliance	M	M	M	H
Need for foreign bogey	M	M	M	H
Power Balance				
Perceived threat	H	M	H	H
Perceived hostility from Western leaders	H	M	L–M	H
Reliance on a military deterrent	L	M	M	H
Foreign allies against détente	M	L	L	L
Secrets to keep from foreigners	M	H	M	H
Divided nation with rival next door	L	L	M	H
Receipt of foreign aid even without détente	L	L	L	M–H

Code: Low, Medium, or High rating in the given year. *Source:* Author's evaluations.

*Each cell summarizes a complicated situation. For example, the Brest-Litovsk Treaty signed away much of Russia's empire, but Lenin persuaded his comrades that this step was essential to save the Soviet regime from a German advance.

Cultural Factors

It has been easier for Americans to understand and deal with Soviet leaders than with those whose languages and cultures arise from different civilizations. Russia's Orthodox heritage, though different in many ways from Western Christianity, is much closer to Western traditions than are the historic paths of Libya and Korea. Most college-educated Americans have been exposed to Russian literary classics and some to ballet, but very few to the diverse influences shaping Libya or Korea. Most educated Russians are quite familiar with Western culture, even if they have never traveled abroad. Relatively few Libyans and even fewer North Koreans have been exposed to Western ways.

Americans tend to be low-context negotiators focused on the bottom line. Christopher Hill compares diplomats to basketball players—each wants to score baskets.[19] Libyans and North Koreans tend to be more concerned with the total context and rely on personal ties built up over time. Professionals such as Robert L. Gallucci and Hill and their DPRK counterparts probably surmounted these stereotypes and learned how to accommodate one another's peculiarities. But the George W. Bush administration's frequent slights to Asian "face" and outright insults made it harder to come to terms with Pyongyang. Washington's reluctance to deal with top Korean leaders at the highest level probably obstructed momentum toward a deal.

A second cultural distinction is that U.S. diplomats tend to be more optimistic—more confident that problems can be solved—than those from authoritarian states and cultures. Americans trust that if all parties are sincere, they can create mutually beneficial accords that open doors to broader realms of cooperation. Far from expecting mutual gain, many authoritarians tend to all politics as a zero-sum struggle. This outlook prevailed for long periods in the USSR and Libya and lives on in North Korea.

Should Democrats Sup with Authoritarians?

Should top leaders of democracies deal one-on-one with despots? There are strong grounds to oppose such meetings. First, heads of state seldom have the time or detailed knowledge needed to negotiate security agreements. Many foreign policy experts believe it wiser to let experts work out the details of any such deal before inviting heads of state to sign off on the final document. Second, democrats may lose moral stature if they treat dictators—especially mass murderers—as equals. Western liberals could only blanche when Richard Nixon toasted Mao Zedong in 1972. The political realist and publicity-seeking Nixon did not object to smiling for photos with a man responsible for at least 30 million unnecessary Chinese and uncounted Tibetan and other minority deaths. We cannot say if the Nixon-Mao encounter was necessary for Henry Kissinger and Zhou Enlai to work out the terms of normalization. But history suggests that many summits between Soviet and U.S. leaders left a very mixed record—some benefit but also much damage to American and world security.[20]

Perhaps negotiations with authoritarians are too important to be left to heads of state. Even Kissinger may have been too political and insufficiently professional to handle the SALT I negotiations in 1971–1972.[21] America's interests would probably have been better served if the dialogue with Moscow had been carried on by diplomats such as George F. Kennan, Charles Bohlen, Raymond Garthoff, and Jack F. Matlock—each a master of Russian language and culture as well as

---

Box 12.1 Dangers at the Summit

The wartime meetings of Franklin Delano Roosevelt and Winston Churchill with Josef Stalin sustained the war against Germany but failed to resolve many important issues (access to Berlin, reparations). They gave rise to some wishful thinking (on liberated Europe) and aggravated mutual suspicions. The 1955 Geneva summit probably convinced leaders from the four countries that none wanted a nuclear war. But Nikita Khrushchev's two visits to the United States and his confrontation with Dwight Eisenhower at the Paris summit stirred up more animosity than goodwill. Khrushchev's Vienna meeting with John Kennedy in 1961 emboldened Khrushchev to send missiles to Cuba but did not prepare him for a steely U.S. response. The meetings between Richard Nixon and Leonid Brezhnev in 1972 and 1973 and between Jimmy Carter and Brezhnev in 1979 added only an illusory veneer to the detailed accords worked out by foreign policy experts. Brezhnev's visit to San Clemente did not prevent a serious confrontation later in 1973. Carter's meeting with Brezhnev in 1979 did not prepare the White House for the Soviet invasion of Afghanistan. The bonhomie of George H. W. Bush and Bill Clinton with Boris Yeltsin gained little for any party. Better policies on the ground might have done more than showy summits to help Russia shift from communism to economic and political freedom. Encounters between George W. Bush and Vladimir Putin generated greater misunderstanding and animus than long-term collaboration. Nevertheless, Ronald Reagan's meetings with Gorbachev conduced to several arms accords and a peaceful end to the cold war. Talks between the chief U.S. and Soviet diplomats, George Shultz and Eduard Shevardnadze, defined the fine print implicit in their presidents' entente.

of the technical issues of arms control. Each understood the big picture as well as the importance of adding or omitting a comma in the text.

People who see President Barack Obama as the hope for humanity might cringe if he shook hands with a Kim Jong Il, a Vladimir Putin, a Mu'ammar Gaddafi, or a Mahmoud Ahmadinejad. If each side's deep interests push them to an accord, is staged amiability necessary or desirable? Nevertheless, there is a case to be made for summit diplomacy. A meeting at the highest level may be necessary to break a cycle of hostility and open the way to normal relations between dangerous adversaries. Authoritarian leaders tend to limit the scope of their diplomats. Dictators want the final say and publicity for themselves. Both Kim Il Sung and Kim Jong Il indicated often that they wanted to deal with their opposite numbers in Washington. It may be that for Koreans, as Stephen Linton puts it, "proof of interest at the highest level is paramount for giving the negotiating process legitimacy."[22]

The role of Jimmy Carter in breaking the momentum toward war with North Korea in 1994 appeared to confirm Linton's thesis. As president, Carter mediated the 1978 Camp David Peace Accords. Having lost the 1980 election, private citizen Carter became the world's best known and most successful mediator in the 1980s and 1990s. Carter believed that judgments about the participants should be left outside the meeting room. A mediator should focus the disputants on whether an agreement can advance their interests. "People in conflict have to be willing to talk about ending it, or at least changing it, and there has to be someone willing to talk to them, however odious they are—and that's where I come in."[23]

Critics objected to the ex-president's meddling in government affairs and his willingness to get friendly and personal with dictators. If results count, however, the record shows that Carter's interventions helped Nicaragua achieve a peaceful transition to democracy and persuaded Haiti's junta to leave office peacefully. But Carter's greatest achievement was to turn the United States and North Korea away from war and outline terms for their official framework agreement in 1994.[24]

Both Carter and Kim Il Sung believed in high-level contacts. If Kim Il Sung could not meet the existing president, he seemed anxious to meet with an ex-president, one who—as president—had reduced the U.S. troop presence in South Korea. Many observers were surprised that a part-time Baptist preacher could find any rapport with a communist dictator. But Carter's faith acknowledged that no humans or regimes are perfect. For his part, Kim Il Sung had enjoyed a positive relationship with his grandmother, a Presbyterian. He permitted some

Christian observances in North Korea so long they did not obstruct the regime's economic and political programs.

When Madeleine Albright met Kim Jong Il in 2000, as we saw in Chapter 8, he expressed the hope that President Clinton would visit, saying that "if both sides are genuine and serious, there is nothing we will not be able to do."

Some leaders may consider their opposite number so repulsive that they find it difficult to sit and talk with them. [25] George W. Bush said that he loathed Kim Jong Il, but, as we saw earlier, he relented enough in December 2007 to write a letter to the DPRK leader addressed as "Dear Mr. Chairman." Rejecting a mere former U.S. vice president, Al Gore, the DPRK Dear Leader sought and got a visit from former president Bill Clinton in June 2009 as part of a deal in which Pyongyang released two imprisoned U.S. journalists (leaving many captured South Koreans, including fishermen who had strayed too far northward, without immediate succor).

How vital is interaction at the summit? This issue is part of larger questions. What is the role of individual free will relative to great forces in history? How important are "principals" (such as presidents) and "agents" (such as diplomats) relative to "structure"? Profoundly inefficient, the Soviet system was bound to collapse, but when and how? Individuals played crucial roles. Had Yegor Ligachev or some other leader been at the helm rather than Gorbachev, the cold war might not have terminated so peacefully. Had Reagan not agreed to meet with Gorbachev, the two would not have developed a kind of mutual trust. Had Jimmy Carter not studied all the issues in great depth and traveled to Pyongyang in 1994—dismissing negative signs and accenting the positive—the U.S.-DPRK confrontation might have become more intense. *Fortuna* was also at play. Had the death of Kim Il Sung occurred several weeks earlier, Carter might have met no one except some stolid foreign ministry officials afraid to budge.

Implications for Dealing with the DPRK

Smart power in dealing with North Korea requires tapping the full range of tools—"diplomatic, economic, military, political, legal, and cultural—picking the right tool, or combination of tools, for each occasion."[26] Effective negotiation with Pyongyang will require interagency coordination in Washington, coordination with allies and other stakeholders, and great skill in negotiating with North Korea.[27]

Underlying conditions set the context, but individuals still shape negotiations and make the final decisions. The structure of U.S.–North Korean relations makes it important and feasible for Washington and Pyongyang—backed by their four negotiating partners—to come together in ways that enhance the deepest interests of each side. A way had to be found for Washington and Pyongyang to negotiate bilaterally, but within a framework that secures the blessing and support of Beijing, Seoul, Tokyo, and Moscow. Professional diplomats should work out the details. If six foreign ministers sign the relevant documents, the moral complications for any democratic signatory would be lessened. If a summit meeting is the price of peace, the U.S. president should meet with the top DPRK leader to seal the deal. Yes, democrats can and should try to deal with authoritarians. The way to get them to "yes," a former U.S. ambassador believes, is not to preach morality or history but to show them how the deal could advance their interests.[28]

CHAPTER THIRTEEN

HOW TO GET TO YES IN KOREA?

Here was interdependence—mutual vulnerability and sensitivity—in spades. As the Obama administration settled into its second year, tough choices and dangers confronted each player in Korea. Every week, if not every day, new challenges and opportunities emerged. But action in any domain depended on what happened in others. Progress toward one goal might advance or set back movement toward other objectives.

Challenges to Washington

Should the United States try to abort or learn to live with North Korea's incipient nuclear arsenal? A broader question: Should Washington and partners seek an accommodation with the DPRK regime, strive to strangle it, or just stall until—like the former USSR—it implodes? The Obama team could ask, *Should we sign a security agreement with Pyongyang if it strengthens the regime and delays its demise? Must we sacrifice human rights for arms control?*

What answers could history provide? Did the Obama administration face a DPRK that resembled more Gorbachev's USSR or Hitler's Germany? One could compromise with Gorbachev but hardly with Hitler. But North Korea in 2010 was not the USSR of Andrei Sakharov. The DPRK lacked known opposition figures hoping to liberalize the system.

Some analysts warned that the DPRK was more erratic than other nuclear aspirants. To be sure, the regime in Pyongyang often talked and sometimes acted like a rogue elephant, but no more than did Mao Zedong's China in the 1960s. Might the leadership in Pyongyang mellow? One or two generations after Mao, China no longer acted the zealot. Its leaders became more pragmatic. Still, future trends were unknown. Beijing in the early twenty-first century steadily increased military outlays and marched backward on human rights. Despite its opening to world trade since 1979, China remained a one-party state struggling to tighten its already severe limits on free thought and expression.

If the Soviet superpower expired after seventy-four years, could the DPRK last much beyond fifty-five or sixty? Communist-led China survived its sixtieth anniversary with a blend of capitalism cum Leninism. But the DPRK leadership seemed unwilling or unable to manage a Chinese-style transformation.

Economic weakness, mounting international isolation, the Dear Leader's fragile health, and the absence of an agreed successor suggested that the DPRK system could not long endure. Yes, Kim Jong Il's sixty-eighth birthday was celebrated with festivities on February 16, 2010. But the government did not dispense gifts of fish and chicken as it did in 2009. Its handouts were instead limited to one kilo of candy, a kilo of biscuits, two bottles of beer, one bottle of *soju,* and two bottles of lemonade. The Dear Leader did not appear for his birthday bash, though some reports claimed he had helicoptered offshore to deliver candy to children on an island.

The United States and South Korea developed contingency plans to cope with any instability in the North, ranging from humanitarian disasters to civil war to potential loose nuclear weapons. They agreed in late 2009 that U.S. forces would take responsibility for safeguarding and then eliminating the North's nuclear weapons. Bound by the Nuclear Nonproliferation Treaty, the ROK could not legally take possession of the North's nuclear assets. The United States, however, could claim a right and duty to do so—as could China and Russia. When combined U.S. and ROK forces conducted exercises in March 2010 to prepare for any contingency in the North, Pyongyang denounced the maneuvers as preparations for an attack and threatened an all-out war in reply.

Here was a dilemma for Washington: Not to prepare for chaos in the North would be irresponsible. But active preparations—for amphibious landings and street warfare—pushed the DPRK leadership to hunker down. Would the North negotiate its disarmament under these conditions?

Despite the North's rigidity in many domains, Pyongyang's diplomacy pushed to open new doors. The DPRK Foreign Ministry in January 2010 reiterated its call to start negotiations for a peace treaty. The ministry averred that, sixty years after the outbreak of the Korean War, the absence of such a treaty fanned distrust.[1] Continually menaced by the United States, the DPRK had acquired nuclear weapons. But Pyongyang was flexible. It was willing to conclude peace with Washington in a bilateral or a multilateral setting. Responding in the same news cycle, U.S. and ROK representatives insisted that before peace talks could begin, North Korea had to return to the six-party talks and improve its human rights record. Both Washington and Seoul worried that starting to talk about a peace treaty would shift attention from arms control and imply acceptance of North Korea as a nuclear weapons state. When Washington and Seoul spurned Pyongyang's appeal for a peace treaty, did this not imply their belief that the end was near for the DPRK regime?

Challenges to Pyongyang

Pyongyang noted that Washington acquiesced in nuclear weapons for India and Pakistan as well as Israel. Would it not eventually do the same with the DPRK? The longer everyone dithered, the stronger North Korea's arsenal could grow.

On the other hand, autarky had failed. The DPRK needed help, but its top elites had to worry: *Can we risk an opening to outsiders that undercuts our regime? And if nuclear disarmament is part of the deal, won't our generals complain we are surrendering the crown jewels? And how can we be sure Washington will not just pocket our concessions and then demand more? Aren't the Americans just stalling until our system falls apart like the Soviet Union?*

Pyongyang got very mixed signals. Nongovernmental actors from the West continued to provide medical and food aid to the people of North Korea. Stanford University scientists worked with DPRK officials to develop the country's first laboratory to test drug-resistant tuberculosis—a project backed also by former senator Sam Nunn, co-chair of the Nuclear Threat Initiative. He explained in 2010 that international cooperation was essential to prevent a TB pandemic that would be catastrophic for global health and security. On the other hand, donor nations to the UN World Food Programme (WFP) lost patience with the

DPRK regime—especially after it expelled U.S. private agencies in March 2009 and blocked monitoring of food distribution in rural districts and inquiries by Korean-speaking aid workers. In early 2010 North Koreans were getting less than $5 in aid per person compared to more than $35 in other needy countries. United Nations officials warned that the decline in donations could compel the WFP to halt operations in North Korea in June 2010. The United States refused to supply more cereals to North Korea until the regime permitted aid agencies to track final recipients. Undermining international pressures on the DPRK, China increased its own food shipments to the North.

The DPRK government on January 1, 2010, promised its people a major improvement in living standards and greater emphasis on light industry and agriculture. But Pyongyang continued to shoot itself in both feet. The regime launched a currency reform late in 2009 that compelled North Koreans to swap existing won notes for new ones at a rate of 100 to one. With a cap of 100,000 won per family ($690 at the official rate, but only $35 on the black market), the reform decimated any private stores of local currency. The reform aimed to curb inflation and crack down on free markets, but aggravated food shortages and drove up prices. The resulting chaos undermined the government's New Year promises and political stability as public protests, unprecedented in the North, erupted. Some protestors held piles of bills rendered worthless by the reform. In February 2010 Premier Kim Yong-il (in this post since 2007) apologized for "recklessly enforcing the latest currency reform without making sufficient preparation." By March 2010 the government permitted private markets to reopen but food prices continued to rise. DPRK media reported that Kim Jong-un, rumored to be next in line to succeed his father, now controlled the Korean Workers' Party finances and had ousted officials blamed for the failed currency reform, one of whom may have been executed.

Off again, on again. Pyongyang continued in 2010 to hint that it would return to six-party talks—conditioned on meaningful talks with Washington and/or an end to UN sanctions. A flurry of reciprocal visits by Chinese and DPRK officials in February 2010 reaffirmed both governments' commitment to denuclearizing the Korean peninsula.[2] But outsiders could not know if all this meant smoke or fire. The highest UN official to visit Pyongyang in years, B. Lynn Pascoe, reported in February 2010 that the DPRK was not eager to return to six-party talks but did not rule them out. Meanwhile, South African authorities acting under UN mandate seized DPRK arms exports in February 2010, as Thai authorities had done in December 2009.

Challenges to Seoul

South Koreans did not want war or chaos on the Korean peninsula. They reckoned, *Our economy might benefit if we could integrate more closely with the North and employ its low-cost labor. But a collapse of the DPRK would cost us dearly. The economic burden for us would be far greater than German unification meant for west Germans.* Nonetheless, South Korean actions added to the economic constraints already facing the DPRK from the tightening noose of UN sanctions. In spring 2010 South Korea decided to phase out imports of sand from the North—the largest legitimate earner of hard currency for Pyongyang, bringing in twice what workers earned at Kaesung. Sand served as a barometer of North-South relations. As détente grew in 2002, the South began to import sand from the North. But the South halted imports in March 2009 to protest a planned missile-firing by the DPRK. The South resumed imports on a much reduced scale in November 2009 only to end them in 2010. The South explained it could now dredge its own sand and declined a DPRK offer to trade sand for other building materials and fuel. Perhaps, observers said, North Korea could sell more sand to builders in Vladivostok.

Stripping away another source of income for the North, authorities in the South suspended tours to Mt. Kumgang and to Kaesung after DPRK troops shot and killed a South Korean tourist in 2008. Seldom lost for words, Pyongyang continued in 2010 to blame the South for the incident. The DPRK leadership seemed to labor under an approach-avoidance syndrome. Determined to restart visits by South Korean tourists, authorities in the North summoned South Korean businessmen to Mt. Kumgang on short notice in March 2010—warning they would lose all their Kumgang assets (worth some $370 million) if they did not appear for what turned out to be a fifteen-minute browbeating. Unless tours resumed promptly, Pyongyang threatened to take "extraordinary measures." While the North wanted visitors to Mt. Kumgang, it also demanded that ROK and U.S. authorities stop journalists from visiting the DMZ or face unpredictable consequences.

Challenges to Beijing

Like South Korea, China valued stability in the Korean peninsula. Its leaders probably thought: *A North Korea dependent on China means economic opportunity for us. Already we have bought up mines and ports in the North. But the DPRK nuclear weapons program must be curtailed or eliminated—lest it provoke Japan and others to develop nuclear arms. We don't like the leadership in Pyongyang. It seems now to be counterfeiting not just dollars but faking "super-yuan"! But the alternatives are worse. The regime's collapse would trigger a mass exodus to China, while a unified Korea could put a dynamic rival on our doorstep—perhaps even a rising nuclear weapons power.* Would China send troops into North Korea if the regime there collapsed? The signs were contradictory, but Beijing probably counted on its growing economic hold on the North—what South Koreans called "Chinese colonialism."

Challenges to Moscow

Like China, Russia saw economic opportunity in Korea. The Kremlin could calculate: *A backward DPRK might be more open to Russian penetration than a unified Korea. Less confrontation and more stability could help us deliver petrol and other Siberian products southward. But nuclear arms on the Korea peninsula means danger. For now, we must back U.S. efforts to disarm the North. For the longer term, however, we must sabotage any arrangements that strengthen U.S. influence in Northeast Asia and try to cultivate our own.*

Challenges to Tokyo

Japan also saw economic opportunity in Korea but faced stiff competition from China and Russia as well as the United States. Some Japanese leaders sought a pretext to go nuclear, but most preferred the relative strategic stability of the early twenty-first century. They joined Washington in trying to eliminate North Korea's weapons of mass destruction. Most Japanese politicians calculated that we *should normalize ties with Pyongyang but must bow to public pressure regarding abductees. We can't endorse any U.S. deal with North Korea unless it meets our concerns.*

Meanwhile, South Korea's pop culture flourished in Japan but Tokyo continued to rub salt in old wounds by discriminatory policies toward ethnic Koreans. South as well as North Koreans complained when Tokyo excluded Korean-language schools from free programs extended to Japanese high schools. In March 2010 Japanese authorities dropped the exclusion policy but discrimination remained in other realms.[3] Many Japanese seemed oblivious to the many contributions that Korea had made to Japan—in religion, the arts, and even in genes. As Japan and South Korea prepared to cosponsor the 2002 World Cup, Emperor Akihito acknowledged the Korean lineage of the Japanese imperial family.[4]

Challenges to Understanding

Policy formulation in Washington and other capitals was the more difficult because information about North Korea was fragmentary and often unreliable. For starters, analysts disagreed on which model or models best explained the North. Was the North shaped by a unique blend of Confucianism and Communism? Was it a Mafia-style family business? Did the *juche* slogan represent a long-standing commitment to self-reliance or mere window dressing to mask other needs? Was the "military-first" orientation the product of strategic military determinism in the nuclear age?[5] Or part of a Clausewitzian use of military force to extend diplomacy by other means?[6] Was the core ideology nothing but a paranoid, racist nationalism—a teaching that the "Korean people are too pure blooded, and therefore too virtuous, to survive in this evil world without a great parental leader"? And was that parent the stern patriarch of a fatherland or the dear and somewhat feminine leader of caring motherland? The latter, according to B. R. Myers, whose evidence included a poster of Kim Jong Il titled "We cannot live far away from his breast." Did Pyongyang fear the United States or despise and ridicule its empty threats? Did North Koreans cross the Tumen River to reach freedom or merely to acquire cell phones and DVD players?[7] Did Kim Jong Il (perhaps like George W. Bush and Woodrow Wilson) have an inferiority complex that pressed him to outdo his own father? Did most of his subjects adore him as a demigod or merely submit to a totalitarian dictatorship? Or, engrossed in daily struggles to get by, did it simply not occur to them to oppose him?[8]

Trying to Fathom "Outliers"

Can we know what is the operational code of the DPRK leadership—its strategies, its expectations, its way of responding to perceived challenges and opportunities? One analyst has tried to deduce Iran's operational code from letters sent by its president to the United States.[9] This effort underscores how difficult it is to understand renegade regimes such as in Iran or North Korea—what President Obama in 2010 called "outliers." For starters, there were probably differences between the nominal top leader in Tehran and in Pyongyang and others who shape policy. Were the curtain pulled back, we would probably find that, as in Iran, the DPRK regime was far from monolithic. In Iran, as in Pyongyang, there were often contradictions between public diplomacy and what the regime told its public. Many DPRK communications to Washington suggested that Pyongyang wanted to deal, while the regime often portrayed conciliatory U.S. policies as abject surrender. It was not clear even if Pyongyang feared Washington or deemed it a paper tiger. And if the regime's line shifted from skepticism to optimism about a possible deal, was the switch driven by internal or external factors? How difficult to know what caused or led to what. When Nikita Khrushchev sought a deal with Washington, his media began to depict the rise of "sober forces" opposed to intransigent "madmen" in U.S. ruling circles. Which came first: political change in Washington or some new factor—a bad harvest, delays in the Soviet ICBM program, ideological challenges from China—that altered Soviet policy? [10]

Coping with Uncertainty

Given these uncertainties, what paradigm should guide the policies of the United States and its partners? Realism teaches that power is and must be the backbone of policy. The powerful do what they can and the weak what they must. By this logic, the world's only superpower should dictate terms and strip North Korea of WMD. Some neorealists, however, reached the opposite conclusion. Since nuclear diffusion adds to stability, they reasoned, outsiders should want North Korea to feel safe behind a minimum nuclear deterrent. If DPRK leaders were also realists—or neorealists—a deal might be achieved on the basis of each side's national interests. If they were paranoid racists, however, a rational quest for mutual gain would be impossible. If they were military opportunists, they might see a deal as a short-term expedient but not as a long-term accommodation.

Liberal idealists want arms control and democracy. Arms control can reduce the likelihood of war, they say, but so can democracy. No authentic democracy, they believe, has attacked another democracy. So liberals face also a dilemma. An arms accord with Pyongyang could help international stability but also serve to prop up a dictatorship.

Constructivists remind us that reality is what we make of it—underscoring that strong wills and minds can sometimes trump power, ideology, and even *fortuna.*[11] All parties should strive to reduce stereotypical thinking and misunderstandings. All should cultivate empathy.

Each of these approaches fits some cases but not others. They oversimplify. A better paradigm combines the insights of interdependence and complexity theory. All the globe's peoples are interdependent—linked so closely that they can harm or help one another. Even a superpower is vulnerable to a failing state equipped with nuclear weapons. How human actors respond to their shared vulnerabilities is up to them. Wise policymakers and diplomats will look for ways to promote mutual gain—even with adversaries. Stronger powers can afford and should take some risks for peace—initiatives to reduce tensions and work toward cooperative accommodations. Doing so, however, they must also guard against abuse of their concessions by the other side.

Complexity theory updates Darwin to define "fitness" as the capacity to cope effectively with complex challenges. For human societies, fitness requires more than merely surviving or claiming and seizing more values. Yes, survival is basic, but fitness also entails an ability to acquire and process information, leverage assets, take advantage of opportunities, and create values. Learning how to cooperate is important not only for survival but also for peace, prosperity, harmony, and cultural richness. One way to measure fitness is the Human Development Index generated each year by the United Nations Development Programme. The index, as we saw in Chapter 2, seeks to measure the conditions that expand human choice within each society.

Fitness, according to complexity theory, is found neither in anarchic conditions nor in the polar opposite of a rigid hierarchy. It is found close to the edge of chaos, where vibrant assets generate creative responses to complex challenges. Such fitness thrives where there is self-organization—not in a top-down dictatorship. No government, by these lights, should treat hard power as a goal in itself. Every society's institutions should be oriented toward enhancing fitness—for its own people and all humanity. Getting to yes on arms control might add to U.S. fitness and that of its negotiating partners, but any long-term accommodation should also be geared to enhancing human development in North Korea.

What Could It Mean to "Get to Yes" in Korea?

Human rights supporters worried that any accommodation with Pyongyang would condemn most North Korans to continued suffering under a totalitarian dictatorship. "The Kim regime essentially holds its people hostage," wrote Hassig and Oh. They complained that Washington appears "much more interested in the hostage taker's weapons of mass destruction than in the fate of his hostages."[12]

Prudence suggested that arms control for global security was more urgent than human rights in North Korea. Peace between Pakistan and India may benefit from their nuclear standoff, but a similar benefit was not likely if North Korea enlarged its nuclear arsenal. Others—Japan, South Korea, and Taiwan—might then take the same route and push China, India, and Pakistan to intensify their arms competitions. If Pyongyang proliferated its WMD, a chain link of catastrophes could ensue.

By 2010 brave North Koreans with cell phones were feeding five Web sites in South Korea to break the news blackout over Kim Jong Il's hermit kingdom.[13] Outsiders labored to reach the minds of North Koreans but external actors could do little to transform the ruling regime in Pyongyang.[14] Change, if it came, would arise mainly from within—as happened across the Soviet empire and in Yugoslavia. Realists and idealists alike could urge the Obama administration to negotiate with Pyongyang—as did presidents Reagan and George H. W. Bush with the USSR. Reagan and Bush engaged the Kremlin despite signs that the evil empire was wilting and that, even under Gorbachev, the Soviet system abused human rights. How soon the Soviet regime would implode could not be known. Meanwhile, Washington and Moscow reached accords in 1987, 1990, and 1991 that benefited their countries and the world. President Obama concluded another strategic arms accord with President Medvedev in 2010, regardless of the Kremlin's difficulties in the North Caucasus and elsewhere.

To be sure, the DPRK regime could collapse virtually overnight, as happened in East Germany. To prepare for such a possibility, the other parties to the six-party talks needed to consult and get to yes among themselves. Washington needed to maintain and deepen its ties with allies in Seoul and Tokyo but also to collaborate with Beijing and Moscow to prevent a mad rush to fill a power vacuum. To stop "loose nukes" falling into the wrong hands, however, U.S. forces would have to promptly take control of the North's nuclear facilities and proceed with the IAEA to dismantle them. The UN Security Council would need to establish a framework by which North Koreans could decide their political future—independence under a provisional government or some kind of confederation or union with the ROK. [15]

Meanwhile, North Korea in April 2010 praised President Obama's commitment to work toward a world without nuclear weapons but complained that the

United States still sought global hegemony and continued to threaten others with its nuclear weapons. Pyongyang's determination to build its own nuclear deterrent was probably deepened when the U.S. *Nuclear Posture Review* released on April 6 left room for use or threat of U.S. nuclear arms against nonsignatories of the NPT or countries deemed by Washington to have violated the treaty.[16]

Many experts believed in 2010 that the DPRK regime, if it survived current difficulties, would never agree to nuclear disarmament. But the stakes were so high and the risks so limited, that the United States and its partners needed to explore every avenue to an accord to eliminate or constrain North Korea's nuclear weapons capacity and prevent it from proliferating nuclear technology, materials, or weapons. "Getting to yes" had to focus on arms control but also

- supplant threats with assurances of nonaggression;
- transform the 1953 armistice into a peace treaty;
- replace economic sanctions with economic and technical assistance;
- open doors to freer trade of goods, services, and ideas;
- liberalize exchanges across the North-South border; and
- normalize political relations between Pyongyang and Seoul, Pyongyang and Washington.

A negative peace—the absence of war—could then expand gradually into a positive peace. A new era could then generate value for all participants in the six-party talks and all East Asians, including the people of Taiwan. Better relations could ensue among China, Russia, and the United States. North Koreans could live better as their government downgraded *juche* and "military first" and permitted them to participate more fully in the global economy and world of ideas. If the parties got to yes in Northeast Asia, new synergies would enhance human development in the region and across the globe. Value-creating would supplant value-claiming.

NOTES

Notes for Chapter 1

1. Gilbert Rozman, "The Geopolitics of the Korean Nuclear Crisis," in Richard J. Ellings and Aaron L. Friedberg, eds., *Strategic Asia 2003–04* (Seattle: National Bureau of Asian Research, 2003), 250–267 at 252.

2. A veteran observer says these qualities are basic to Korean culture, North and South, but he also catalogs a whole series of tough negotiating DPRK tactics meant to coerce, offend, manipulate, confound, and obstruct. He also refers to tactics meant to persuade and encourage cooperation. Richard Saccone, *Negotiating with North Korea* (Elizabeth, NJ: Hollym, 2003); and Richard Saccone, *The Business of Korean Culture* (Elizabeth, NJ: Hollym, 1994). The fistfights that occasionally break out in the ROK Diet presumably represent a deviation from the genteel features of Korean culture.

3. Princeton Seminars, February 13, 1954, quoted in Robert L. Beisner, *Dean Acheson: A Life in the Cold War* (New York: Oxford University Press, 2006), 323.

4. Current Intelligence Staff Study Sino-Soviet Competition in North Korea (ESAU XV-61), April 5, 1961, declassified May 2007, Summary page i.

5. Yang Yung in *People's Daily*, October 24, 1960, quoted in ibid., 14.

6. Bill Gates, "The Facts Depend on Where You Are Coming From," *Business Times*, http://www.btimes.co.za/97/0406/tech/tech6.htm, accessed June 1, 2007.

7. Gavan McCormack and Wada Haruki, "Forever Stepping Back: The Strange Record of 15 Years of Negotiation between Japan and North Korea," in John Feffer, ed., *The Future of U.S.-Korean Relations: The Imbalance of Power* (London: Routledge, 2006), 81–100 at 87.

8. Selig S. Harrison, "Did the U.S. Provoke N. Korea?" *Newsweek*, October 16, 2006.

9. Quoted in David Drake, *Sartre* (London: Haus, 2005), 88.

10. Frank McCourt, interviewed by Terry Gross in 1996, replayed on NPR, July 20, 2009.

11. Korean Central News Agency, May 27, 2009, Juche 98, http://www.kcna.co.jp/index-e.htm, accessed July 20, 2009.

12. North Korea's leaders could have learned from Lenin how to use arms control negotiations to shield their country's weaknesses and divide enemy ranks. Soviet diplomacy tried to expose the futility of disarmament negotiations so long as capitalist regimes remained in power and pursued their vested interests. Walter C. Clemens Jr., "Lenin on Disarmament," *Slavic Review* 23, no. 3 (September 1964): 504–525.

13. Roger Fisher and William Ury, *Getting to Yes: Negotiating Agreement without Giving In*, 2d ed. (New York: Penguin, 1991). For related works, see John P. Holdren, *Getting to Zero: Is Pursuing a Nuclear-Weapon-Free World Too Difficult? Too Dangerous? Too Distracting?* (Cambridge, MA: Belfer Center for Science and International Affairs, Harvard University, 1998); William Ury, *Getting Past No: Negotiating Your Way from Confrontation to Cooperation*, rev. ed. (New York: Bantam, 1993); William Ury, *The Power of a Positive No: How to Say No and Still Get to Yes* (New York: Bantam, 2007).

14. A positional bargainer might begin by demanding $1,000 for her used car. If the potential buyer offers $500, she might be willing to split the difference at $750. But what if the seller must leave town tomorrow and the buyer refuses to bid higher than $500? The seller's *interest* may require her to ignore her bargaining position and sell the car at any price—as happened to investment bank Bear Stearns in 2008 when compelled to sell its stock for $10 a share rather than the recent value of $133.

15. Howard Raiffa, *The Art and Science of Negotiation* (Cambridge, MA: Harvard University Press, 1982); David A. Lax and James K. Sebenius, *The Manager as Negotiator: Bargaining for Cooperative and Competitive Gain* (New York: Free Press, 1986); Howard Raiffa et al., *Negotiation Analysis: The Science and Art of Collaborative Decision Making* (Cambridge, MA: Harvard University Press, 2002); Michael Watkins, *Shaping the Game: The New Leader's Guide to Effective Negotiating* (Boston: Harvard Business School Press, 2006); Max Bazerman and Deepak Malhotra, *Negotiation Genius: How to Overcome Obstacles and Achieve Brilliant Results at the Bargaining Table and Beyond* (New York: Bantam, 2007); Gary Friedman and Jack Himmelstein, *Challenging Conflict: Mediation through Understanding* (Chicago: American Bar Association Section on Dispute Resolution, 2008). For additional references, see http://www.pon.harvard.edu/hnp/; also *Conflict Resolution Quarterly, Journal of Conflict Resolution, International Negotiation,* and *Negotiation Journal.*

16. Walter C. Clemens Jr., *Dynamics of International Relations: Conflict and Mutual Gain in an Era of Global Interdependence,* 2d ed. (Lanham, MD: Rowman and Littlefield, 2004), chaps. 1, 2, 16.

17. Walter C. Clemens Jr., *Can Russia Change? The USSR Confronts Global Interdependence* (New York: Routledge, 1990).

18. Hard power is the ability to command or coerce others using military or economic assets; soft power is the ability to inspire or persuade others to act as one would like. Conversion power is needed to activate these assets and use them to shape others' behavior. See Joseph S. Nye, *The Powers to Lead* (New York: Oxford University Press, 2008). Many academics thought that, of their number, Nye had the greatest influence on U.S. foreign policy.

19. Clemens, *Dynamics of International Relations,* chaps. 1, 16.

20. See, for example, http://www.nautilus.org/energy/2006/beijingworkshop/index.html, accessed July 15, 2007. The Northeast Asia Peace and Security Network brings together nonproliferation specialists, regional security experts, and nongovernmental organizations to analyze energy and other issues of peace and security in Northeast Asia. A daily report is available from napsnet@nautilus.org

21. Robert O. Keohane and Joseph S. Nye, *Power and Interdependence,* 3d ed. (New York: Longman, 2001), 9–17.

22. See Walter C. Clemens Jr., "Toward a New Paradigm for International Studies: The Interdependence of Complexity," presented at the International Studies Association

Annual Meeting, San Diego, California, 2006; and the essays by Walter C. Clemens Jr. and others in Neil Harrison, ed., *Complexity in World Politics: Concepts and Methods of a New Paradigm* (Albany: State University of New York Press, 2006).

23. There are several approaches to complexity studies. Neo-Darwinians analyze the fitness of all kind of organisms—from fruit flies to states to international networks. See Stuart A. Kauffman, *Origins of Order: Self-Organization and Selection in Evolution* (New York: Oxford University Press, 1995); and Walter C. Clemens Jr.; *The Baltic Transformed: Complexity Theory and European Security* (Lanham, MD: Rowman and Littlefield, 2001). Researchers at the New England Complex Systems Institute look for patterns, as in Mark Klein et al., "Negotiating Complex Contracts," at http://cci.mit .edu/klein/papers/gdn-02.pdf, accessed July 14, 2007.

24. A. A. Golovin and A. A. Nepomnyashchy, eds., *Self-Assembly, Pattern Formation and Growth Phenomena in Nano-Systems* (Berlin: Springer, 2006).

25. Peter Matthiessen, *The Birds of Heaven: Travels with Cranes* (New York: North Point, 2001).

Notes for Chapter 2

1. Descended from Tungusic (Manchurian) tribes, Koreans, like Japanese, probably migrated from the Northeast Asian mainland. Their language may be tied to the Ural Altaic family, which includes Mongolian, Hungarian, Turkish, Finnish, and, possibly, Japanese. The Korean and Japanese languages share a similar grammar but little more.

2. http://hdr.undp.org/en/media/HDR_20072008_EN_Complete.pdf, accessed April 20, 2009. Rankings are based on data from two or three years earlier.

3. Purchasing power parity rank versus HDI rank was −10 for the United States and +6 for the ROK.

4. Blaine Harden, "At the Heart of North Korea's Troubles, an Intractable Hunger Crisis," *Washington Post*, March 6, 2009.

5. "The Failed State Index," *Foreign Policy* (July–August 2009): 80–85; and http:// www.fundforpeace.org/web/index.php?option=com_content&task=view&id=326& Itemid=492, accessed July 14, 2009.

6. Václav Havel and Kjell Magne Bondevik, "North Korea's Crimes against Humanity," *Boston Globe*, September 19, 2008.

7. Andre Vornic, "North Korea Executes Christians," *BBC News*, July 24, 2009.

8. Chung Young Chul, "Society in Disarray: Crime, Corruption, and Deepening Cognitive Dissonance in North Korea," *Global Asia* 4, no. 2 (Summer 2009).

9. Andrei Lankov, "Turning Back the Clock: Attempts to Regain Control in North Korea after 2004," lecture at US-Korean Institute at SAIS, February 11, 2009, http:// uskoreainstitute.org/pdf/spring09/Lankov%20Transcript%20021109%20edit.pdf, accessed 04/30/09.

10. Harden, "At the Heart of North Korea's Troubles."

11. Blaine Harden, "North Korea Tightening Its Restrictions on Markets, Food Aid," *Washington Post*, July 14, 2009.

12. Junhoon Moon et al., "The Impact of IT Development on Rural Communities in Korea," *International Studies Review* 10, no. 1 (June 2009): 99–115.

13. The president of another government with Confucian traditions, Taiwan's Chen Shui-bian, and his wife were indicted in 2009 on charges of forgery and money laundering. But no religious faith guarantees honesty. Top leaders in Muslim Afghanistan, Protestant England, and Catholic Boston were also accused of economic crimes in 2009.

14. L. M. Wortzel, "North Korea's Connection to International Trade in Drugs, Counterfeiting, and Arms," testimony before the Government Affairs Subcommittee, U.S. Senate, May 20, 2003.

15. Chul, "Society in Disarray."

16. http://www.sgi-network.org/index.php, accessed June 10, 2009.

17. http://www.worldvaluessurvey.org/, accessed June 10, 2009.

18. South Korea's exports rose by 10 percent in October 2008—their slowest pace in thirteen months, as shipments to China fell for the first time since 2002, adding to concern that the ROK economy was headed for its first recession in a decade.

19. *The Economist*, April 27, 2009.

20. Daniel Gomà Pinilla, "Border Disputes between China and North Korea," *China Perspectives* no. 52 (2004), http://chinaperspectives.revues.org/document806.html, accessed March 31, 2009.

21. Several legal scholars opined that the line was a useful temporary conflict avoidance device but said that treating it as a permanent maritime boundary could not be supported by legal principles and precedents. Jon M. Van Dyke et al., "The North/South Korea Boundary Dispute in the Yellow (West) Sea," *Marine Policy* 27, no. 2 (March 2003): 143–158.

22. César Ducruet and Jin Cheol Jo, "Coastal Cities, Port Activities, and Logistics Constraints in a Socialist Developing Country: The Case of North Korea," *Transport Review: A Transdisciplinary Journal* 28, no. 1 (January 2008): 1–25. See also Sung-Hoon Llim and Kang-Taeg Lim, "Special Economic Zones as Survival Strategy of North Korea," *North Korean Review* 2, no. 2 (Fall 2006): 47–61.

23. Eugene J. Palka and Francis A. Galgano, *Geographic Perspectives: North Korea* (New York: McGraw-Hill/Dushkin, 2004).

24. Peter Hayes, "Unbearable Legacies: The Politics of Environmental Degradation in North Korea," *Global Asia* 4, no. 2 (Summer 2009): 33–39.

25. "Land of Morning Brightness," in Frances Carpenter, *Tales of a Korean Grandmother* (Boston: Tuttle, 1973), 27–35.

26. Another version holds that Kija left China because the Chou dynasty had replaced Kija's relatives in the Shang dynasty.

27. Casting doubt on this story, the Bronze Age in Korea was quite different from that in China.

28. Scott Snyder, *China's Rise and the Two Koreas: Politics, Economics, Security* (Boulder, CO: Lynne Rienner, 2009).

29. Max Weber, *The Protestant Ethic and the Spirit of Capitalism* (New York: Scribner, 1976).

30. JaHyun Kim Haboush and Martina Deuchler, eds., *Culture and the State in Late Choson Korea* (Cambridge, MA: Harvard University Press, 2002).

31. Many of the features he attributes to Korea are exaggerated, according to Yurim Yi, or not unique to Korea.

32. Lucian W. Pye, *Asian Power and Politics: The Cultural Dimensions of Authority* (Cambridge, MA: Harvard University Press, 1985), esp. chaps. 2 and 8. See also

Lucian W. Pye, "Political Culture Revisited," *Political Psychology* 12, no. 3 (September 1991): 487–508.

33. Pye, *Asian Power*, 75.

34. This sentence and several other qualifications of Pye's views in these pages were suggested by Yurim Yi.

35. Pye, *Asian Power*, 86.

36. Ibid., 84.

37. Gilbert Rozman, "Can Confucianism Survive in an Age of Universalism and Globalization?" *Pacific Affairs* 75, no. 1 (Spring 2002): 11–37; and Gilbert Rozman, *Northeast Asia's Stunted Regionalism: Bilateral Distrust in the Shadow of Globalization* (New York: Cambridge University Press, 2004).

38. See the debate between Patrick McEachern, "Interest Groups in North Korean Politics," and Jacques E. C. Hymans, "Assessing North Korean Nuclear Intentions and Capacities: A New Approach," in *Journal of East Asian Studies* 8, no. 2 (May–August 2008): 235–258 and 259–292.

39. Ra Kyung-jun, "Early Print Culture in Korea," *Korean Culture* (Summer 1999): 13–21.

40. He wrote: "The sounds of our language differ from Chinese and are not easily communicated by using Chinese ideographs. Therefore, many are ignorant ... unable to communicate [by writing]" (ibid.). Known as a Confucian humanist, Sejong also composed music for wind and string instruments still played in the twenty-first century on ceremonial occasions.

41. More than 50 percent of all Korean vocabulary is derived from Chinese loan words. In many cases there are two words—a Chinese loan word and an indigenous Korean word with the same meaning. Compounding foreign influences, under Japanese rule (1910–1945), large numbers of Chinese character compounds that were coined in Japan to translate Western scientific vocabulary came into use in Korea. American influence since 1945 is reflected in the many English words also absorbed—often quite oddly—into Korean. For example, because Korean lacks an F, "fashion" is rendered as "passion"—as in "passion stores." Though "stress" can be readily rendered with Korean words, some contemporary writers prefer the English word "stress" spelled with Korean letters.

42. Deviating somewhat from Marxist-Leninist dogma, *Kullo-ja* includes all kinds of workers. There is a separate word for physical or "blue-collar" workers, "Nodong-ja."

43. http://www.declan-software.com/korean.htm#Origins, accessed July 6, 2009.

44. Hymans, "Assessing North Korean Nuclear Intentions," 266.

45. Like a fractal, this pattern holds true on many levels throughout the chain of being, from large groups and entire organisms down to the heartbeat of an individual. See the Web sites of the Santa Fe Institute, New England Complex Systems Institute, and David Suzuki Foundation. For applications in politics, see Neil Harrison, ed., *Complexity in World Politics* (Albany: State University of New York Press, 2006); and Walter C. Clemens Jr., *The Baltic Transformed: Complexity Theory and European Security* (Lanham, MD: Rowman and Littlefield, 2001).

46. D. Lawrence Kincaid and June Ock Ym, "The Needle and the Ax—Communication and Development in a Korean Village," in Wilbur Schramm and Daniel Lerner, eds., *Communication and Change: The Last Ten Years—and the Next* (Honolulu: University Press of Hawaii, 1976), 83–97.

47. Jeeyang Rhee Baum, *Responsive Democracy: Increasing State Accountability in East Asia* (Ann Arbor: University of Michigan Press, forthcoming), chap. 1. Her primary data come from the 1990, 1994, and 2001 waves of the "World Values Survey"; the 1996 and 2001 waves of the Korea Barometer Surveys; and the 2001 and 2002 waves of the East Asia Barometer.

48. Some cultures are "progress-prone," whereas others are "progress-resistant." See Lawrence E. Martin, *The Central Liberal Truth: How Politics Can Change a Culture and Save It from Itself* (New York: Oxford University Press, 2006).

49. Thomas Kalinowski, "From Developmental State to Developmental Society? The Role of Civil Society Organizations in Recent Korean Development and Possible Lessons for Developing Countries," *International Studies Review* 10, no. 1 (June 2009): 53–71.

50. When two rescuers swam to help a family stranded on the roof, the worker father gave them "not his children" but portraits of the long dead "president" and his son, the Dear Leader. Other such exploits were proudly recorded by Korean Central News Agency (KCNA) on August 9, 2006.

51. Dramatically documented in the National Geographic film *Inside North Korea* (2007), available on DVD. Dr. Sanduk Ruit is an ophthalmologist in Katmandu and a director of the Himalayan Cataract Project, which works far and wide. See www.cureblindness.org, accessed June 4, 2009. For his service to humanity, Dr. Ruit in 2007 received Australia's highest honor for a foreign national.

Notes for Chapter 3

1. Quoted in Yur-Bok Lee, "A Korean View of Korean-American Relations, 1882–1940," in Yur-Bok Lee and Wayne Patterson, eds., *Korean-American Relations, 1866–1997* (Albany: State University of New York Press, 1999), 11–34 at 15.

2. William Franklin Sands, *Undiplomatic Memories* (New York: McGraw-Hill, 1930), 56. On the conflicts between an idealistic American chargé d'affairs in Seoul and an insouciant State Department, see Samuel Hawley, ed., *America's Man in Korea: The Private Letters of George C. Foulk, 1884–1887* (Lanham, MD: Lexington Books, 2008).

3. The number amounted to 16,814 full texts or extracts according to *Korean Review* (May 1902): 223–224.

4. Isabella Bird Bishop, *Korea and Her Neighbors* (New York: Fleming H. Revell, 1897).

5. Lee, "A Korean View."

6. Quoted in Yur-Bok Lee, "Korean-American Diplomatic Relations, 1882–1905," in Yur-Bok Lee and Wayne Patterson, eds., *One Hundred Years of Korean-American Relations, 1882–1982* (Tuscaloosa: University of Alabama Press, 1986), 12–45 at 23.

7. Wayne Patterson and Hilary Conroy, "Duality and Dominance: An Overview of Korean-American Relations, 1866–1997," in Yur-Bok Lee and Patterson, *Korean-American Relations*, 1–10 at 5.

8. Details can be found in the next chapter.

9. Paul Gauguin's painting with this title in French hangs in the Museum of Fine Arts, Boston.

10. The Korean title for such a person is *Hungsun Taewongun*.

11. *A Historical Summary of United States–Korean Relations, with a Chronology of Important Developments, 1834–1962* (Washington, DC: U.S. Department of State, 1962), 3.

12. Fred Harvey Harrington, "An American View of Korean-American Relations," in Lee and Patterson, eds., *One Hundred Years,* 46–67 at 50–51.

13. Quoted in Yur-Bok Lee, *Diplomatic Relations between the United States and Korea, 1866–1887* (New York: Humanities Press, 1970), 29.

14. Harrington, "An American View," 51.

15. http://www.presidency.ucsb.edu/ws/index.php?pid-29512&st-korea&stl-grant, accessed July 11, 2009. This database permits a researcher to search for "Korea" and the name of a president or the relevant year and quickly find the full text with "Korea" marked in red.

16. *A Historical Summary,* 4.

17. Huang Tsunhsien quoted in Chae-Jin Lee, *A Troubled Peace: U.S. Policy and the Two Koreas* (Baltimore, MD: Johns Hopkins University Press, 2006), 11.

18. http://en.wikipedia.org/wiki/Empress_Myeongseong#The_American_ Expedition, accessed June 12, 2007.

19. http://www.presidency.ucsb.edu/ws/index.php?pid-29512&st-korea&stl-grant, accessed July 10, 2009.

20. http://www.presidency.ucsb.edu/ws/index.php?pid-29529&st-cleveland&stl-korea, accessed July 10, 2009.

21. Lee, *A Troubled Peace,* 12.

22. Lee, "Korean-American Diplomatic Relations," 18.

23. One delegate stayed on in Massachusetts to study at the Governor Dummer Academy. Moon-Hyon Nam, "Early History of Electrical Engineering in Korea: Edison and First Electric Lighting in the Kingdom of Corea," in *Singapore 2000: Promoting the History of EE,* January 23–26, 2000, 1–9, http://www.ieee.org/portal/cms_docs_ iportals/iportals/aboutus/history_center/conferences/singapore/Nam,-Early_History .pdf, accessed June 1, 2007.

24. Michael Adas, *Dominance by Design: Technological Imperatives and America's Civilizing Mission* (Cambridge, MA: Harvard University Press, 2006), 1–31.

25. http://www.presidency.ucsb.edu/ws/index.php?pid=29530&st-korea&stl-, accessed July 13, 2009.

26. http://www.presidency.ucsb.edu/ws/index.php?pid-71083&st-korea&stl-, accessed July 13, 2009.

27. *Opisanie Korei,* 3 parts (St. Petersburg, 1890).

28. http://www.presidency.ucsb.edu/ws/index.php?pid-29535&st=korea&stl-, accessed July 13, 2009.

29. Text at http://www.isop.ucla.edu/eas/documents/1895shimonoseki-treaty.htm, accessed May 4, 2009.

30. William Reed, "Information, Power, and War," *American Political Science Review* 97, no. 4 (November 2003): 633–641.

31. http://www.presidency.ucsb.edu/ws/index.php?pid-29544&st-great+ oriental+ empire&stl-roosevelt, accessed July 10, 2009.

32. See *Krasnyi arkhiv* documents cited in Walter C. Clemens Jr., "From Nicholas II to SALT II: Change and Continuity in East-West Diplomacy," *International Affairs* 49, no. 3 (July 1973): 385–401.

33. Report from Lloyd C. Griscom, U.S. Legation in Tokyo, to the Secretary of State

John Hay on January 8, 1904, in *Foreign Relations of the United States* [hereinafter *FRUS*] *1904* (Washington, DC: GPO, 1905), 410. A few days later, in reply, Tokyo demanded that St. Petersburg recognize that Korea and its littoral were outside Russia's sphere of interest (411). All editions of *FRUS* referred to in this book were published in Washington, DC, by the GPO. *FRUS* from 1861 through 1960 may be found at http://digicoll.library.wisc.edu/cgi-bin/FRUS/FRUS-idx?type-browse&scope-FRUS.FRUS1, accessed July 14, 2009.

34. Translation from *Japan Times* reprinted in *FRUS 1904,* 414.

35. See Article IV of text delivered on February 26, 1904, to the Secretary of State by the Japanese legation in Washington in *FRUS 1904,* 437.

36. Griscom to Secretary of State Hay, March 17, 1904, in *FRUS 1904,* 438.

37. Hay to Horace N. Allen, U.S. Legation in Seoul, April 6, 1904, in *FRUS 1904,* 452. The Korean Minister of Foreign Affairs then expressed his apologies to Mr. Allen (453). As late as January 1905, however, Roosevelt sent to Congress a State Department report on reforms of the U.S. "extraterritorial judicial system in China and Korea, with … a draft of an act providing for the establishment of a district court of the United States for China and Korea."

38. Tyler Dennett quoted in *FRUS 1950* (Washington, DC: GPO, 1976), 7:625 n5.

39. See Rhee's letter to President Harry Truman on May 15, 1945, in *FRUS 1945* (Washington, DC: GPO, 1968), 6:1028–1029 and n31.

40. A. A. Gromyko, *Pamiatnoe,* 2 vols. (Moscow: Politizdat, 1988), 1:189.

41. "*khitryi i mudryi,*" in ibid., 1:17.

42. In 1908 Roosevelt reported that the State Department often received appeals to stop mistreatment abroad of various groups—blacks, whites, Christians, Jews, Armenians, Koreans, and others. Only in exceptional cases, he said, should the United States act in their behalf.

43. All this was documented in Japanese government ordinances and Japanese newspaper accounts sent by the U.S. Legation in Tokyo to the secretary of state on January 19 and July 6, 1906. See *FRUS 1906* (Washington, DC: GPO, 1909), part 2: 1023–1026 and 1044–1046.

44. *FRUS 1906,* part 2:999–1005.

45. Japan treated Taiwan, annexed in 1895, much better, in part because many Japanese looked up to Chinese civilization but down on Korean. Equally or more important, Taiwan was administered by enlightened naval officers; Korea, by rather brutal army personnel. A century or more later, ties between Taiwan and Japan were cordial and respectful, whereas Korean resentments to Japan still bristled. In 2007 Tokyo continued to deny that Japan had abused Korean and other Asian women in World War II.

46. Before Cheng arrived at the colony in 1942, however, another Japanese commander treated the lepers "like his family." When he died, residents purchased a cenotaph in his memory. Norimitsu Onishi, "A Korean Bridge Must Span Years of Bias and Sadness," *New York Times,* August 9, 2007, A4.

47. http://www.presidency.ucsb.edu/ws/index.php?pid-29551&st-korea&st1-, accessed July 13, 2009.

48. http://www.presidency.ucsb.edu/ws/index.php?pid-29552&st-korea&st1-, accessed July 13, 2009.

49. The inquiry dealt with three issues concerning Japan—including Japanese "interests in Eastern Asia and the Pacific"—and more than a dozen issues concerning China,

including the Open Door Policy. The inquiry asked the American consul in Seoul (!) to report on Japanese politics. *The Paris Peace Conference, FRUS 1919* (Washington, DC: GPO, 1942), 1:72, 90. The inquiry occupied pp. 9–220 of this volume, but "Korea" did not appear in the Index.

50. Ibid.

51. *A Historical Summary*, 8.

52. Cordell Hull, *The Memoirs of Cordell Hull*, 2 vols. (New York: Macmillan, 1948), 1:270.

53. All quotes and paraphrasing as rendered in the report from the U.S. Embassy in Tokyo to the secretary of state, dispatched on November 27, 1918, but not received in Washington for nearly a month—December 23. See *FRUS 1919*, 1:490–491.

54. John K. Fairbank in 1968 quoted in Dean Acheson, *Present at the Creation: My Years on the State Department* (New York: Norton, 1987), 740.

55. This sentence is not quoted and its legal justification is omitted in David F. Schmitz, *Henry L. Stimson: The First Wise Man* (Wilmington, DE: SR Books, 2003), 102–107. The book mentions Korea once, in passing, on 103.

56. William J. H. Hough III, "The Annexation of the Baltic States and Its Effect on the Development of Law Prohibiting Forcible Seizure of Territory," *New York Law School Journal of International and Comparative Law* 6, no. 2 (Winter 1985), entire issue. Even though the Stimson doctrine did not help Korea, the doctrine later encouraged Washington and most Western countries to defy Soviet annexation of the Baltic republics.

Notes for Chapter 4

1. See letters by Syngman Rhee and other Korean leaders to President Harry Truman and subsequent exchanges between Rhee and other U.S. officials in *FRUS 1945* (Washington, DC: GPO, 1969), 6:1028–1037. All editions of *FRUS* cited here were published in Washington, DC, by the GPO.

2. Roosevelt gave little thought to Korea. He could hope, however, that the promise of eventual independence for Korea would appeal to some U.S. voters. See Stephen E. Pelz, "U.S. Decisions on Korean Policy, 1943–1950: Some Hypotheses," in Bruce Cumings, ed., *Child of Conflict: The Korean-American Relationship, 1943–1953* (Seattle: University of Washington Press, 1983), 93–132 at 97–101.

3. Notes by the Chinese delegation show that, meeting with Roosevelt in Cairo on November 23, 1943, Chiang Kai-shek stressed the need to grant independence to Korea. The next day, however, Roosevelt told Churchill he had no doubt that China "had wide aspirations which included the re-occupation of Manchuria and Korea." *The Conferences at Cairo and Tehran, FRUS 1943*, 325 ff.

4. See Soviet and U.S. sources analyzed in Walter C. Clemens Jr., *Baltic Independence and Russian Empire* (New York: St. Martin's Press, 1991), 297–298. The extent of Roosevelt's appeasement, if not myopia and perfidy, seems not to have penetrated the minds of the many historians who rank him as one of the greatest U.S. presidents in foreign policy. One secretary of state, however, considered Roosevelt superficial as well as haughty. See Dean Acheson, *Present at the Creation: My Years in the State Department* (New York: Norton, 1987).

5. Andrei A. Gromyko, *Pamiatnoe*, 2 vols. (Moscow: Politizdat, 1988), 1: 189–190.

6. General Wang Peng Sheng, an adviser to Chiang Kai-shek's government, worried about a Soviet takeover of Korea. He stressed that peace in the Far East depended on resolving the problem of Korea. Comments transmitted by U.S. chargé d'affaires George Atcheson Jr. in Chungking to Washington on August 14, 1943, in *FRUS 1943*, 3:1095–1096.

7. C. E. Gauss in Chungking to the secretary of state, December 6, 1943, in ibid.

8. Chu Hein-ming, chief of the Russian Department, Ministry of Information, May 20, 1945, in *FRUS 1945*, 7:870–876 at 873.

9. For U.S. statements on April 3, 1945, and a related internal discussion on June 11, 1945, see *FRUS 1945*, 1:191 and 1242.

10. Memorandum by G. M. Elsey, Assistant to the president's naval aide, transmitted to Admiral William D. Leahy on July 1, 1945, and subsequently transmitted to Truman. See *The Conference of Berlin FRUS 1945*, 2 vols., 1:309–310.

11. Ibid.

12. Notes by U.S. ambassador W. Averell Harriman in Moscow, in *The Conference of Berlin*, part 1:46–47.

13. Ibid., part 1:310.

14. Report by Harriman in Moscow to President Truman and Secretary of State James F. Byrnes, July 3, 1945, in *FRUS 1945*, 7:912–914.

15. *The Conference of Berlin*, part 1:310–315, 924–926.

16. Stimson to Truman, July 16, 1945, in *FRUS 1945* (1960), 2:631.

17. This act violated Moscow's April 13, 1941, neutrality pact with Tokyo, which bound each side to respect the other's territorial integrity for at least five years. The Kremlin denounced the 1941 treaty in April 1945, but it probably remained legally binding until April 1946.

18. Rusk's recollections in a July 12, 1950, memorandum, *FRUS 1945*, 6:1039.

19. *FRUS 1945*, 6:1038 n48.

20. Ibid., 6:1038.

21. Gerhard Keiderling, ed., *"Gruppe Ulbricht" in Berlin, April bis Juni 1945: von den Vorbereitungen im Sommer 1944 bis zur Wiederbegründung der KPD im Juni 1945: eine Dokumentation* (Berlin: Berlin Verlag A. Spitz, 1993).

22. A former minister in the provisional government based in Shanghai and then in Chungking, Yu-pil Lee (Yi) had headed the Self-Rule Council. When the communists took control, he moved south but died en route. The great grandfather of Yurim Yi, she learned Yu-pil Lee's story from her own father.

23. Pelz, "U.S. Decisions on Korean Policy, " 107–109.

24. *FRUS 1945*, 6:1065-1071.

25. *FRUS 1945*, 2:697–705.

26. Ambassador Harriman in Moscow to Soviet Foreign Commissar Molotov, November 8, 1945, in *FRUS 1945*, 2:627. His message ignored the brusque rejection of U.S. overtures by Soviet authorities in Korea.

27. Hodge in Seoul to MacArthur in Tokyo, October 12, 1945, in *FRUS 1945*, 6:1072–1073.

28. *FRUS 1945*, 2:699–700 and 716–717.

29. Named Kim Sung Joo (or Kim Song-ju) by his Presbyterian parents, the future

leader took the name Kim Il Sung ("become the sun") in 1935. Some skeptics say he lifted it from a legendary hero believed to have fought for Korean independence several decades earlier.

30. *FRUS 1946*, 1:1145–1160 at 1148 and 1153.

31. *FRUS 1947*, 1:736–750 at 746.

32. Hickerson to the secretary of state, March 6, 1948, in *FRUS 1948*, 3:779–780 at 780.

33. *FRUS 1948*, 1:14–15.

34. In January 1950 the chief of the U.S. Advisory Group, Brigadier General William L. Roberts, and several ROK officers made a good case to U.S. ambassador-at-large Philip C. Jessup "for at least a few aircraft and antiaircraft guns." Tanks were less urgent. Jessup memorandum, January 14, 1950, in *FRUS 1950*, 7:1–7 at 2.

35. See Se-Jin Kim, ed., *Documents on Korean-American Relations, 1943–1976* (Seoul: Research Center for Peace and Unification, 1976).

36. http://www.asiasource.org/society/syngmanrhee.cfm, accessed May 5, 2009.

37. Normimitsu Onishi, "Korea's Tricky Task: Digging Up Past Treachery," *New York Times*, January 5, 2005.

38. *New York Times*, March 2, 1949.

39. Long excerpts in Kim, *Documents on Korean-American Relations*, 83–89.

40. Ibid.

41. Acheson, *Present at the Creation*, 356–358.

42. Rhee to U.S. ambassador-at-large Philip C. Jessup. See Jessup memorandum.

43. Putative archival material quoted in the *DPRK Report* (Moscow), no. 23 (March–April 2000), in Jussi M. Hanhimäki and Odd Arne Westad, eds., *The Cold War: A History in Documents and Eyewitness Accounts* (New York: Oxford University Press, 2003), 185–186.

44. Gromyko, *Pamiatnoe*, 2:128–131.

45. For some two dozen recent sources on the Korean War, see Walter C. Clemens Jr., "North Korea and the World: A Bibliography of Books and URLs in English, 1997–2007," *Journal of East Asian Studies* 8 (2008): 293–325 at 297–299.

46. For analysis, documents, and bibliography, see "New Evidence on North Korea," *Cold War International History Project Bulletin* 14–15 (Winter 2003–Spring 2004), which includes the work of Beijing-based scholar Shen Zhihua, "Sino-Soviet Korean Conflict and Its Resolution during the Korean War" (9–24), and other findings based on archives in Budapest, Berlin, and Moscow. For a digest of the new evidence and citations to her own work, see Kathryn Weathersby, "Introduction" (5–7). See also Sergei N. Goncharov, John W. Lewis, and Xue Litai, *Uncertain Partners: Stalin, Mao, and the Korean War* (Palo Alto, CA: Stanford University Press, 1993); and William Stuek, ed., *The Korean War in World History* (Lexington: University of Kentucky Press, 2004).

47. http://www.wilsoncenter.org/index.cfm?topic_id=1409&fuseaction=va2.document&identifier=E4474099-B4AD-4067-B4A88B9C7643B3BE&sort=Collection&item=The%20Korean%20War, accessed June 4, 2009.

48. Kennan to Acheson on August 21, 1950, in *FRUS 1950*, 7:623–628.

49. Ibid.

50. Paul Nitze, proponent of building up U.S. forces, agreed with Kennan that the Korean War overextended U.S. forces and, with Kennan, opposed UN forces advancing

into North Korea. See Nicholas Thompson, *The Hawk and the Dove: Paul Nitze, George Kennan, and the History of the Cold War* (New York: Henry Holt, 2009), chap. 8.

51. Alexandre Y. Mansourov, "Stalin, Mao, Kim, and China's Decision to Enter the Korean War, September 16–October 15, 1950: New Evidence from the Russian Archives," *Cold War International History Project Bulletin* 6–7 (Winter 1995–1996): 94–119 at 100.

52. Ibid.

53. William Taubman, *Khrushchev: The Man and His Era* (New York: Norton, 2003), 332 and 732 n30.

54. See, for example, Draft Memorandum Prepared by the Policy Planning Staff, Department of State, July 25, 1950, in *FRUS 1950*, 7:469–473 at 471.

55. Much of the foregoing derives from Shen Zhihua, "Alliance of 'Tooth and Lips' or Marriage of Convenience? The Origins and Development of the Sino–North Korean Alliance, 1946–1958," Working Paper Series, WP-08–09 (Washington, DC: US-Korea Institute at SAIS, 2008); and Kathryn Weathersby, "Dependence and Mistrust: North Korea's Relations with Moscow and the Evolution of Juche," Working Paper Series, WP-08–08 (Washington, DC: US-Korea Institute at SAIS, 2008).

56. *Encyclopedia of Asian History*, http://www.asiasource.org/society/syngmanrhee .cfm, accessed June 23, 2007.

57. Geoffrey Perret, *Commander in Chief: How Truman, Johnson, and Bush Turned a Presidential Power into a Threat to America's Future* (New York: Farrar, Straus and Giroux, 2007), 6.

58. Ibid., 7.

Notes for Chapter 5

1. The following is a list of documents used in Chapter 5. All are available from the Woodrow Wilson International Center for Scholars, Cold War International History Project, Virtual Archive 2.0, Subject: Korea, DPRK, Nuclear Program, at http://www .wilsoncenter.org/index.cfm?topic_id=1409&fuseaction=va2.browse&sort=Subject& item=Korea%2C%20DPRK%2C%20Nuclear%20Program, accessed May 30, 2009.

Document 1: Conversation Between Soviet Ambassador in North Korea Vasily Moskovsky and the German Ambassador, August 26, 1963.

Document 2: Conversation Between Soviet Ambassador in North Korea Vasily Moskovsky and Soviet Specialists in North Korea, September 27, 1963.

Document 3: Report, Embassy of Hungary in North Korea to the Hungarian Foreign Ministry, January 11, 1964.

Document 4: Report, Embassy of Hungary in North Korea to the Hungarian Foreign Ministry, March 13, 1967.

Document 5: Report, Embassy of Hungary in North Korea to the Hungarian Foreign Ministry, February 29, 1968.

Document 6: Report, Embassy of Hungary in the Soviet Union to the Hungarian Foreign Ministry, November 12, 1969.

Document 7: Report, Embassy of Hungary in North Korea to the Hungarian Foreign Ministry, July 30, 1975.

Document 8: Memorandum, Hungarian Foreign Ministry, February 16, 1976.

Document 9: Report, Embassy of Hungary in North Korea to the Hungarian Foreign Ministry, February 18, 1976.

Document 10: Report, Embassy of Hungary in North Korea to the Hungarian Foreign Ministry, April 15, 1976.

Document 11: Telegram, Embassy of Hungary in North Korea to the Hungarian Foreign Ministry, June 25, 1976.

Document 12: Memorandum, Branch Office of the Hungarian Ministry of Foreign Trade in Pyongyang to the Hungarian Ministry of Foreign Trade, August 9, 1976.

Document 13: Memorandum, Hungarian National Commission of Atomic Energy to the Hungarian Foreign Ministry, August 31, 1976.

Document 14: Report, Embassy of Hungary in North Korea to the Hungarian Foreign Ministry, December 8, 1976 (part of the virtual archive but not cited here).

Document 15: Telegram, Embassy of Hungary in the Soviet Union to the Hungarian Foreign Ministry, January 20, 1977.

Document 16: Memorandum, Hungarian Foreign Ministry, February 16, 1977.

Document 17: Report, Embassy of Hungary in North Korea to the Hungarian Foreign Ministry, November 21, 1977.

Document 18: Telegram, Embassy of Hungary in North Korea to the Hungarian Foreign Ministry, February 17, 1979.

Document 19: Report, Embassy of Hungary in North Korea to the Hungarian Foreign Ministry, March 12, 1981.

Document 20: Report, Embassy of Hungary in North Korea to the Hungarian Foreign Ministry, April 30, 1981.

Document 21: Memorandum, Hungarian Academy of Sciences to the Hungarian Foreign Ministry, March 7, 1983.

Document 22: Letter, Hungarian Foreign Ministry to the Hungarian Academy of Sciences, April 6, 1983.

Document 23: Report, Embassy of Hungary in North Korea to the Hungarian Foreign Ministry, March 9, 1985.

Document 24: Report, Embassy of Hungary in North Korea to the Hungarian Foreign Ministry, May 30, 1988.

Additional details of many events described in this chapter—names, official positions, dates, places, and documentary references—are given in Walter C. Clemens Jr., "North Korea's Quest for Nuclear Weapons: New Historical Evidence," *Journal of East Asian Studies* 10, no. 1 (January–April 2010): 127–154.

2. Jacques E. C. Hymans, "Discarding Tired Assumptions about North Korea," *Bulletin of the Atomic Scientists,* May 28, 2009, http://www.thebulletin.org/node/7115, accessed June 3, 2009. For more details, see Jacques E. C. Hymans, "Assessing North Korean Nuclear Intentions and Capacities: A New Approach," *Journal of East Asian Studies* 8, no. 2 (May–August 2008): 259–292.

3. Michael J. Mazarr, *North Korea and the Bomb: A Case Study in Nonproliferation* (New York: St. Martin's Press, 1996), 17.

4. Walter C. Clemens Jr., *The Arms Race and Sino-Soviet Relations* (Palo Alto, CA: Hoover Institution, 1968).

5. Nie Rongzhen, *Nie Rongzhen hui yi lu,* 3 vols., 2d ed. (Beijing: Zhan shi chu ban she, 1983), vol. 3.

6. IAEA, "In Focus: IAEA and the DPRK," http://www.iaea.org/NewsCenter/Focus/IaeaDprk/fact_sheet_may2003.shtml, accessed July 15, 2009.

7. Mazarr, *North Korea and the Bomb,* 25.

8. Weathersby, "Dependence and Mistrust."

9. Ibid.

10. William C. Potter, Djuro Miljanic, Ivo Slavs, "Tito's Nuclear Legacy," *Bulletin of the Atomic Scientists* 56, no. 2 (March–April 2000): 63–70.

11. Don Oberdorfer, *The Two Koreas: A Contemporary History* (Reading, MA: Addison-Wesley, 1977), 253.

12. Andrei Lankov, "The Troubled Russia–North Korea alliance," *Asia Times Online,* December 25, 2004, http://www.atimes.com/atimes/Korea/FL25Dg01.html, accessed April 29, 2009.

13. IAEA, "In Focus."

14. Robert A. Wampler, ed., *North Korea and Nuclear Weapons: The Declassified U.S. Record, National Security Archive Electronic Briefing Book no. 87* (2003), documents 1 and 2, http://www.gwu.edu/~nsarchiv/NSAEBB/NSAEBB87/#docs, accessed January 2, 2009.

15. Hymans, "Assessing North Korean Nuclear Intentions," 274–275.

16. North Korea's attack on ROK leaders in Rangoon in October 1983 killed twenty-one persons and wounded forty-six.

17. Michael J. Mazaar, "Predator States and War: The North Korean Case," in Tong Whan Park, ed., *The U.S. and the Two Koreas: A New Triangle* (Boulder, CO: Lynne Rienner, 1998), 75-95 at 85.

18. Weathersby, "Dependence and Mistrust," 21.

19. Seung-Ho Joo, "Moscow-Pyongyang Relations under Kim Jong-il: High Hopes and Sober Reality," *Pacific Focus* 24, no. 1 (April 2009): 107–130.

Notes for Chapter 6

1. Chuck Downs, *Over the Line: North Korea's Negotiating Strategy* (Washington, DC: American Enterprise Institute, 1999). For instruction in hard-line diplomacy, see John Illich, *Power Negotiating: Strategies for Winning in Life and Business* (Reading, MA: Addison-Wesley, 1980).

2. Iranian diplomacy in the early twenty-first century was also confused and confusing—the product of shifting coalitions trying to shape policy decisions. Some factions in Tehran wanted to negotiate seriously on nuclear issues; others opposed any compromise. Some Europeans concluded the Iranians were just stalling; more likely, they had no agreed strategy.

3. On TFT at Panmunjom, see Alfred D. Wilhelm Jr., *Chinese at the Negotiating Table: Style and Characteristics* (Washington, DC: National Defense University Press, 1994), 161.

4. *Sympathy* prompts a person to offer the first favor, particularly to someone in need. *Anger* protects the giver against cheaters who accept a favor without reciprocating. *Gratitude* impels a beneficiary to reward those who helped in the past. *Guilt* prompts a cheater in danger of being found out to repair the relationship. Steven Pinker, "The Moral Instinct," *New York Times Magazine,* January 13, 2008.

5. *American Heritage Dictionary of the English Language,* 4th ed. (Boston: Houghton Mifflin, 2000), 2013–2114, 2035.

6. Ji Chaozhu, *The Man on Mao's Right: From Harvard Yard to Tiananmen Square, My Life Inside China's Foreign Ministry* (New York: Random House, 2008), 102–108.

7. My paraphrase based on Robert Axelrod, *The Evolution of Cooperation* (New York: Basic Books, 1984).

8. For a history of the Joint Security Area and the many events that occurred there, see http://www.newworldencyclopedia.org/entry/Joint_Security_Area#Staffing_and_Purpose. Photos of the Swiss camp are at http://www.vtg.admin.ch/internet/vtg/en/home/themen/einsaetze/peace/korea/fotos.html, both sites accessed March 13, 2009.

9. Reuters, July 20, 2009; KCNA, July 23, 2009.

10. Joshua S. Goldstein and John R. Freeman, *Three-Way Street: Strategic Reciprocity in World Politics* (Chicago: University of Chicago Press, 1990).

11. Charles E. Osgood, *An Alternative to War or Surrender* (Urbana: University of Illinois Press, 1962).

12. Author's interview at Panmunjom. See Walter C. Clemens Jr., "GRIT at Panmunjom: Conflict and Cooperation in Divided Korea," *Asian Survey* 13, no. 6 (June 1973): 531–59 at 548.

13. To win over European pacifists, Lenin advised Soviet diplomats in 1922 to avoid "terrible words" such as "inevitable violent revolution" at the Genoa Economic Conference.

14. I have never met a U.S. official who had even heard of GRIT or Osgood.

15. The Kennedy speech was printed in full in *Pravda* and *Izvestiia,* June 13, 1963; Khrushchev's comments on the speech were published in *Pravda,* June 15, and *Izvestiia,* June 16, 1963. Quickly grasping the significance of these exchanges, China referred to them as "Kennedy's Big Conspiracy," *Peking Review* 6, no. 26 (June 28, 1963): 12–14. For the Kennedy speech and analysis, see Walter C. Clemens Jr., *Toward a Strategy of Peace* (Chicago: Rand McNally, 1965). The Foreword by Robert F. Kennedy explains the background to the speech.

16. See Lincoln P. Bloomfield, Walter C. Clemens Jr., and Franklyn Griffiths, *Khrushchev and the Arms Race: Soviet Interests in Arms Control and Disarmament, 1954–1964* (Cambridge, MA: MIT Press, 1966), 209–224; for background, see Vincent P. Rock, *A Strategy of Interdependence* (New York: Scribner's, 1964).

17. Walter C. Clemens Jr., "Gorbachev's Role in International Détente: True GRIT?" *Soviet and Post-Soviet Review* 20, no. 1 (1993): 51–76.

18. Each man and his qualities are debated. See, for example, Gao Wenquian, *Zhou Enlai: The Last Perfect Revolutionary* (New York: Public Affairs, 2009); Fredrik Logevall and Andrew Preston, eds., *Nixon in the World: American Foreign Relations, 1969–1977* (New York: Oxford University Press, 2008), with a chapter on the opening to China by Margaret MacMillan.

19. Henry Kissinger, *The White House Years* (Boston: Little, Brown, 1979), 173, 192–193.

20. When Taiwanese agents blew up the plane on which Zhou was scheduled to fly to the Bandung Conference in 1955, they may well have had help from the CIA. Getting wind of the plot, Zhou took a different plane, leaving the passengers on the scheduled

flight to die in an explosion. Windell L. Minnick, "Target: Zhou Enlai," *Far Eastern Economic Review* (July 13, 1995): 54–55; Steve Tsang, "Target Zhou Enlai: The 'Kashmir Princess' Incident of 1955," *China Quarterly* 139 (September 1994): 766–782.

21. Kissinger, *The White House Years*, 187–188.

22. In 1970 I gave a talk in Taiwan and spoke not of Red China or the PRC but (I had hoped, diplomatically) of "mainland China." Later I learned that my Taiwanese translator had rendered my turn of phrase as "five-bandit regime."

23. While in Japan, a U.S. player hitched a ride with a Chinese van and received a gift. He reciprocated with a gift the next day and hinted at a desire to play in Beijing. Soon the PRC Foreign Ministry was debating the issue. According to Chinese sources, the Foreign Ministry leaned toward inviting U.S. journalists rather than ping-pong players. Zhou asked Mao what to do. He was silent for days, leading the Foreign Ministry to phone Japan and say no. When Mao changed his mind and said yes, the Foreign Ministry switched gears.

24. Kissinger, *The White House Years*, 712.

25. Ibid.

26. Without naming the USSR, the document denounced efforts by any country to establish "hegemony" or "collude" with other countries to "divide up the world into spheres of interest." In effect, Washington pledged not to cooperate with Moscow against China. Declassified documents show Kissinger less concerned to protect the interests of Taiwan than do his memoirs. See William Burr, ed., *The Kissinger Transcripts: The Top-Secret Talks with Beijing and Moscow* (New York: Free Press, 1999); and additional documents in William Burr, ed., *National Security Archive Electronic Briefing Book*, no. 66, February 27, 2002, http://www.gwu.edu/~nsarchiv/NSAEBB/NSAEBB66, accessed July 19, 2009.

27. Ji Chaozhu, *The Man on Mao's Right*, 243–245, 257–258.

28. Had Mao been more prescient about how to signal Nixon, he might have chosen a U.S. journalist without Snow's leftist reputation.

29. On "The Myth of America's Lost Chance in China," see Chen Jian, *Mao's China and the Cold War* (Chapel Hill: University of North Carolina Press, 2001), chap. 2.

30. When Taiwan became more prosperous and confident, Taipei began in 1986 to respond more positively to Beijing's overtures. See Jun Zhan, *Ending the Chinese Civil War: Power, Commerce, and Conciliation between Beijing and Taipei* (New York: St. Martin's Press, 1993).

Notes for Chapter 7

1. B. R. Myers, "To Beat a Dictator, Ignore Him," *New York Times*, April 2, 2008, A27.

2. See Lawrence E. Harrison, *The Central Liberal Truth: How Politics Can Change a Culture and Save It from Itself* (New York: Oxford University Press, 2006).

3. Alastair Iain Johnston, *Cultural Realism: Strategic Culture and Grand Strategy in Chinese History* (Princeton, NJ: Princeton University Press, 1995), 1.

4. Kenneth B. Pyle, "Reading the New Era in Asia: The Use of History and Culture in the Making of Foreign Policy," *Asia Policy* 3 (January 2007): 1–11 at 11.

5. Harrison, *The Central Liberal Truth*, xvii.

6. Lucian W. Pye, "Political Culture Revisited," *Political Psychology* 12, no. 3 (September 1991): 487–508.

7. Raymond Cohen, *Negotiating Across Cultures: International Communication in an Interdependent World*, rev. ed. (Washington, DC: United States Institute of Peace, 2002).

8. Stephen W. Linton, "Approach and Style in Negotiating with the D.P.R.K.," lecture at the Center for Korean Research, Columbia University, New York, April 6, 1995. Linton grew up in a Presbyterian missionary family in South Korea. He first visited North Korea in 1979 as an observer to an international table tennis meet. Later, while studying and teaching Korean religion at Columbia University, he met twice with DPRK leader Kim Il Sung as an interpreter for Billy Graham. When the DPRK asked for assistance in 1995, Linton left Columbia and founded the Eugene Bell Foundation to coordinate shipments of donated food. In 1997 the DPRK Ministry of Public Health asked Linton to focus the organization's work on tuberculosis. By 2003 Linton had visited North Korea more than sixty times, traveling into every district. See Stephen W. Linton, Testimony before the Senate Subcommittee on East Asian and Pacific Affairs, June 5, 2003; see also http://www.eugenebell.org/, accessed March 24, 2009.

9. Stephen W. Linton, email to Clemens, November 8, 2009.

10. Ibid.

11. Charles W. Freeman interviewed in Nancy Bernkopf Tucker, ed., *China Confidential: American Diplomats and Sino-American Relations, 1945–1996* (New York: Columbia University Press, 2001), 429–430.

12. Karen Elliot House, "Let North Korea Collapse," *Wall Street Journal*, February 21, 1997, A14.

13. Myers, "To Beat a Dictator."

14. Scott Snyder, *Negotiating on the Edge: North Korean Negotiating Behavior* (Washington, DC: United States Institute of Peace, 1999). Another well-balanced interpretation is that of Richard Saccone, *Living with the Enemy: Inside North Korea* (Elizabeth, NJ: Hollym, 2006); and Richard Saccone, *Negotiating with North Korea* (Elizabeth, NJ: Hollym, 2003).

15. Snyder, *Negotiating on the Edge*, 65–96.

16. Adapted from comments by Yurim Yi in June 2009.

17. Richard H. Solomon, *Chinese Negotiating Behavior: Pursuing Interests through "Old Friends"* (Washington, DC: United States Institute of Peace, 1999).

18. Henry Kissinger, *The White House Years* (Boston: Little, Brown, 1979), 1056.

19. Anna Fifield, "Kim Comes Off the Fence," *Financial Times*, May 15, 2005, 7.

20. Myers, "To Beat a Dictator."

21. B. R. Myers, "Stranger Than Fiction," *New York Times*, February 13, 2005, E15.

22. Michael Harrold, *Comrades and Strangers: Behind the Closed Doors of North Korea* (Hoboken, NJ: John Wiley, 2004).

23. Barry K. Gills, "Prospects for Peace and Stability in Northeast Asia: The Korean Conflict," *Conflict Studies* 278 (February 1995): 17–18.

24. William W. Maddux and Adam D. Galinsky, "Cultural Borders and Mental Barriers: The Relationship between Living Abroad and Creativity," *Journal of Personality and Social Psychology* 96, no. 5 (2009): 1047–1061.

Notes for Chapter 8

1. For a detailed chronology of North Korea and disarmament diplomacy, see http://armscontrol.org/factsheets/dprkchron, accessed May 10, 2009.

2. DPRK-PRC communiqué on September 2, 1994, quoted in Larry Niksch, "North Korea's Campaign against the Korean Armistice," Congressional Reference Service Report for Congress, 95–1187 F, December 11, 1995.

3. See Michael J. Mazarr, *North Korea and the Bomb: A Case Study in Nonproliferation* (New York: St. Martin's Press, 1997), 94–99.

4. IAEA, "In Focus: IAEA and the DPRK," http://www.iaea.org/NewsCenter/Focus/IaeaDprk/fact_sheet_may2003.shtml, accessed July 15, 2009.

5. Carter was accompanied by retired ambassador Marion V. Creekmore Jr., who describes the event in *Moment of Crisis: Jimmy Carter, the Power of a Peacemaker, and North Korea's Nuclear Ambitions* (New York: Public Affairs, 2006).

6. Michael Watkins and Susan Rosegrant, *Breakthrough International Negotiation: How Great Negotiators Transformed the World's Toughest Post–Cold War Conflicts* (San Francisco: Jossey-Bass, Wiley, 2001), 89.

7. Text at http://www.kedo.org/pdfs/AgreedFramework.pdf, accessed April 8, 2009.

8. Executive agreements are binding under international law but avoid the ratification process required for treaties.

9. Watkins and Rosegrant, *Breakthrough International Negotiation,* 105; also 128–129.

10. The 1991 agreement distinguished between facilities to produce highly enriched uranium (HEU), suitable for weapons manufacture, and low enriched uranium (LEU), sufficient to power light-water reactors. See Selig S. Harrison, "Did North Korea Cheat?" *Foreign Affairs* 84, no. 1 (2005): 99–110. But an enrichment facility dedicated to producing LEU can be reconfigured to produce HEU. In this sense it is misleading to speak of fundamentally different facilities, wrote former U.S. official Larry Scheinmann in 2005, commenting on a draft of this chapter. By 2005 the Bush administration worried that any "civilian" nuclear reactor could be diverted.

11. IAEA, "In Focus."

12. Dinshaw Mistry, *Containing Missile Proliferation: Strategic Technology, Security Regimes, and International Cooperation in Arms Control* (Seattle: University of Washington Press, 2003).

13. James Goodby and William Drennan, "Koreapolitik," *Strategic Forum* 29 (May 1995): 2.

14. Joseph Cirincione et al., *Deadly Arsenals: Tracking Weapons of Mass Destruction* (Washington, DC: Carnegie Endowment for International Peace, 2002), 247.

15. Huge questions loomed. How would the LWR be integrated into North Korea's electric grid? Where was the necessary backup power supply? How would insurance for builders and third parties be handled and financed? How could world-class safety standards be assured? Who would take the spent fuel from the old gas-graphite reactor? How would more comprehensive IAEA inspections be arranged? David Albright and Kevin O'Neill, eds., *Solving the North Korean Nuclear Puzzle* (Washington, DC: Institute for Science and International Security Press, 2000); Joel Wit, "Viewpoint: The Korean Peninsula Energy Development Organization:

Achievements and Challenges," *Nonproliferation Review* 6, no. 2 (Winter 1999): 59–69.

16. Nicholas N. Eberstadt, "Korea," in Richard J. Ellings and Aaron L. Friedberg with Michael Wills, eds., *Strategic Asia 2002–03: Asian Aftershocks* (Seattle: National Bureau of Asian Research, 2002), 130–182 at 149.

17. "A Fabulous Appeal," *Korea Herald,* August 27, 2003, editorial.

18. Asan reported in August 2008 that it had paid US$675,250 to North Korea to cover costs accrued by 10,380 South Korean tourists who had visited the mountain resort on July 1–11, until the tours halted after a South Korean tourist was shot and killed by a North Korean soldier at Mt. Kumgang. According to *Choson Ilbo,* August 8, 2008, Asan sent the payment at the end of each month, at the rate of $30 per person for a one day tour, $48 for two days, or $80 for three days. Later in August 2008 Asan was expected to pay a further $928,560 to the North to cover the cost of trips to another tourist destination, Kaesong City. The cumulative payments Asan made to the North for the first six months of 2008 amounted to $10.7 million for the Mt. Kumgang tour and $5.1 million for the Kaesong tour.

19. Indeed, the Soviet government under Mikhail Gorbachev gave the Reagan administration more than a year to respond to unilateral Soviet moves. And having a surfeit of intermediate-range nuclear forces (INF) missiles and conventional arms, the Kremlin ultimately made larger concessions than the U.S. or other NATO allies to reach the 1987 ban on INF and the 1990 treaty on conventional forces in Europe.

20. The dilemma and how to cope with it were suggested by Chung-In Moon and Tae-Hwan Kim, "Sustaining Inter-Korean Reconciliation: North-South Korea Cooperation," and Dae-Sung Song, "A Peace Regime and Arms Control on the Korean Peninsula: Challenges and Alternatives in the Beginning of the 21st Century," *Journal of East Asian Affairs,* 15, no. 2 (Fall–Winter 2001): 203–245 and 246–269, respectively.

21. Kim Chin, "Pukhan 'Taeryukkan Missile P'ogi,'" *Joongang Ilbo,* August 5, 2000, http://www.joins.com/, accessed July 23, 2009.

22. http://www1.korea-np.co.jp/pk/149th_issue/2000101402.htm, accessed July 23, 2009.

23. Madeleine Albright, *Madame Secretary* (New York: Hyperion, 2003), 459–472.

24. North Korea's top diplomat since 1998, he died in 2007 at age seventy-eight.

25. Albright also liked symbols—famous for wearing a decorative pin suited to the occasion and her own frame of mind. When she saw Jo again in Pyongyang, he wore a pin bearing the image of Kim Il Sung; she, her largest stars and stripes pin.

Notes for Chapter 9

1. For a view from inside the State Department, see Charles L. Pritchard, *Failed Diplomacy: The Tragic Story of How North Korea Got the Bomb* (Washington, DC: Brookings Institution, 2007). For a parallel narrative by a CNN reporter, see Mike Chinoy, *Meltdown: The Inside Story of the North Korean Nuclear Crisis* (New York: St. Martin's Press, 2008).

2. For a detailed chronology of North Korea and disarmament diplomacy, with frequent updates, see http://armscontrol.org/factsheets/dprkchron, accessed April 19, 2009.

3. Bob Woodward, *Plan of Attack* (New York: Simon and Schuster, 2004), 31–32.

4. See, e.g., Kang Chol-hwan and Pierre Rigoulot, *The Aquariums of Pyongyang: Ten Years in the North Korean Gulag* (New York: Basic Books, 2001).

5. Madeleine Albright, *Madame Secretary* (New York: Hyperion, 2003), 470.

6. "Bush Tells Seoul Talks with North Won't Resume Now," *New York Times*, March 8, 2001; and detailed analysis in Chae-Jin Lee, *A Troubled Peace: U.S. Policy and the Two Koreas* (Baltimore, MD: Johns Hopkins University Press, 2006), 212–214.

7. Barton Gellman, *Angler: The Cheney Vice Presidency* (New York: Penguin, 2008), 228–229.

8. Glenn Kessler, *The Confidante: Condoleezza Rice and the Creation of the Bush Legacy* (New York: St. Martin's Press, 2007), 65–87.

9. Gellman, *Angler*, 209.

10. Selig S. Harrison, "Did North Korea Cheat?" *Foreign Affairs* 84, no. 1 (January–February 2005): 99–110 at 106–107.

11. Cheney's view as summarized by Aaron Friedberg, Cheney's deputy national security adviser, 2003–2005, quoted in Chinoy, *Meltdown*, 194.

12. Interview with Bolton in 2004, quoted in Gellman, *Angler*, 373.

13. Kessler, *The Confidante*, 71.

14. Ruediger Frank, "Dreaming an Impossible Dream? Opening, Reform, and the Future of the North Korean Economy," *Global Asia* 4, no. 2 (Summer 2009): 18–32 at 21.

15. The president altered the law of the land without participation by the legislature (needed to make a treaty or any other law). More than thirty members of the House of Representatives sued the administration in the District of Columbia District Court for violating Article II, Section 2, of the Constitution. The court dismissed their suit as a nonjusticiable political question.

16. See the Justice Department memoranda released by the American Civil Liberties Union, http://www.aclu.org/safefree/general/olc_memos.html, accessed April 18, 2009.

17. For the *Nuclear Posture Review*, see http://www.globalsecurity.org/wmd/library/policy/dod/npr.htm, accessed April 19, 2009.

18. Despite the Bush team's public assertions about Saddam Hussein's WMD, Washington expected to oust his regime without major incidents. Woodward, *Plan of Attack*, 31–32.

19. Robert W. Nelson, "Low-Yield Earth-Penetrating Nuclear Weapons," *Science and Global Security* 10, no. 1 (January–April 2002): 1–20.

20. Excerpts released by the White House in *Congressional Record*, July 21 and 23, 2003.

21. International Institute for Strategic Studies, *The Military Balance, 2003–2004* (London: Oxford University Press, 2004), 19, 28, 163, 177–179.

22. The treaty permitted each side to keep—not destroy—the nuclear warheads withdrawn from its deployed arsenal. The U.S. Senate approved the treaty in March 2003, as did the Russian Duma three months later, when the newspaper *Moskovskii Komsomolets* (May 15, 2003) ran the headline "A Nuclear Bomb in Stars and Stripes." The article declared that even though the treaty "does not actually bind Russia to anything, the obligations of the United States under it are even less binding than Russia's."

23. Article in the authoritative newspaper *Rodong Sinmun*, September 1, 2003.

24. For India the decision to proceed with nuclear weapons derived as much from Hindu nationalism as from worries about foreign threats. See George Perkovich, *India's Nuclear Bomb: The Impact of Global Proliferation* (Berkeley and Los Angeles: University of California Press, 1999).

25. William C. Potter et al., "Tito's Nuclear Legacy," *Bulletin of the Atomic Scientists* 56, no. 2 (March–April 2000): 63–70 at 69.

26. Albright, *Madame Secretary,* 469.

27. James Goodby, "America's Mixed Signals in Korea," *Financial Times,* June 11, 2004. See also "American Forces in South Korea: The End of an Era?" *Strategic Comments* 8, no. 5 (July 2003): 1–2.

28. According to a former ROK prime minister, South Korea' direct aid consisted mainly of food and medical supplies. As of early 2005, the industrial zone in North Korea, where fifteen ROK companies had begun operations, occupied just twenty-three acres. These companies paid their DPRK workers $57 about month—a wage so low that it helped them compete with industries in China. Goh Kun, "U.S.-ROK Alliance and the North Korean Problem," lecture at John F. Kennedy Forum, Harvard University, Cambridge, Massachusetts, March 16, 2005.

29. Kessler, *The Confidante,* 71.

30. Hill later said that DPRK negotiators, though tough, were no match for the Serbian negotiators with whom he had tangled in the 1990s.

31. IAEA, "In Focus: IAEA and the DPRK," http://www.iaea.org/NewsCenter/Focus/IaeaDprk/fact_sheet_may2003.shtml, accessed July 15, 2009.

32. John Bolton, quoted in ibid., 376.

33. Senate Hearings in April 2009 on whether to approve Hill as U.S. ambassador to Iraq. He won approval—73 to 23.

34. Goh Kun, "U.S.-ROK Alliance."

35. Kessler, *The Confidante,* 86 and interviews by Gellman, *Angler.*

36. On April 24, 2008, U.S. intelligence officials reported their assessment that the Syrian facility was a nuclear reactor being built with North Korean assistance. A CIA-produced video included photographs taken from inside and around the facility at various times during its construction, as well as satellite images and digital renderings of certain elements of the reactor's operations.

37. Siegfried S. Hecker report, March 14, 2008, http://iis-db.stanford.edu/pubs/22146/HeckerDPRKreport.pdf, accessed May 16, 2009.

38. Winston Lord and Leslie H. Gelb, "Yielding to North Korea Too Often," *Washington Post,* April 26, 2008.

39. For a history and analysis, see Terence Roehrig, "North Korea and the U.S. State Sponsors of Terrorism List," *Pacific Focus* 24, no. 1 (April 2009): 85–106.

40. John R. Bolton, "The Tragic End of Bush's North Korean Policy," *Wall Street Journal,* June 30, 2008.

41. Larry A. Niksch, "North Korea: Terrorism List Removal?" Congressional Reference Service, February 02, 2009, http://opencrs.com/document/RL30613/, accessed May 10, 2009.

42. Leon V. Sigal, "Punishing North Korea Won't Work," *Bulletin of the Atomic Scientists,* May 28, 2009, http://www.thebulletin.org/web-edition/op-eds/punishing-north-korea-wont-work, accessed June 12, 2009.

43. Frank, "Dreaming an Impossible Dream."

Notes for Chapter 10

1. For analysis of many classic and recent theories, see Jennifer Sterling-Folker, ed., *Making Sense of International Relations Theory* (Boulder, CO: Lynne Rienner, 2006).

2. Jonathan Haslam, *No Virtue like Necessity: Realist Thought in International Relations since Machiavelli* (New Haven, CT: Yale University Press, 2002); Michael Smith, *Realist Thought from Weber to Kissinger* (Baton Rouge: Louisiana State University Press, 1990).

3. Kenneth N. Waltz, *Theory of International Politics* (New York: McGraw-Hill, 1979); Robert O. Keohane, ed., *Neorealism and Its Critics* (New York: Columbia University Press, 1986); David A. Baldwin, ed., *Neorealism and Neoliberalism: The Contemporary Debate* (New York: Columbia University Press, 1993).

4. Leslie H. Gelb, *Power Rules: How Common Sense Can Rescue American Foreign Policy* (New York: HarperCollins 2009).

5. The first case occurred in 1963, when Moscow's signature on the 1963 nuclear test ban led to large imports of U.S. grain. Of course, other factors also played a role. Moscow and Washington sought conditions that would make another Cuban missile confrontation less likely.

6. Food aid to North Korea increased by nearly seven times in 1997/8 relative to 1996/7 and remained at high level until 2005, when it fell to less than in 1997/8. It is difficult to correlate need with foreign aid because of the inherent lags between demand and supply. See the tables recording humanitarian assistance to North Korea from 1996 to 2005 in Stephan Haggard and Marcus Noland, *Famine in North Korea: Markets, Aid, and Reform* (New York: Columbia University Press, 2007), Appendixes 2.1–2.4.

7. Cary Nederman, "Niccolò Machiavelli," in Edward N. Zalta, ed., *The Stanford Encyclopedia of Philosophy*, http://plato.stanford.edu/entries/machiavelli/#3, accessed February 27, 2009.

8. Hindsight bias is the inclination to see events that have occurred as more predictable than they in fact were before they took place. Hindsight bias has been demonstrated experimentally in many settings, including politics and medicine. In psychological experiments of hindsight bias, subjects tend to remember their predictions of future events as having been stronger than they actually were, in those cases where those predictions turn out correct.

9. Nassim N. Taleb, *The Black Swan: The Impact of the Highly Improbable* (New York: Random House, 2007).

10. One polymath argues the inadequacies of any reductionism. The evolution of the universe and of humankind does not violate the laws of physics but cannot be explained by them. Stuart A. Kauffman, *Reinventing the Sacred: A New View of Science, Reason, and Religion* (New York: Basic Books, 2008).

11. Innovators in tiny Israel compete and cooperate with those in Silicone Valley.

12. Miles J. Unger, *Magnifico: The Brilliant Life and Violent Times of Lorenzo de' Medici* (New York: Simon and Schuster, 2008), 118.

13. Ibid., 125–126.

14. For other cases, see Philip E. Tetlock, Richard Ned Lebow, and Geoffrey Parker, eds., *Unmasking the West: "What-If" Scenarios That Rewrite World History* (Ann Arbor: University of Michigan Press, 2006).

15. Counterfactual history is not the same as historical revisionism (negationism) or alternative history. See Niall Ferguson, ed., *Virtual History: Alternatives and Counterfactuals* (New York: Basic Books, 1999).

16. Following the U.S. example, no West European country except Sweden and, for a short time, New Zealand ever recognized Baltic annexation.

17. Choong Nam Kim, *The Korean Presidents: Leadership for Nation Building* (Norwalk, CT: Eastbridge, 2007), 142.

18. Diplomatic relations between the two countries were restored in April 2007. Soon, reports surfaced that Pyongyang had sold rocket launchers to Myanmar and increased DPRK purchases of raw materials from Myanmar.

19. The Korean Central News Agency, October 16, 2008 (*Juche* 97), assured readers that "the Korean people are entrusting their destinies entirely to the great revolutionary party and are implementing the Party's lines and policies by displaying boundless loyalty and devotion with the revolutionary faith 'the Party decides, so we do!'"

20. For complexity theory references, see Chapter 1, n. 22–24.

21. Immanuel Kant, *Political Writings* (New York: Cambridge University Press, 2006); Michael W. Doyle, *Ways of War and Peace: Realism, Liberalism, and Socialism* (New York: Norton, 1997); Walter C. Clemens Jr., *Dynamics of International Relations: Conflict and Cooperation in an Era of Global Interdependence*, 2d ed. (Lanham, MD: Rowman and Littlefield, 2004), 351–385.

22. Herodotus made a similar point as he compared Persian autocracy with Athenian democracy.

23. The cult of personality nearly paralyzed North Korea. Seeking to report on honors for its Dear Leader, the KCNA proudly reported in October 2007 that a Kim Jong Il essay on *juche* (June 19, *Juche* 86 [1997]) was recently published as a pamphlet in Aruba. An even greater feat was broadcast on October 16, 2008. Kim Jong Il's work "Our Socialism Centered on the Masses Shall Not Perish" was brought out as a pamphlet by the Party for Peace and Unity of Russia. The work, first published on May 5, *Juche* 80 (1991), purported to clarify the sure victory of Korean-style socialism, key to the solidity and invincibility of socialism in the DPRK and its essential characteristics. A "book-releasing ceremony" took place in Moscow on October 9, 2008.

24. Alexander Wendt, *Social Theory in International Politics* (New York: Cambridge University Press, 1999); Daniel M. Green, ed., *Constructivism and Comparative Politics* (Armonk, NY: M. E. Sharpe, 2002); Stafano Guzzini and Anna Leander, eds., *Constructivism and International Relations: Alexander Wendt and His Critics* (London: Routledge, 2006).

25. The DPRK delegate to the United Nations demanded that any "antiterrorism" activities be conducted in conformity with the principles of the UN Charter and international law. Speaking to the General Assembly on October 8, 2008, he emphasized the need not to allow some specified states to use the antiterrorism struggle as leverage for seeking their political and economic purposes. To remove the root cause of terrorism, he said, it is necessary to eradicate social inequality and poverty while establishing fair international relations on the basis of mutual respect, equality, friendship, and cooperation whereby all countries and nations can fully exercise their rights to live and develop independently.

26. Alexander J Motyl, email from Rutgers University, October 30, 2008.

27. Malcolm Gladwell, *Outliers: The Story of Success* (Boston: Little, Brown, 2008).

Notes for Chapter 11

1. Stephen Jay Gould, *The Structure of Evolutionary Theory* (Cambridge, MA: Harvard University Press, 2002).

2. Stephan Haggard and Marcus Noland, *Famine in North Korea: Markets, Aid, and Reform* (New York: Columbia University Press, 2007), 222–223.

3. The process took decades. Moscow acted quickly and with massive force to crush the East German *Aufstand* in 1953; it took weeks before sending tanks into Budapest in 1956; it debated for months before invading Czechoslovakia in 1968, with almost no loss of life; it permitted the Polish communist regime to impose martial law against Solidarity in the 1970s; it did nothing to stop East Europe's withdrawal from the Soviet empire in the late 1980s; it killed fewer than fifty Balts as they drove to split from the USSR in 1988–1991. However, the Soviet regime did kill many Kazakhs in 1986 and some twenty Georgians in 1989.

4. Adrei Lankov, "The Troubled Russia–North Korea Alliance," *Asia Times Online* December 25, 2004, at http://www.atimes.com/Korea/FL25Dg01.html, accessed April 29, 2009.

5. Haggard and Noland, *Famine*, 225–226.

6. Ibid., 212–216.

7. *Human Development Report, 2007/2008,* based on 2005 data, http://hdr.undp.org/en/media/HDR_20072008_EN_Indicator_tables.pdf, accessed March 21, 2009.

8. See the "Report of the Commission to Assess the Threat to the United States from Electromagnetic Pulse (EMP) Attack" (2004), http://www.empcommission.org/docs/empc_exec_rpt.pdf; and (2008); and "Critical National Infrastructures" (2008), http://www.empcommission.org/docs/A2473-EMP_Commission–7MB.pdf, both accessed on March 30, 2009.

9. Scott Snyder, *China's Rise and the Two Koreas: Politics, Economics, Security* (Boulder, CO: Lynne Rienner, 2009).

10. "$12.7bn Record for S Korean Bonds," *Financial Times,* June 4, 2009.

11. Martin Fackler, "So Close, yet So Far Away: At Border, South Koreans Heed a Blustery Neighbor," *New York Times,* June 4, 2009, A8.

12. Haggard and Noland, *Famine*, 221–222.

13. Gilbert Rozman, *Northeast Asia's Stunted Regionalism: Bilateral Distrust in the Shadow of Globalization* (New York: Cambridge University Press, 2004). See also relevant Working Papers at the Washington, DC–based US-Korea Institute at SAIS: Im Hyug Baeg, "How Korea Could Become a Regional Power in Northeast Asia: Building a Northeast Asian Triad" (WPS-08–4); Carla P. Freedman, "In Pursuit of Peaceful Development in Northeast Asia: China, the Tumen River Development Project, and Sino-Korean Relations" (WPS-08–2); Walter Andersen, "Korea: An Important Part of India's Look East Policy" (WPS-08–1); and Yoon Sung-hak, "Strategic Opportunities for South Korean Development of Energy Resources in Central Asia" (WPS-09–02).

14. Gilbert Rozman, "Can Confucianism Survive in an Age of Universalism and Globalization?" *Pacific Affairs* 75, no. 1 (Spring 2002): 11–37.

15. These maxims are inferred from the case histories of this book and from the negotiating handbooks cited in Chapter 1. On transformation, see Chaesung Chun, "Moving from a North Korean Nuclear Problem to the Problem of North Korea," *Policy Forum Online* 09–047, June 11, 2009, http://www.nautilus.org/fora/security/09047Chun .pdf, accessed June 12, 2009.

16. Christopher Oliver, "Seoul Drafts $40bn North Korea Plan," *Financial Times*, July 21, 2009, 4; Bloomberg News, July 22, 2009.

17. Reuters, July 19, 2009.

Notes for Chapter 12

1. Leslie H. Gelb, "In the End, Every President Talks to Bad Guys," *Washington Post*, April 27, 2008.

2. Russia's foreign minister, Sergei Lavrov, said the UN sanctions were not constructive. Nevertheless, he received a cold *nyet* when he visited Pyongyang in April 2009 and tried to persuade the DPRK leaders to return to the six-party talks. He advised: "We should not give way to emotions, instead we should concentrate on what we have already achieved."

3. Letter of POTUS to M. S. Gorbachev, January 23, 1990. James A. Baker III Papers, Seeley G. Mudd Manuscript Library, Princeton University, MC#197, Series B: Secretary of State, Box 109, quoted in Darius Furmonavicius, "The Price of Freedom," *Lituanus* 54, no. 1 (2008): 12.

4. However, Reagan proposed a summit meeting to Chernenko not long before the latter's death.

5. Pavel Podvig, "Did 'Star Wars' Help End the Cold War? Soviet Response to the SDI Program," presentation at the Harvard University Davis Center for Russian and Eurasian Studies, January 22, 2009, based on Soviet archives and the papers of weapons designer V. L. Kataev. Open sources available in the 1980s suggested similar interpretations in Walter C. Clemens Jr., *Can Russia Change? The USSR Confronts Global Interdependence* (New York: Routledge, 1990), chaps. 7–10.

6. Douglas Martin, "George C. Minden, Who Smuggled Books in a Cold War of Words, Is Dead at 85," *New York Times,* April 23, 2006, 29. Minden's center sent several hundred copies of this author's book *Baltic Independence and Russian Empire* (New York: St. Martin's Press, 1991) to readers in the Baltic countries and in Moscow.

7. Edward Reed, "Books Open Doors in North Korea," undated report, Korea representative of the Asia Foundation. For the big picture, see http://www.asiafoundation .org/program/overview/books-for-asia, accessed May 12, 2009.

8. Bruce W. Jentleson and Christopher A. Whytock, "Who 'Won' Libya? The Force-Diplomacy Debate and the Implications for Theory and Practice," *International Security* 30, no. 3 (Winter 2005–2006): 47–86.

9. Tripoli's disarmament was also a success story for the U.S. intelligence community, which uncovered and halted some of the assistance Libya was being provided by the nuclear smuggling network led by Pakistani nuclear official Abdul Qadeer Khan.

10. Gaddafi's son stated that the December 19, 2003, agreement with the United

States was a "win-win" deal for both sides. "Our leader believed that if this problem were solved, Libya would emerge from the international isolation and become a negotiator and work with the big powers to change the Arab situation."

11. Flying hours for DPRK air forces amounted to just 20 hours or less, compared to 150 for Japan and more than 200 for the United States. International Institute for Strategic Studies, *The Military Balance, 2004–2005* (London: Oxford University Press, 2004), 19, 28, 163, 177, 178, 179.

12. Patrick McEachern, "Interest Groups in North Korean Politics," *Journal of East Asian Studies* 8, no. 2 (May–August 2008): 235–258.

13. Pyongyang's experiences with Moscow and Beijing as well as recollections of U.S. bombing and subsequent threats shaped the regime's worldview. See Kathryn Weathersby, "Dependence and Mistrust: North Korea's Relations with Moscow and the Evolution of Juche," Working Paper Series, WP-08-8 (Washington, DC: US-Korea Institute at SAIS, 2008).

14. Charles Armstrong, "Necessary Enemies: Anti-Americanism, Juche Ideology, and the Tortuous Path to Normalization," Working Paper Series, WP-08-3 (Washington, DC: US-Korea Institute at SAIS, 2008).

15. See *The Amartya Sen and Jean Drèze Omnibus: Comprising Poverty and Famines, Hunger and Public Action, India: Economic Development and Social Opportunity* (New Delhi: Oxford University Press, 1999); and Amartya Sen, "Foreword," to Stephan Haggard and Marcus Noland, *Famine in North Korea: Markets, Aid, and Reform* (New York: Columbia University Press, 2007).

16. Uri Ra'anan, ed., *Flawed Succession: Russia's Power Transfer Crises* (Lanham, MD: Lexington Books, 2006).

17. Marshall I. Goldman, *Petrostate: Putin, Power, and the New Russia* (New York: Oxford University Press, 2008).

18. Natan Sharansky, "Death of a Dissident," *Washington Post*, May 28, 2009.

19. "The Interview," BBC broadcast, January 21, 2009.

20. See also Gordon R. Weihmiller and Dusko Doder, eds., *U.S.-Soviet Summits: An Account of East-West Diplomacy at the Top, 1955–1985* (Lanham, MD: University Press of America, 1986).

21. Kissinger's use of the back channel undercut the U.S. negotiators working directly with their Soviet counterparts. In the end, he probably allowed the Soviets more room to expand their submarine-based missile forces than needed. See Gerard Smith, *Double Talk: The Story of SALT I* (Lanham, MD: University Press of America, 1985).

22. Stephen W. Linton, "Approach and Style in Negotiating with the D.P.R.K.," lecture at the Center for Korean Research, Columbia University, New York, April 6, 1995.

23. Jim Wooten, "The Conciliator," *New York Times Magazine*, January 29, 1995.

24. Marion V. Creekmore, *A Moment of Crisis: Jimmy Carter, the Power of a Peace-maker, and North Korea's Nuclear Ambitions* (New York: Public Affairs, 2006).

25. One diplomat pictured the late Serbian president Slobodan Milošević as "the sleaziest person you've ever met" and armed with an IQ of 160. Many mediators have felt uneasy dealing with suspected genocidists but did so as part of the job. Nevertheless, Lord Owen (trained as a physician) could not bring himself to discuss medicine with Bosnian Serb leader Radovan Karadžic, a former psychiatrist but also an accused war criminal. Owen's partner in Balkan mediation, Cyrus Vance, believed that a mediator should not see anyone as evil incarnate. But he also thought that compromise with persons so evil

as Adolf Hitler was impossible. Vance added, however, that with Saddam Hussein "we probably should have given talks more time." Leslie H. Gelb, "Vance: A Nobel Life," *New York Times*, March 2, 1992, A15.

26. Eni F. H. Faleomavaega, chairman, Subcommittee on Asia, the Pacific, and the Global Environment, "Smart Power: Remaking U.S. Foreign Policy in North Korea," February 12, 2009, http://www.internationalrelations.house.gov/111/faleo021209 .pdf, accessed March 19, 2009.

27. Scott Snyder testimony, http://www.internationalrelations.house.gov/111/ sny021209.pdf, accessed March 19, 2009.

28. Donald Gregg, president of the Korea Society, conversation on February 7, 2009.

Notes for Chapter 13

1. When an ROK warship burst in two in March 2010, the ROK Defense Ministry speculated that it might have struck one of the 4,000 mines put down by North Korea during the war or, more ominously, a more recently planted DPRK floating mine.

2. First, Wang Jiarui, the Chinese Communist Party international affairs chief, met with Kim Jong Il. KCNA reported that Wang transmitted a "verbal message from President" Hu Jintao and that both governments reaffirmed their "dedication to the denuclearization of the Korean peninsula." On his return flight to Beijing, Wang was accompanied by the North's lead nuclear negotiator, Minister Kim Gye-Gwan, and the DPRK official in charge of American affairs, Li Gun, scheduled to meet with their Chinese counterpart, Wu Dawei, named special representative on Korean peninsular affairs in February—the same month in which he met Obama's envoy for Korean affairs, Stephen Bosworth, in Beijing.

3. For their parts, many South Koreans discriminated against refugees from the North. See, e.g., Choe Sang-hun, "Fury of Girl's Fists Lifts Up North Korean Refugee Family," *The New York Times*, October 26, 2008, 16. B. R. Myers portrayed North Korea as a racist society in his book *The Cleanest Race: How North Koreans See Themselves and Why It Matters* (Brooklyn: Melville House, 2010).

4. Holland Cotter, "Japanese Art and Its Korean Secret," *The New York Times*, April 6, 2003.

5. Such a determinism appeared to explain China's arms and arms control policies in the 1960s—and probably later as well. See Walter C. Clemens, Jr., *The Arms Race and Sino-Soviet Relations* (Stanford, CA: Hoover Institution, 1968).

6. A Japanese analyst portrayed this as North Korea's consistent approach since the 1960s. See Narushige Michishita, *North Korea's Military-Diplomatic Campaigns, 1966–2008* (New York: Routledge, 2010). For political-science fiction depicting a panicked U.S. response to North Korea's military exploits, see Ben Bova, *Able One* (New York: Tor, 2010).

7. B. R. Myers wrote that the DPRK regime inculcated a racist nationalism, similar to that of imperial Japan, and that most North Koreans accepted it. See his *The Cleanest Race*.

8. This last explanation is the view of Ralph C. Hassig and Kongdan Oh, *The Hidden People of North Korea: Everyday Life in the Hermit Kingdom*. (Lanham, MD: Rowman

& Littlefield, 2009). Another picture is painted by a journalist who tracked the lives of six North Koreans—how they fell in love, raised families, nurtured ambitions, and struggled for survival in an Orwellian world. One by one, they realized that their government had betrayed them. See Barbara Demick, *Nothing to Envy: Ordinary Lives in North Korea* (New York: Spiegel & Grau, 2009). Proof that at least some Americans hunger for information about the world, by February 2010 some thirty-six subscribers had placed a hold on Demick's book at the public library in Lexington, Massachusetts.

9. Balkan Devlen, "Dealing or Dueling with the United States? Explaining and Predicting Iranian Behavior During the Nuclear Crisis," *International Studies Review* 12, no. 1 (March 2010): 53–68. See also Devlen, *Renegade Regimes and Foreign Policy Crises: Understanding Saddam Hussein, Slobodan Milosevic, and Kim Il-Sung* (Saarbrucken: VDM Verlag, 2008).

10. Lincoln P. Bloomfield, Walter C. Clemens, Jr., Franklyn Griffiths, *Khrushchev and the Arms Race: Soviet Interests in Arms Control and Disarmament, 1954–1964* (Cambridge, MA: The M.I.T. Press, 1966).

11. General Stanley McChrystal believed that human agency could overcome history. See Robert D. Kaplan, "Man Versus Afghanistan," *The Atlantic* 305, no. 3 (April 2010): 60–71.

12. Ralph C. Hassig and Kongdan Oh, *The Hidden People of North Korea: Everyday Life in the Hermit Kingdom* (Lanham, MD: Rowman & Littlefield, 2010).

13. Choe Sang-hun, "North Koreans Use Cellphones to Bare Secrets," *The New York Times,* March 29, 2010, 1, 10.

14. Of 8,400 agents sent north by the ROK from 1953 to 1994, only one in four returned. Ibid.

15. The German model utilized rudiments of democracy absent in North Korea. In November 1989 East Germans broke through the Berlin Wall and were welcomed by compatriots. In March 1990 East Germans voted in the first free parliamentary elections ever held in the German Democratic Republic. Some 48 percent voted for a conservative coalition that favored accession to the Federal Republic of Germany. Social Democrats, who wanted a more evolutionary approach with a joint constitution, won just 22 percent. A reunification treaty between the GDR and FRG was negotiated in mid-1990 and approved by large majorities in the legislatures of both countries in September. The result was not a third country but the enlargement of the same FRG founded in 1949. Citizens of a united Germany voted for a new parliament in December 1990. In March 1991 the 4 + 2 (France, UK, USA, USSR + FRG, GDR) treaty on unified Germany entered into force. The expanded German state retained the treaty rights and obligations from before. If the ROK absorbed the DPRK in a similar manner, the expanded ROK would still be bound by the NPT.

16. The review stated that "the United States will not use or threaten to use nuclear weapons against non-nuclear weapons states that are party to the Nuclear Non-Proliferation Treaty and in compliance with their nuclear non-proliferation obligations."

INDEX

ABOUT THE AUTHOR

Walter C. Clemens Jr. is Professor of Political Science at Boston University and Associate, Harvard University Davis Center for Russian and Eurasian Studies. He is the author (with Pulitzer Prize–Winning Editorial Cartoonist Jim Morin) most recently of *Ambushed! A Cartoon History of the George W. Bush Administration* (Paradigm 2009), and sole author of *America and the World, 1898–2025: Achievements, Failures, Alternative Futures* (2000). His op-eds have appeared in the *Christian Science Monitor, Los Angeles Times, The New York Times, Wall Street Journal,* and *Washington Post.*